Land Warfare since 1860

A Global History of Boots on the Ground

Jeremy Black
University of Exeter

ROWMAN & LITTLEFIELD
Lanham • Boulder • New York • London

Published by Rowman & Littlefield
An imprint of The Rowman & Littlefield Publishing Group, Inc.
4501 Forbes Boulevard, Suite 200, Lanham, Maryland 20706
https://rowman.com

Unit A, Whitacre Mews, 26-34 Stannary Street, London SE11 4AB, United Kingdom

Copyright © 2019 by The Rowman & Littlefield Publishing Group, Inc.

All rights reserved. No part of this book may be reproduced in any form or by any electronic or mechanical means, including information storage and retrieval systems, without written permission from the publisher, except by a reviewer who may quote passages in a review.

British Library Cataloguing in Publication Information Available

Library of Congress Cataloging-in-Publication Data
Names: Black, Jeremy, 1955– author.
Title: Land warfare since 1860 : a global history of boots on the ground / Jeremy Black, University of Exeter.
Description: Lanham, MD : Rowman and Littlefield, [2018] | Includes bibliographical references and index.
Identifiers: LCCN 2018012997 (print) | LCCN 2018013509 (ebook) | ISBN 9781442276895 (hardcover : alk. paper) | ISBN 9781442276901 (pbk. : alk. paper) | ISBN 9781442276918 (ebook)
Subjects: LCSH: Military history, Modern—20th century. | Military history, Modern—19th century. | Military art and science—History. | War—History—20th century. | War—History—19th century.
Classification: LCC D431 (ebook) | LCC D431 .B533 2018 (print) | DDC 355.02—dc23
LC record available at https://lccn.loc.gov/2018012997

♾ ™ The paper used in this publication meets the minimum requirements of American National Standard for Information Sciences Permanence of Paper for Printed Library Materials, ANSI/NISO Z39.48-1992.

Printed in the United States of America

*For Kate and Dominic Powell
With Much Affection*

Contents

Preface	vii
Abbreviations	ix
1 Introduction	1
2 A New Age of War? 1860–80	11
3 Different Types of Conflict, 1880–1913	41
4 The First World War, 1914–18	57
5 Between the Wars, 1918–39	89
6 The Second World War, 1939–45	111
7 The Cold War, 1945–71	149
8 The Cold War, 1972–89	179
9 After the Cold War, 1990–Today	201
10 Into the Future	233
11 Conclusions	245
Notes	251
Selected Further Reading	265
Index	273
About the Author	281

Preface

This book is designed both to stand on its own and as part of a series that includes, in order of publication, *Air Power: A Global History*, *Insurgency and Counterinsurgency: A Global History*, *Naval Warfare: A Global History since 1860*, and *Fortifications and Siegecraft: Defense and Attack through the Ages*. These are complementary but also stand on their own and, as a result, there is some similar coverage but also much new material. For greater coverage of certain topics, readers should consult the relevant books.

Several challenges face this work. First and foremost will be providing enough information and analysis for those who know little or nothing about the subject, primarily students, while also offering a rewarding analysis to those who are familiar with the history. Second, there is the need to avoid excessive duplication with the other volumes in the series while still providing the necessary coverage. Third, given its theme, there is the problem of coverage. And fourth, the very descriptive scope—a global coverage—and the very analytical approach, one that emphasizes variety in developments around the world, create considerable conceptual, organizational, and methodological difficulties.

All that allowed for, this is a very exciting challenge, and notably as the late 2010s offer a good time to address the subject and to look at the period since 1860, a year that began a decade that saw the American Civil War, the Wars of German Unification, the War of the Triple Alliance, and the continuation of the Taiping Rebellion. The revival of great-power confrontation in the 2010s has led to a shadowing of the earlier conviction that all wars, present and future, would be "among the people," and, in that light, a reexamination of the entire period is appropriate.

The major theme of the book will be that, on a global level looking at the period since 1860, there is no one essential character of warfare. The resulting situation created problems for planners and commentators in the past, and it invalidates notions of clear-cut developmental patterns, as well as the related clichés, such as total war, industrial war, and wars among the people.

There are also clear regional and national dimensions. From the viewpoint of the 2010s, the history of China appears of much greater relevance than it did during the period covered by this book down certainly to the 1970s, if not later. Now, the story of how China became a republic, remained united, held off Japan, and was won by the Communists emerges as one of the key strands of modern military history. Earlier episodes in Chinese military history emerge as significant, not least, but not only, in terms of this strand. In the 1920s, the defeat of regionalism, in the shape of the warlords, was a key development in Chinese history, as it left the Guomindang (Chinese Nationalists) and Communists to battle for control over a country that both wished to keep united, a unity achieved in 1949 with the exception of continued Guomindang control in Taiwan. Moreover, the military history of China offers other perspectives, both of relative importance and of general relevance. For example, consideration of the scale of conflict in China in the 1920s and 1930s serves as a corrective to any focus on the contemporary situation within Europe. Furthermore, the role of the warlords in China serves as a corrective to the tendency to consider modern warfare in terms of modern states. Instead, the divisive tendencies seen in many countries recently and currently, notably Lebanon, Afghanistan, Congo, Iraq, Syria, and the Ivory Coast, were also present earlier. They both helped provoke and reflected civil conflict.

I have benefited from opportunities to develop ideas offered here provided by invitations to lecture at the Royal College of Defence Studies, the University of Oxford, the New York Historical Society, Radley College, the World Affairs Council of Delaware, and to the D Group. The advice on a previous draft from Stan Carpenter, Guy Chet, Luigi Loreto, Albert Nofi, Kaushik Roy, Anthony Saunders, Mark Stevens, Harold Tanner, and Heiko Werner Henning has been of great value. It is a great pleasure to dedicate this book to Kate and Dominic Powell.

Abbreviations

AWM	Canberra, Australian War Memorial
BL Add	London, British Library, Department of Western Manuscripts, Additional Manuscripts
JMH	*Journal of Military History*
LH	London, King's College, Liddell Hart Archive
NA	London, National Archives
RGS	Royal Geographical Society
RUSI	Royal United Services Institute

Chapter One

Introduction

Is land warfare obsolescent? That might appear to be the conclusion of a consideration of the period from 1860 to the present. In these years, the results of war were apparently repeatedly dictated by the respective weight of the resources deployed by the two sides, before being superseded, from 1945, by nuclear, and then thermonuclear, capability. This book will consider these points, and will, however, suggest a very different conclusion.

There are important conceptual, methodological, and historiographical issues involved in the historical study of land warfare, as with other branches of history, not least the dominance of master narratives.[1] Told from the present, looking back, history, including military history, inevitably shifts to reflect changing perspectives. It does so in a number of respects. In part, it is because at each point in the present, and therefore in the past, people are looking forward and considering their options and problems in that light. There are the questions to consider, the emphasis placed on specific ones, the relationships discerned between particular factors, and the methods adopted to analyze and explain them. This movable, moving, and to be moved perspective is taken further because the past is classically shaped in order to produce narratives and explanations of change. As a result, there are not only implicit notions of the significance of particular episodes, but also wider understandings of their mutual relationship through time.

To query the standard understanding of a particular war, or even not to regard it as of wider significance, both militarily and politically, is therefore often to challenge broader explanatory accounts. These accounts take on further importance in terms of the intellectual (and career) capital invested in them by academics and with reference, even more significantly, to military doctrine and to strategic, operational, and tactical discussion and training. "Learning from the past" is never value free or passive, even though that is the implication of the term *learning*.

There is the related issue of timing. For those considering the history of war during the late twentieth century, which was a period of major worldwide expansion in higher education, historical publications, and formal military education, the subject was very much defined by recent major wars between similarly armed powers. Only "major powers" could afford a decent military infrastructure. This situation encouraged a focus on the history and needs of these powers. Many commentators, moreover, had served in the Second World War (1939–45) or, at least, lived through it. Similarly, previous generations had served in the First World War (1914–18) or, indeed, in other conventional struggles, notably the Franco-Prussian (1870–71) and Russo-Japanese (1904–5) Wars. Moreover, these conflicts and the analysis of them, with lessons learned based on best practice, affected patronage practices and promotion structures within the military, both then and subsequently.

Although there was no similar conflict after 1945, the impact of the Cold War made such a focus on major wars appear appropriate. This was particularly so in the form of preparation for a full-scale struggle between NATO (the North Atlantic Treaty Organization founded in 1949) and the rival Soviet-directed Warsaw Pact. This was founded in 1955 by the Soviet Union and incorporated its Eastern European satellite states. It was dissolved in 1991 with the end of the Soviet Union and of Communism in Eastern Europe. Such a struggle would probably have been a cataclysmic Third World War. The focus of such a struggle on land would have been Europe, and that focus in planning and preparation made recent large-scale conflicts in Europe appear the necessary historical context for a discussion of war.

Linked to this, a clear chronological pattern in the type and vocabulary of warfare was drawn, that of the rise of modern, supposedly total war. This warfare was generally presented as having its genesis within the period covered in chapter 2, in the decade 1861–71, namely in the American Civil (1861–65) and Franco-Prussian (1870–71) Wars, then coming to fruition in the two world wars, and subsequently serving as the backdrop to the development and planned use of nuclear weaponry. In practice, nuclear weaponry, although extensively deployed, was not employed after 1945, or, rather, it has not hitherto been used in conflict.

In addition, it is unclear why modern warfare, as opposed to other periods of warfare, deserves the description "total." The destructiveness of modern warfare is striking, notably in the 2010s in countries such as South Sudan and Syria, but in percentage terms of population lost, it is not notably greater than that in many earlier periods, for example, in the wide-ranging conquests of the Mongol leader Genghis Khan in the early thirteenth century and those of Timur two centuries later. Moreover, some ancient battles, such as Cannae (216 BCE), had very heavy death tolls. Modern war itself is a curious concept and is something of a movable feast. The start of the industrialization of warfare is hard to pin to a specific period. It can be argued that, without the mass-production of the tools of war, war is not total. In this case, however, how industrial must manufacture be to be termed mass-production? In practice, the mass-production of weapons went through several phases going back centuries before the Industrial Revolution that began in the late eighteenth century. Saxon and Viking warriors were armed with mass-produced weapons and armor, arrowheads were mass-produced by new techniques in England during the Wars of the Roses in the late fifteenth century, and Tudor armorers mass-produced weapons in England in the sixteenth. Separately, sometimes so-called new technologies are reinventions or versions of older ones, albeit with a more efficient manufacturing process.

Perhaps, therefore, modern war has more to do with different ways of thinking about tactical, operational, and strategic problems than it does with weapons. And yet, that is not helpful either, as similar tactical, operational, and strategic solutions have been found more than once in the past, and often long before the advent of so-called modern war.

A more profound critique is that the commonplace notion that history can be neatly pigeonholed into discrete episodes that fit together linearly is not supported by evidence. Moreover, the problem with categorizing and trying to make things fit into a system is that there are always exceptions that will not fit, plus inconvenient overlaps. The danger is that making things fit becomes an end in itself. With Iraq, Afghanistan, and Syria, however, the West's enemies do not share the West's views on waging war according to categories. Categories only really work when all the protagonists follow the same war-making rules. That is uncommon, as the Vietnam War showed in the 1960s and early 1970s. In conceptual terms, variety is the key concept. As a result, knowing what happened in n different cases does not allow the prediction of how $n + 1$ will look or work. All n cases are, nevertheless, of interest to prepare us better to understand the $n + 1$ case when it comes along.

The idea of clear historical development was strongly offered in the 1990s, not least with the concept of "the end of history." The collapse of the Warsaw Pact and the Soviet Union in 1989–91 without war came as a major surprise. Given that China was then in effect a de facto American ally, and that an American-led coalition readily defeated the Soviet-equipped and doctrinally influenced Iraqi army in 1991, the route of large-scale conventional warfare appeared closed, by and with the development of American hegemony. This hegemony was frequently referred to as constituting a unipolar world, as opposed to the bipolar world of the Cold War. Commentators focused on this situation and therefore produced a military lexicon to match the geopolitical counterpart, with the United States referred to as reaching the position of a "hyperpower," in order to distinguish it from the merely great powers of the past.

There was a clear military counterpart to this greatness and unmatched dominance, what was called a "Revolution in Military Affairs," later termed a "Transformation," one in which technological, organizational, and conceptual advances had apparently given the United States a capacity to visit a military—that is, precise—version of total war on its opponents rather than an antisocietal version. A modern, cutting-edge military could deliver results without a mass conscript army or the use of nuclear weaponry. War appeared obsolescent to some commentators, notably American ones. Why seek to oppose the United States?

A reaction to this situation and the prevailing views of it, however, gathered pace in the 1990s and burst into full prominence in the 2000s. This reaction principally involved what were termed "wars among the people," namely intractable and bloody sectarian struggles motivated by a range of factors, but energized and made particularly violent by racial and religious hatred. These conflicts, notably those in Rwanda (1994) and in the former Yugoslavia from 1992 to 1999, but also elsewhere, for example in the Caucasus, suggested a different narrative and analysis of war.

This approach was given a particular slant and energy by those arguing that a more global approach to war needed to be adopted. This thesis had two purposes, first to understand the context, experience, and consequences of war as a whole, and second to bring non-Western perspectives into play to examine Western capabilities and the distinctiveness of the Western trajectory.

These ideas were galvanized in the 2000s by the acute difficulties faced by American-dominated Western forces operating in Afghanistan and Iraq once the postconquest phase was over in each case, in 2001 and 2003, respectively. These difficulties gave force to the call for an approach to war that, first, was not focused on technology and on the resulting real or apparent related capability gaps, but, second, instead addressed the issues involved in asymmetric warfare in a more perceptive fashion.[2]

That was scarcely a new call, as it had long been heard, not only by those concerned to resist Western force, but also, within the West, from politicians and commentators keen to emphasize the role of willpower in military capability and effectiveness. These commentators tended to focus on the "people under arms." In theory, the latter were the armed civilian population, although in practice many former conscripts or retired military personnel were included. The "people under arms" were supposed to provide willpower as well, rather than simply the numbers necessary for modern war.

More particularly, the American experience in the Vietnam War had encouraged an awareness in the late 1960s and early 1970s of the limitations in specific contexts of being the "cutting-edge," conventional military power or powers. This had implications for the very concept of being cutting edge.

This awareness was downplayed subsequently as the American (and British) military reverted to a Cold War focus on conventional conflict in the late 1970s.[3] However, the awareness was revived in response to conflict in Iraq and Afghanistan in the 2010s. The reexamination of the past in a search for new significances and resonances was further accelerated in the early 2010s as the "Arab Spring" of 2011 led to bitter and intractable civil conflicts in Libya and Syria.

Yet, by the mid-2010s, there were also signs of a new narrative in place. Alongside alarm due to North Korean atomic and missile plans and the threatening unpredictability of the North Korean decision-making process, confrontation between China and Japan deepened. As a result, there was increasing talk of an Asian arms race and of possible confrontation between China and the United States. This tendency was further encouraged by Russian aggression in Ukraine and by the possibility that such aggression would also be seen in the Baltic, thereby creating a fundamental crisis for NATO, that of defending vulnerable member states, particularly Estonia.

These issues led to a movement, in tasking, strategy, procurement, doctrine, and training, back toward conventional warfare, similar to that of the Cold War but without its mass. However, Russian operations in Crimea and Ukraine in the 2010s led to an interest in what, in the 2000s, was defined first as "compound warfare" and then, more successfully, as "hybrid warfare," that involving conventional forces alongside irregulars. In Crimea and Ukraine, the Russians provided "weekend" volunteers and, in practice, mercenaries paid and instructed by Russia. An understanding of the past in light of what was supposedly relevant was therefore ripe for revision,[4] although this understanding was seen more commonly among the military, with its instrumentalist, and often short-term, approach, than in academe.

Separately, there was the continuing issue of particular service perspectives. Navies and air forces were, and are, far more prone to focus on conventional warfare, while armies have tended, notably since 1990, to devote far more attention to counterinsurgency warfare or COIN. This again is a contrast between services that greatly affects readings of the past—a contrast, moreover, seen more generally across time. More broadly, questions of prioritization, with all that they entail, are scarcely new. They helped determine strategic planning and all that went with it.[5] Military history cannot be safely abstracted from these questions.

Learning from the past for the benefit of the future is the key element in military education. Clearly, the future is the element for which militaries prepare. That is their purpose and need. Yet there is no data set for the future, nor any language devised for it other than that based on the past. The present may appear to offer an alternative, but the present is simply a moment on the cusp of time between past and future. Moreover, as a consequence, the values and experiences of the present are necessarily understood in terms of what came earlier, while the present is prepared for in what to it is the past.

Yet, if the past necessarily offers what will be studied, that, as already indicated, does not leave clear how it should be studied. At the most basic level, there is the question of what past? Indeed, if the past is to be the guide, there are the issues of what past should be scrutinized, of how it should be understood in the present, and of what future is being envisaged. These issues are different but linked in dynamic interaction, for the past that is considered is set in part by anticipations of the future, and by the extent to which the near-future rapidly becomes the past.

The present day provides a classic instance. In the period covered by most military experience, both of the serving military and of their educators, there have been abrupt changes in the present, thereby resulting in very different accounts of a searchable past. Most crudely, as already noted, the Western powers have moved from a concern with symmetrical conflict in the 1980s to asymmetrical in the 1990s–2000s, and then back, on a smaller scale, to symmetrical, although with an ongoing commitment to asymmetrical conflicts. That account of recent changes itself can be refined to reflect a considerable variety in each category, while any process of change is also greatly affected by drag processes and factors, as well as by the more concrete forms of legacy structures and practices.

THE OPERATIONAL DIMENSION

Nevertheless, this account captures a fundamental problem with the presentation of operational experience. In particular, there is a tendency to look at past episodes that most conform to present concerns, and/or to interpret the former in light of these concerns. There are related complications stemming from the absence of value-free analysis. More particularly, the competing nature of service interests very much affects the reading of operational experience, both in terms of the questions asked and the answers given. This is the case at the strategic, operational, and, indeed, tactical levels.

Here it is worth adding the caveat that distinguishing between these levels can be nebulous, indeed flawed. So also with the important question of the direction of influence between these levels. There is the more particular point that success at one level does not preclude overall failure due to difficulties at other levels. That is one of the key lessons for, and of, the operational dimension, as also for the tactical and the strategic: it is necessary to pursue an autonomous approach to each, while also being aware that such an approach has its limitations and that the multiple interactions of these levels should take center stage.

THE EXAMPLE OF AMPHIBIOUS ASSAULTS

Some of the issues involved in learning at the operational level are fully displayed in the case of joint operations in the form of amphibious assaults. These were long the crucial instance of joint operations and, in part as a result, an element of land warfare that was downplayed, because analytical "ownership" was partly, even largely, held by navies and marines. It is clear that tactical proficiency was crucial to operational and strategic success in amphibious assaults, as, indeed, in land warfare as a whole, for example in 1918, the last year of campaigning in the First World War. The powers that were most successful in amphibious assaults—Britain, the United States, and, briefly in 1941–42, Japan—were thus both because of their naval strength and because of the proficiency they developed in large part through practice. This can be seen in terms of learning curves. Each amphibious assault became a lesson for the others.

Moreover, this process took place in a context made dynamic by the learning practices of opponents. Thus, in the Second World War, the Japanese came, from 1943, to learn that it was foolish to contest the Americans on the beaches, as they were most exposed there to American firepower. For a similar reason, charges at American positions led to heavy casualties. Instead, the Japanese came to favor an attritional operational stance based on not contesting the landing beaches but, instead, on digging in in difficult terrain, especially by means of caves and tunnels. Adopted from 1944, this approach posed tactical, operational, and strategic problems for the Americans, not least in terms of both casualties and the time taken by individual campaigns. Having mastered an operational approach based on the contested landing, the Americans now had to do the same based on successful exploitation, a situation in which land warfare was to the fore, as in 1945 on Iwo Jima and Okinawa.

The Americans and British learned from landings in the Mediterranean in 1943 and early 1944 that it was difficult to deploy sufficient units to fend off counterattacks. Indeed, in Italy, at Salerno (1943) and Anzio (1944), German counterattacks were held off essentially by the use of air power and naval support. This problem encouraged the effort in Normandy in 1944 to seal the area of operations from German armor by means of bombing, particularly of bridge and rail links, although that was less successful than might have been hoped. Delay, not prevention, was obtained, and the combat with German armor and antitank guns had to be settled on the ground.

Another instance of learning from experience was provided by the bombardment of invasion beaches, a key instance of the use of artillery. The British preferred to focus on heavy naval fire, the Americans on air support. The latter, however, proved inadequate against the ferroconcrete defenses at Omaha Beach in Normandy: in this case, they had learned the wrong lessons from the bombardments necessary in the Pacific campaign. In Normandy, naval fire proved more appropriate as warships could stay in the area and deliver more ordnance than aircraft, and, because they had good air cover, they could do so without danger to themselves. However, in most cases of attack on bunkers and casemates, the assault had to be by ground troops, the situation that still pertains today.

Airborne attacks, in order to deploy and place troops for land combat, also improved with practice and experience, in part due to the determination to learn lessons. This was seen in the improvements from Sicily (1943) to Normandy (1944), and then to the Rhine crossing (1945). This learning process had its corollary on the Western Front in the First World War.

In October 1949, General Omar Bradley, the chairman of the American Joint Chiefs of Staff, speaking to a congressional committee discussing the reorganization of the American military, argued that the nuclear bomb had made large-scale amphibious assaults unlikely in the future.[6] Ironically, one was to be used successfully the following year by the Americans at Inchon, causing a major development in the Korean War, one from which significant strategic consequences followed.

More generally, Bradley's remark, and the very different Inchon outcome, reflected the folly of assuming at any one stage that there was, is, or will be an "ur" or fundamental state of military proficiency, and that planning and procurement should be organized accordingly. Such an approach, which is all too common, appears to make the learning of lessons an easy process, but it is mistaken. The strategic context in 1949 had been altered by atomic weaponry, and the lesson of 1945 was that this had prevented the need to rely on the large-scale landing on the main Japanese Home Islands planned by the Americans for 1946 had the Second World War not been ended by their use of atomic weapons. However, thereafter the Americans repeatedly relied on power projection in which landings played a part, including in Lebanon (1958), Grenada (1983), and Panama (1989). Moreover, proficiency again improved with practice, as the contrast between Grenada and the far-better-handled Panama operation indicated, or, again, between the Shi'a militia in Iraq defeated by Islamic State (IS) in 2014–15 and those that were more battle hardened by 2017.

Very differently, the salience of politics, and of the strategic issues involved in, and stemming from, political considerations, emerged clearly from the Somalia commitment in 1992–93: the deployment of American forces was successful, but there was a failure to confront the likely level of difficulties, including casualties that, in comparative terms, were in practice very low. As a result, the Americans withdrew in 1994 without having fulfilled their goals.[7]

This trajectory prefigured problems that were to be faced in the 2000s. Indeed, with regard to the latter, it can be argued that the Americans (and also the British) failed to assess adequately the dependence of strategic planning, and even operational-level action, on political considerations, which were significant and dynamic, both in the area of operations and in the homeland. This dependence, more generally, has been a lesson that the military has been reluctant to accept, but it is necessary for them to build it into operational learning and strategic planning, rather than keeping the latter somehow separate.

CONCLUSIONS

Broader political issues about the nature of military planning will be further developed in the future due to the current need to respond to the prospect of great-power confrontation. In particular, that prospect poses serious strategic issues of prioritization. These issues are accentuated by the limited size of the available forces. Operational-level issues of command and control in which the cohesion of forces will be challenged by techniques of cyber warfare are a more specific concern looking to the future and one emphasized by the rapid progress made in recent years. Revisiting the ground of past conflict can be useful when addressing such issues, and it is certainly encouraged in the military learning process in many states, including the United States, where the process is highly professional.

This process needs to be fully sensitive to changing political-strategic contexts and to the multiple consequences of these contexts. These points can readily be grasped. Nevertheless, it is striking how frequently writers do not discuss the specific impact of the particular contexts, whether chronological, national, and/or service, within which everyone and, notably, they themselves are thinking and writing. As a consequence, there can be a somewhat unreflective character to military history. Possibly it is because some writers appear to consider themselves almost as "warriors" at one remove in assessing military matters, a process encouraged by the focus on the individual approach to war in the "face of battle" paradigm.

That is not the intention here. We, writers and readers, are all taking part in a thinking process, and my task is to make clear that choices have been made in what to cover and how to do it. Moreover, other approaches could readily be taken. Such reflection is necessary as we face the future.

Chapter Two

A New Age of War? 1860–80

The variety of war was clear from the outset. This period saw state-to-state conflicts, notably the Franco-Prussian War (1870–71) and, less prominently for contemporaries outside South America, the Paraguayan War of 1864–70. It also saw conflicts within states, particularly the American Civil War (1861–65) and the Taiping Rebellion in China (1851–66). The impact of these varied contexts, political, geographical, economic, and social, and of the particular goals they entailed, on military means and outcomes, are readily apparent. At the same time, alongside the variety, major themes can be discerned even if they sometimes led to the grouping together of very different conflicts. Empire building sat alongside empire preservation; each related more closely to the other than might be readily apparent. Each also was seen across a range of state types and sizes.

Both empire building and empire preservation were also related to struggles over the existence, identity, and character of states, of states that wished to be empires, and of would-be states that sought by fighting for independence to resist the process of imperial incorporation. These struggles could be short term, largely taking the form of seizures of power or abortive rebellions, but, as indicated, there were also protracted civil wars, notably in China and the United States.

SOCIOECONOMIC CONTEXTS

Systemic factors encouraged warfare between, and within, states. These factors included mass politicization in an age of spreading nationalism, and rapidly rising population on a then unprecedented scale, and also the assertion, often violent, to which this nationalism frequently gave rise. The scale and volatility of major social changes were also significant, notably large-scale urbanization. So also with economic transformation, particularly the industrialization that made it easier than hitherto to mass-produce large quantities of armaments speedily and to retool rapidly for new specifications, as well as major improvements in transportation and a significant rise in agricultural production. Politicization was also focused on specific policy goals and related rifts. They could include state formation, as in Germany and Italy, and state division, as in the American Civil War and the Polish rising against Russian imperial rule in 1863.

Benefiting from economic and population growth, states were willing, and able, to deploy plentiful resources for, and to, war. Government direction over the population was expressed in mobilization for war: mobilization of manpower and of the tools for war. The directing element was scarcely new but was strengthened by nationalism. It was assumed that the bulk of the male population would serve if required, and on terms that they did not influence. Their views were not sought on the purposes and methods of warfare as a whole, or of individual wars. In this respect, civil wars were different, notably the American Civil War. More generally, however, the encouragement of enthusiasm by means of stirring up nationalist values helped produce a change in commitment.

Even if there was a lack of such commitment, that did not mean that rulers and commanders were oblivious to the condition of their forces or to casualties. Although adequate provision was difficult to secure, especially on campaign, commanders were well aware that poor food and accommodation could lead to debilitating disease. Concern about casualties might encourage caution in risking battle. Nevertheless, such concern did not prevent leaders from seeking it. Indeed, the ethos of the period placed a great premium on military success and on bravery and boldness in command. There was nothing inherently cautious about generalship or concerning ideas about generalship.

Élan was expected of commanders and troops alike. It was encouraged in military literature and training manuals. Élan was expected to carry the day irrespective of obstacles such as charging into destructive rifle fire. There was a lack of willingness to face the fact that technological change in the form of mass-produced rifled weapons (available from the 1840s), along with pointed bullets that expanded in the barrel to make a gas-tight seal (notably the Minié bullet), meant higher rates of fire and greater accuracy than had been considered when the manuals were first written. The battles of the American Civil War and the Wars of German Unification, for example, Gravelotte-Saint Privat in 1870, demonstrated this by the number of casualties inflicted by bolt-action rifles firing pointed bullets.

The rise of the plan was also a key element in the psychology of war, notably the belief in the possibility that everything could be calculated, understood, and planned. This belief in large-scale plans was encouraged by the large size of the armies involved. The plan became an aspect of boldness and thus of bravery.

QUESTIONS OF SIGNIFICANCE

Beginning this book in 1860 both captures a sense among contemporaries that major changes were occurring and, inevitably, places an emphasis on those, rather than on changes over previous decades. For example, simply to take land warfare, those decades had seen revolutionary advances in transportation with railroads and steam-propelled ships; the use of the telegraph to send messages; the introduction and diffusion of more lethal infantry weaponry, notably the percussion cap for ignition and, subsequently, the "needle gun"; and the experience of symmetrical conflict and a form of trench warfare in the Crimean War of 1854–56 between Russia on the one hand and a coalition of Britain, France, Piedmont, and Turkey on the other. Moreover, in terms of the global dimension, the British suppression of the Indian Mutiny in 1857–59 was the most significant episode in Indian military history prior to the world wars.

So, there is a degree of foregrounding a particular account of the West, and, indeed, the world, in putting an emphasis on the American Civil War (1861–65) and on the Wars of German Unification (1864–71), to employ terms that were only valid in hindsight: the conflicts could have become the War of Southern Independence and Prussia's failed drive for hegemony. Certainly, the achievement of Italian unification in 1859–60 contrasted with failure in 1848–49. The emphasis on these conflicts, moreover, emerged partly only in hindsight. Although followed by foreign observers,[1] the American Civil War, in particular, attracted less attention among commentators outside America, then and later, than it arguably merited. Whereas British, French, and, in particular, German military advisers and models were very important elsewhere in the world over the following decades, this was not the case with their American counterparts. Even in nearby Latin America, there was an emphasis instead on emulating Europe. Such emulation tended to focus on France until its complete defeat by Germany in 1870–71, and then on Germany, the latter notably so for the armies of Chile and Japan.

In part, this stress was a matter of consequences. Although important for the development of the United States, the Civil War confirmed its already existing unity and apparent destiny. It would have been more interesting to contemporaries had the Civil War led to an independent Confederacy and, even more, had Britain and France intervened, or had the victorious Union thereafter fought Britain in Canada and/or France in Mexico in order to confirm and demonstrate a regional superiority. None of these outcomes materialized, despite much speculation about their possibility and concerning their likely consequences, speculation that included British planning and preparations for the defense of Canada. The American Civil War did not become the wide-ranging international struggle that it might have become and that appeared a serious prospect in 1861–62 when both Britain and France considered intervention.

This point serves as a reminder of the great significance of counterfactuals (what-ifs) in the history of war. This significance can be greatly underplayed if a historical approach that focuses only on what occurred is adopted. In practice, military planning, procurement, and training have to deal with counterfactuals.

The Wars of German Unification, in contrast to the American Civil War, radically altered European power politics and the hierarchy of states, were easy to report, and delivered rapid, as well as dramatic, results. Prussian successes appeared to reflect the professionalism of war, and all of these factors encouraged attention. It was as if the triumphs of Napoleon I of France in 1796–1809 had been repeated, but more rapidly and with more lasting effect. The problems of war, tactical, operational, and strategic, appeared to have been overcome. Campaigning could be decisive, and rapidly so.

This was an illusion. Unable to prevail, either in offensive or in defensive warfare, Napoleon failed in 1812 and 1813 and was overthrown in 1814 and again in 1815; Germany lasted longer as a great power but totally failed in 1918 and, again, after a revival in military fortunes in 1939–42, in 1945. After the Franco-Prussian War of 1870–71, Germany's total failure in its next international (as opposed to colonial) war, the First World War

(1914–18), was to show that campaigning could not be rapidly decisive in a planned fashion.

This illusion, nevertheless, had meanwhile encouraged the idea that there were particular lessons to learn and that, if German methods were understood and emulated, then success was likely. To this end, recent military history acquired a far greater degree of purpose, which in turn led to a rereading and rewriting of earlier periods. In a reversion, after the focus on Revolutionary and Napoleonic France in 1792–1815, to interest in the Prussia of Frederick the Great (r. 1740–86), Germany appeared as the paradigm power for land warfare, an assessment encouraged by the notion that Britain was very clearly so at sea. Particular attention was devoted to the Prussian/German General Staff system and to its apparent formulaic ability to implement plans effectively. Recent military history served as a form of education for, and in, this staff system, alongside war-gaming through maneuvers.

In practice, there was no one type of conflict on land in the 1860s and 1870s, and no one means of ensuring success. Armies operated in specific political, social, economic, and environmental contexts, and notions of best practice, and of technological and organizational capability, have to be understood accordingly. This is made abundantly clear by considering, alongside Europe, Latin America and China, in each of which there were important conflicts that came to a conclusion. In Mexico, a civil war that included large-scale foreign intervention ended with a total Republican victory in 1867. The Paraguayan War, or War of the Triple Alliance, of 1864–70 saw complete defeat for Paraguay. In China, the Taiping were crushed. These conflicts were not more generally studied, which meant that the lessons they offered received far less attention. The states involved had no tradition of a "modern" military education system.

Each conflict, however, saw a mixture of conventional warfare with insurgency and counterinsurgency campaigning. The interplay of the two elements helped ensure that a speedy victory was not possible. Considered differently, this interplay ensured that victory in part depended on definition and, in particular, the willingness, having won a conventional victory, to accept a degree of guerrilla opposition.

CHINA

The Taiping Rebellion, a large-scale revivalist movement, that of the Heavenly Kingdom of Peace aimed at the overthrow of the ruling Manchu dynasty, was the most destructive of all civil wars, with a death toll of twenty to thirty million, indeed a death toll and a length that each far exceeded those of the American Civil War. It remains one of the least-known major wars. As with the jihad in West Africa in the early nineteenth century, ideological conviction during the rebellion was an important tool in battle and on campaign. Such conviction both helped lead troops to cross the killing ground in the first case, and encouraged persistence in the face of inadequate logistics in the latter. These factors remain pertinent today.

Ideological conviction made the Taiping reckless of their lives and thus formidable in battle, although their seriously divided leadership was badly flawed. Taiping armaments were not modern, and the Taiping relied heavily on spearmen, halberdiers, and matchlock muskets, with the last placed in the final line in battle,[2] but Taiping numbers were considerable. About three-quarters of a million men took the major city of Nanjing on March 19, 1853: mines created breeches in the wall, through which the outer city was stormed, and human wave attacks carried the inner city's walls. However, there was no inevitable closure in success, as the inability to capture Beijing with a northern expedition begun in 1853, and the, somewhat different, failure to take the city of Shanghai in 1860 and 1862, indicated. In each case, Anglo-French firepower proved significant in the successful defense against the Taiping. In addition, foreigners, the American Frederick Townshend Ward, the Frenchman Prosper Giquel, and the British Charles Gordon, organized and led largely Chinese forces, trained and equipped in a Western fashion, that played a major role in gaining the initiative in successful advances. The Foreign Rifle Corps, the Ever Triumphant Army, and the Ever Victorious Army, as they were called, also benefited from Western artillery.[3] The Taiping were affected by civil war, notably in 1856, and by an inability to maintain their dynamic and therefore the initiative. Nanjing was lost in 1864, and the last Taiping force was defeated in 1866.

Success for the Chinese government took much longer than in the American Civil War, but the scale of operations in China was great, while it was difficult for each side to mobilize resources. Moreover, in America, it proved possible to reach a negotiated peace, in that the Confederate armies all surrendered in 1865 and there was no turn to guerrilla warfare despite the urgings of the Confederate president, Jefferson Davis. In addition, the compromise was taken forward so that, in 1873, federal troops were withdrawn from the former Confederacy, and white supremist governments then ran all the states there. This compromise was in line with the ethos and practice of

American federalism. That was a key element in the strategies of conflict and governance in the United States. No such option was possible for either side in China, no more than it was to be in the civil war of 1946–49.

CHANGES IN WARFARE

Instead of looking at irregular warfare, both counterinsurgency conflict and, somewhat differently, the warfare of Western expansionism, commentators preferred to focus on conflicts in which Western powers operated against each other in a conventional fashion. The strategic and operational means they considered might look back to Napoleonic warfare, which was extensively taught, as at West Point, the army academy in the United States, and the supposed lessons of which were deployed by military commanders and consultants in the shape of former officers who were hired elsewhere for their alleged experience.

However, there had been, and were, important changes in military and other technologies, changes that made the Napoleonic example less valid. These were, first, partly a matter of weaponry, but also, secondly, of a more profound development in the organizational and industrial technologies that made it possible to wage war with greater effectiveness, at least in terms of rapidly applied scale. As far as the first was concerned, there was a marked increase in the accuracy and rate of fire of handheld firearms, and therefore in their lethality. As far as the second was concerned, railways, steamships, and the telegraph made it possible to deploy, control, and supply troops more readily than in the past, and the combination was highly significant. Industrial and agricultural development provided more resources. State revenues rose, as did population size.

The range of technologies involved was great. For example, improvements in medical knowledge and application, in mechanical water distillation, and in the preparation and storage of provisions—notably with canned meat, dried milk powder, and margarine—made it easier for units to operate with lower rates of noncombat casualties.

Without general economic growth, business and institutional capacity, and a pro-entrepreneurial culture, the specific technological improvements would have made far less difference. However, thanks to this background, it was possible, in response to a search for what was seen as best practice, to apply and afford the large-scale use of what were judged advances. The last were in part driven in an action-reaction cycle by the need not only to pursue the newly possible but also to respond to other advances. Many difficulties were encountered, not least in testing out ideas. Nevertheless, a continued process of change now appeared as a reality as well as a possibility. This process was a key characteristic of modernity. All existing tools, arrangements, and even ideas appeared tentative and open to revision, for example, the very role of cavalry, for long a crucial arm. It was still possible to write of immutable principles in warfare, but this approach appeared less helpful or, as with the cult, notably but not only in Germany, of the Prussian general and military commentator Carl von Clausewitz, as one that had to be more abstract, given the pace of change.

Feedback mechanisms were many, varied, and cumulative in their impact, while also posing problems of strategic assessment. For example, rising population numbers made it possible to face higher casualties, and thus to use new, more lethal weaponry, rather than letting the latter serve as a deterrent to campaigning in order to preserve smaller forces. In some states, rising population numbers could be tapped not only by conscription but also by developing systems of reservists so that continued military value could be derived from those who had been trained while conscripted.

Greater firepower certainly affected tactical practice, challenging established assumptions and equations between attack and defense. However, the extent to which greater firepower apparently increased casualty rates is not straightforward, since battles from long before the age of firearms could result in high, indeed very high, casualties. While casualty rates rose during the nineteenth century as firepower increased, the percentage of casualties to men engaged in a battle probably did not.

More generally, the relationship between firepower and casualties is not a simple equation because of the many other factors involved. These included the relationships between the types of firepower, most crudely artillery and rifles. This complexity affected the accuracy of contemporary readings about the extent to which general and specific advances in firepower had made particular formations and tactics more or less viable, and thus responsible for victory or defeat. Generals and commentators struggled to come to terms with weapons, tactics, and casualty rates, for example accepting that cavalry was increasingly vulnerable. The operational and strategic consequences of the tactical possibility of higher casualty rates were not to the fore, a situation, however, that was eventually to change during the First World War.

AMERICAN CIVIL WAR, 1861–65

The American Civil War was a bloody one, with over one million dead or wounded, although with relatively little loss of life among civilians. The fighting was limited to a comparatively small part of the country, indeed a smaller percentage than that in many civil wars, for example that in Spain in 1936–39 and China in 1946–49, but there was a great variety of conflict in the Civil War. This included set-piece battles, large-scale sieges, naval and riverine warfare, guerrilla and counterinsurgency operations, raiding, and trench warfare.

Increasingly destructive weapons gave troops little or no time to find shelter. And in a culture of attack such as that in the nineteenth century, the cost could be high. The idea that the attack would always win if the attackers had sufficient resolve was based on a poor understanding of changing firepower. As an alternative to the advance of the entire force in regular formations, notably lines and columns, rushes forward and going to ground while another part of the attacking force rushed forward, the whole process repeated as necessary to force the enemy back, was one way to reduce casualties. However, it was not always well applied in practice due to poor discipline. Battlefield discipline was a constant problem because of poor training and confusion, notably over uniforms and where the enemy was located or concentrated.

The high military casualties reflected the degree to which the popularly grounded determination of the two sides, based on a conviction of righteousness, was underlined by military factors. In part, this was a matter of the use of new firearms. The percussion-lock rifle and the Minié bullet fired from rifled (rather than smoothbore) muskets were deadly, and notably so at the expense of frontal assaults, which tended to take the form of mass attacks by close-packed units. Casualty rates are a function of the size of the lethal zone, which increased in depth with the increasing range and accuracy of rifled firearms. This meant that an attacker was subjected to deadly fire for longer than hitherto with smoothbore muskets. Even if a bullet missed soldiers at the front of an attacking wave, it could still kill those behind. The lethal zone with rifled muskets at the time of the American Civil War was about five hundred yards deep. A smoothbore had a range of no more than two hundred yards and was only accurate for about fifty to seventy-five yards. The rifle was accurate to about six hundred yards.

Defenders who stood their ground could cut down an attack before it reached them. This undermined infantry tactics as taught at West Point. The accuracy of rifled muskets moved tactics away from the use of volley fire in order to meet an attack. Volley fire made up for the inaccuracy of smoothbore muskets. In contrast, men armed with rifled muskets could take aim at individuals if they chose, which had not been a realistic proposition hitherto. This was aided by the provision of better sights than were fitted to smoothbores. As a consequence, battles could lead to more wounded and worse wounds, putting pressure on medical care.

Battle ranges were rarely greater than three hundred yards, especially if the terrain was difficult, such as in the Battle of the Wilderness on May 5–7, 1864, and often one hundred yards or even less. Some exchanges of fire were at no more than thirty yards. The situation was complicated by the huge variety of weapons that armed the two sides. Although the Enfield 1853 rifled musket was an important weapon, others came from France and Austria (the 1854 Lorenz rifle), and the Union made the Springfield 1855 and 1861 models. There were also repeating breechloaders such as the 1860 Henry, the Spencer (1860), and the Colt revolving rifle (1855). The issue of rates of fire is complicated by the use of some magazine-fed breechloaders, such as the Henry and the Spencer, which could fire faster than muskets whether rifled or smoothbore. The rate of fire of a rifled musket was marginally quicker than a smoothbore because the former needed only seventeen actions to load and fire, compared to the smoothbore, which needed eighteen. In practical terms, this was probably insignificant as the rate of fire depended on the calmness (steadiness) when charged or receiving fire, and that calmness (steadiness) came with experience.

So also with the artillery, the location of which was crucial to the course of many battles. For example, on January 2, 1863, in the Battle of Stones River, a Confederate advance against retreating Union forces was blocked by concentrated artillery fire from fifty-eight guns that caused 1,800 casualties and obliged the Confederates to retreat. Earlier, on December 31, 1862, on the first day of that battle, Union infantry and artillery had eventually beaten off Confederate attacks. Moreover, the Confederate Army of Northern Virginia suffered a casualty rate of 20 percent or more at each of the Battles of Seven Days, Second Bull Run, Antietam, and Chancellorsville, leading to ninety to one hundred thousand battle casualties in Robert E. Lee's first year in command (1862–63).

More generally, the Confederacy mobilized 80 percent of its military-age whites, but by the end of the war, a quarter of this manpower pool was dead and another quarter maimed. These casualty rates were far greater than those in the European wars of the 1860s, in part because the latter were far shorter and were fought over a smaller area, the length being the key issue. One-campaign conflicts, such as the Austro-Prussian War of 1866, could be deadly, but they were also limited wars.

In the American Civil War, the determination to persist strategically, and the attritional quality of the fighting at the tactical and, sometimes, operational levels, were important. Signs of what were later to be seen as total war were also significant. Alongside a willingness, crucially on both sides, to take heavy casualties, there was an ability to employ large quantities of resources. However, there was an unwillingness on the Confederate side to use the manpower offered by slaves.

The Napoleonic Wars, as then taught, notably at West Point, following the maxims of Antoine-Henri, Baron Jomini, did not provide a ready guide for fighting the Civil War or, indeed, a helpful one for later analysis of it. Although the Napoleonic Wars had been lengthy as a whole, individual conflicts between France and either Austria or Prussia had been short in the 1800s and the early 1810s. Moreover, after the Napoleonic Wars finally ended in 1815, Western commentators had become used to short wars, such as those in Europe in 1821, 1823, 1830–31, 1848–49, 1854–56, and 1859–60. Indeed, the 1815 campaign that ended Napoleon's attempt to regain power can be seen as the first in this process. It was expected that, in future conflicts, there would be a major battle that would prove a decisive encounter, and that at any rate, even if not, the conflict would be short. This assumption was to be apparently vindicated by the wars waged in Europe between the Polish rising in 1863 and the end of the Second Balkan War in 1913.

A quick war was sought by both sides in 1861 for political and military reasons. Neither was prepared for a lengthy struggle, and the pattern sought was that of the Mexican-American War of 1846–48, the most recent conventional conflict (as opposed to fighting with Native Americans) in which America had been involved and one in which many American commanders on both sides had taken part. There was no cultural, ideological, political, social, or institutional commitment in the United States to a long war, one requiring a large-scale mobilization of resources. There was, moreover, a lack of mental flexibility in assessing alternatives.

The American Civil War could have gone that way and have been the short struggle that the First World War was to be for the Americans (1917–18), although that itself was a formidable effort for them. As a reminder of the indeterminacy of sides, events, and outcome, political and military factors could have gone in very different directions in 1861. It was not certain which slave states would join the Confederacy. Missouri, Kentucky, Maryland, Delaware, and the parts of Virginia that became West Virginia did not do so; and it was initially unclear that North Carolina and Virginia would. Had the latter two remained outside the revolutionary secession, it would have been far less threatening. The extent to which British North America had divided in 1775–83, with Canada, Florida, and, indeed, the West Indies not following the Thirteen Colonies into revolution, indicated the contingent character of such episodes. This was more generally the case with civil wars in particular, and also with coalition warfare.

As another instance of contingency, the Union forces subsequently might have been sufficiently successful in the early stages to persuade or force the Confederacy to end the war. On the Union side, pressure for a one-campaign outcome led to an advance into Virginia and an encounter battle at First Bull Run/Manassas on July 21, 1861. This was a battle in part determined by the arrival of reinforcements. The battle demonstrated that neither side had an army that matched the seriousness of their task, while Union command proved particularly flawed.[4] The Mexican War of 1846–48 and policing operations against Native Americans were not effective training grounds for the Civil War. Many officers had cut their teeth in the Mexican War, but it was very different, militarily, organizationally, and politically, to the Civil War. In 1861, the US army was only fourteen thousand strong. Neither the Union nor the Confederacy was prepared for a major conflict in 1861: this was as true of the attitudes of their commanders as of the resources available; the ability to make effective use of large numbers of troops had not been developed in peacetime.

Indeed, 1861 saw both the creation of a new military structure, that of the Confederacy, and the massive expansion of the military of the American state, the Union side. As such, it was a significant expansion in overall Western military capability, although it was only to be a temporary one. The Confederacy's remarkable feat of eventually mobilizing virtually every man of military age was strongly rooted in its slave-based economy. Proportionally, the manpower turnout was probably only ever matched by the Romans during the Second Punic War and the Germans in the Second World War, both of whom relied heavily on slave labor for their economy.

Having been defeated at First Bull Run/Manassas, the Union reorganized its forces in the East into the Army of the Potomac, developing a well-disciplined, well-equipped, and large army. However, that in turn created problems because its commander, the young and arrogant, as well as politically partisan, Major General George McClellan, also replaced Winfield Scott, the perceptive general in chief, thus adding overall strategic direction to his command of the Union's largest field army. This situation further increased the Union focus on the Eastern Theater and encouraged a narrowing of strategy to the goal of capturing Richmond, the Confederate capital.[5] Nevertheless, that was not immediately apparent as, after the battle, there was a lull in the fighting in Virginia. This reflected not simply the problems of developing effective field armies, but also the lack of drive of the commanders, especially McClellan, although his opposite number, Joseph Johnston, was not at the forefront of offensive command.

Subsequently, McClellan's advance on Richmond along the James River in May 1862, after a landing to the east of the city, could have been a decisive blow. However, he was better at organizing for battle than at winning it. More specifically, McClellan lacked the fixity of purpose and ability to give rapid operational effect to strategic planning, and he also greatly overestimated Confederate strength, which led him to accentuate his natural caution. Johnston's successor, Robert E. Lee, succeeded in blocking McClellan's cautious advance in the Seven Days Battles (June 26–July 2, 1862) and went on to regain the initiative. This success on land made the Union ability to move troops by sea far less relevant.

Thanks to the Confederate revival in 1862, it became clear that there would be a longer war. This realization led, notably on the part of the Union, to the mobilization of resources and to changes in strategy, the two processes being linked, but also different. The North had far more resources to mobilize, and did so to great effect, a process aided by the maritime blockade of the Confederacy, which was an operation on an impressive scale that was an important counterpoint to the land war. Yet there were also major issues in effectiveness, in the utilization of resources, in the establishment of predictable and regular operating systems, and in the creation of battle-winning armies.

As in other wars, an advantage in overall resources, while extremely useful, notably in recovering from failure, did not prove easy to turn into capacity and capability, let alone into success. Although far more markedly so due to a lack of preparation in 1861, there was a parallel with elements of the First World War, in that it proved difficult to raise large forces for effective use in the field, despite being easy to provide the mass of armed numbers. In the Civil War, indeed, there were serious problems of supply, training, and command. Training was particularly deficient in infantry-artillery coordination. An emphasis on will, morale, and character as the means to victory, an emphasis that drew on the presentation of the French example, notably that of Napoleon I's campaigns, proved no substitute for such training and for experience.

As a result, too many assaults lacked coordination, both between units and between arms (infantry, artillery, and cavalry). Poor planning, and an inability to implement plans, notably the interaction of moves within a planned time sequence, repeatedly emerged, as did command flaws at a number of levels. In part, this failure was due to inadequate generals on both sides. In addition, the basis for a systematic process of effective and rapid decision making was absent, as was one for the implementation of strategic plans in terms of timed operational decisions and interrelated tactical actions. As a consequence, strategies frequently lacked implementation, while operations could be poorly judged, and piecemeal tactics led to battles without overall direction.

Staff training and doctrine were inadequate on both sides in the Civil War, and they certainly did not match that in Prussia/Germany. Neither side had an effective high command, many campaigns were poorly conceived and managed,[6] and most generals failed to develop staffs up to the challenges of moving and controlling large forces and providing reliable operational planning. As a result, those commanders, such as Ulysses Grant, who were able to provide organizational sophistication, operational grasp, and tactical grip under pressure, did well. Moreover, generals needed to be able to adapt their forces to new weaponry; other technology, particularly the railroads; and tactical possibilities.

Yet, those were not the sole problems. The difficulty in coordinating attacks, at all levels, not least due to the slow nature of communications, was exacerbated by the extent of wooded cover and by terrain issues, for example watercourses on the battlefield of Shiloh,[7] and was accentuated by the extent to which subordinate commanders might not carry out their instructions. The legacy of the prevalent interpretation of the Napoleonic Wars encouraged an emulation of what were taught as the methods of Napoleon I. As a result, there was an operational emphasis on moving on interior lines and on defeating opponents in detail (i.e., separately), which, in practice, was not easy to achieve; while there was also a tactical stress on turning the opponent's flank. The first case can be seen in the Second Manassas/Bull Run campaign, in which, in the battle, which was fought on August 28–30, 1862, Lee sought to attack the Army of Virginia under John Pope while the Union forces were divided between that and the Army of the Potomac. In turn, Pope tried to destroy Stonewall Jackson's corps while it was separated from that under Longstreet.

Flanking movements by units whose speed was no greater than that of defenders frequently led, instead, to frontal assaults on defenders who had rapidly altered deployment. Linked to this, speed and surprise could not be readily achieved with inexperienced troops and commanders and in the complex simultaneity of battle. In the Battle of Fredericksburg (December 13, 1862), Ambrose Burnside, McClellan's successor in command of the Army of the Potomac, sought to turn Lee's right in order to cut his direct route to Richmond and thus cause him to fall back. In practice, however, the Union forces attacked positions on the Confederate right, were inadequately supported, and were repelled. Instead, in the battle, the Union army came to focus on frontal attacks on the Confederate left, which fell victim, with heavy casualties, to well-positioned musket and cannon fire. There was also much dependency on the weather. In January 1863, Burnside tried to move around Lee's left, only for what became the "Mud March" to be brought to a halt by heavy rain.

In early May 1863, Union attempts to outflank Lee were lost to cautious generalship, and Union forces retreated north to the other bank of the Rappahannock River. This proved that superiority in men and equipment, and the increased organizational sophistication of the Army of the Potomac,[8] could not yet be translated into an effective army capable of defeating the leading Confederate army, the Army of Northern Virginia, under Lee. As yet, it was not possible both to bring Union force to bear and to outfight the Confederates.

The war is generally presented as a triumph for Union resources, which makes the outcome somehow inevitable and can then be used to prefigure the result in the Second World War. In practice, each side had a viable strategy, and that of the Confederacy looks more viable in light of American success in the War of Independence of 1775–83 and the War of 1812 against the mighty (and far more mighty) military and fiscal resources of Britain. The

Confederacy faced the challenge of persuading its opponents that they could not win and outside observers that it was worth providing support. Taking the initiative was designed to serve one or both of these purposes, and it appeared to do so in 1862 and 1863 when Confederate forces moved north. In 1864, fighting on also provided the possibility that Abraham Lincoln, an opponent of compromise peace, would lose the presidential election to McClellan, the Democrat candidate, who was ready to negotiate with the South.

The campaigning was decisive in that it thwarted those goals: the Confederate strategy could not be implemented. Confederate moves north were blocked in battle at Antietam (1862) and Gettysburg (1863). Moreover, in each case, heavy casualties were imposed on Lee, in large part due to the consequences of mass frontal Confederate attacks on defenses that had not been suppressed by artillery. These losses forced Lee to be cautious in exploitation, both during the battles and subsequently.

In turn, the success of Union forces around Atlanta in July–September 1864, a success that owed much to poor Confederate generalship,[9] helped Lincoln win the election. The war was then over within six months: both the political and the military equations had changed fundamentally, and these dimensions were closely linked.[10]

Success around Atlanta brought to fruition the war in the West, which had become a war in the South. The force-space ratio in the West was very different from that in the East. This created both problems and opportunities for commanders. There was a greater need for mobility and more opportunity for it. The Cumberland, Mississippi, and Tennessee Rivers provided the Union forces with invasion routes, but that did not guarantee success. Instead, Grant was to create opportunities for mobility, both in 1862 with his advance into Tennessee and in 1863 around Vicksburg, the crucial Confederate fortress on the Mississippi. Once he made the campaign there fluid, Grant gained opportunities to achieve concentrations of strength that enabled him to take successful initiatives and drive the Confederates in on the city where they could be besieged. With the surrender of Vicksburg on July 4, 1863, Confederate resources west of the Mississippi were cut off. In effect, Winfield Scott's 1861 plan for an "Anaconda" strategy that included bisecting the Confederacy on the Mississippi axis had been achieved, although it had scarcely been a speedy process. The Union forces sustained their strategic advantage in November 1863 by defeating the Confederates at the key rail junction of Chattanooga, which provided an opportunity for further advance into the South, especially toward Atlanta. The move into the Confederate rear was now possible, and in a very different context from that of amphibious assaults.

The campaigns in the West also saw a more ruthless means of war adapted to operational ends. In the East, Pope had claimed in 1862 that it was legitimate to confiscate and destroy Confederate property. Grant did the same in order to hit Confederate supplies and, thus, war making. While a parallel to the naval blockade, this approach was more direct and obvious. A harsh approach to private property, as well as his emphasis on necessity, enabled Grant to live off the land. In 1863, he used this practice in order to maneuver round Vicksburg.[11]

The following year, William Tecumseh Sherman destroyed $100 million worth of property as he set out to destroy the will of Confederate civilians by making "Georgia howl." His march from Atlanta in November and December 1864 did indeed, in his words, "cut a swath through to the sea," in the shape of the Atlantic Ocean. This was land warfare to a clear strategic purpose in which ideology and will played major roles as "just war" was defined and implemented in a domestic context.[12] Sherman set out to punish the Confederates and to cripple their morale, as well as to destroy their infrastructure, and, with far more opportunities, he did so far more effectively than Confederates who tried to affect Union opinion by raids, notably Jubal Early. The ability to spread devastation unhindered across the Southern hinterland helped to destroy Confederate civilian faith in the war, and it also made the dire penalties that could follow guerrilla warfare readily apparent.[13]

The strategic challenge posed by the size of the Confederacy was thereby destroyed and the Confederacy undermined. The contrast with the failure, in a far larger area, of attempts in the 1930s by, first, Nationalist and, then, Japanese forces to suppress opposition in China is instructive. As with other comparisons, this one directs attention to the specific nature of crucial factors in particular contexts.

Sherman's advance was the culmination and application of the earlier Union success in the Western Theater. In 1862 and 1863, Union pressure and triumphs there had not prevented Lee from advancing in, and from, Virginia. To a considerable extent, it had been possible indeed for the Confederacy to trade space in the West for time with which to attack in the East. This potentially war-winning formula, however, did not succeed. After that, the Union forces were able to exploit their success in the West in order to attack what could otherwise have been the defense in depth that the Confederacy enjoyed in the East.

Political will was accompanied by military means in what at last became a fusion of first-rate leadership.[14] Grant, general in chief of the Union army from 1864, a promotion gained through success, defeated Lee, still commander of the Army of Northern Virginia, with an attritional pounding. Grant worked through the experience of the war and added a strategic purposefulness and impetus to Union military policy, one that matched the ability of Union soldiers to accustom themselves to warfare and continue to provide effective service. There were high desertion rates, but general success in familiarizing the citizenry with conflict.[15]

Grant subordinated the individual battle to the repeated pressure of campaigning against the Confederates and inflicting cumulative damage. High-tempo fighting was imposed on Lee who, instead, exemplified the Napoleonic focus on battlefield victory, as with his attacking attempts at Gettysburg in 1863. The comparison may be too pat, but it captures an important dimension of difference between Lee and Grant. By late 1864, the Confederates were without a viable strategy, military or political, while the Union had not only that of Grant but also the ability of Sherman to operate across the Confederate hinterland, thus showing that Confederate forces could not protect their people and that the war could be directly brought to areas that had hitherto avoided such devastation. Strategy and operations were in synergy for the Union. This was greatly helped by their strength in resources, but did not flow automatically from it.

LATIN AMERICA

There was much civil war elsewhere in the Americas, which, indeed, helped make the United States more similar to Latin America than to the Wars of German Unification. Conflict between Liberals and Conservatives occurred not only in the United States in the shape of the American Civil War, but also in Argentina, Guatemala, Mexico, and Uruguay, among other states. Unlike in the American Civil War, foreign intervention was a key element, with France (and Austria) intervening in Mexico and Brazil in Uruguay. The latter intervention helped broaden out the war in Uruguay into a wider regional struggle, the Paraguayan War, or the War of the Triple Alliance, of 1864–70. In response to Brazilian intervention, President Francisco López of Paraguay invaded first Brazil and then Argentina. This was a bitter conflict, characterized by serious logistical problems. Disease, especially cholera, hit the combatants hard, affecting operations. Once their opponents, especially Brazil, had mobilized their forces, the heavily outnumbered Paraguayans were in a very difficult situation. Frontal assaults on entrenched Paraguayan forces led to heavy casualties, as with the Argentinean attack at Curupaity (1866) and the Brazilian attacks at Ytororó (1868) and Itá-Ybaté (1868). Envelopment, however, proved a more effective technique, being used successfully at Piribebuy in 1869.

With the Paraguayans defeated in the field, the war, unlike with the American Civil War, then became a guerrilla struggle as the Brazilians tried to hunt down López in the barren vastness of northern Paraguay, an area of conflict again in the Gran Chaco, Bolivian-Paraguayan, War of 1932–35 (see chapter 5). In the end, as with other counterguerrilla struggles, success required the adoption of more flexible operational units, specifically flying columns, and the development of an effective intelligence system. The combination of the two led to López being surprised in his encampment in 1870, defeated, and killed.

In Mexico, foreign intervention was not sustained to the same degree, while the Republican opposition had more space in which to maneuver and the resources of a wealthier society on which to draw. The struggle between Republicans and Conservatives saw Napoleon III of France intervene from 1861 on behalf of the latter, but this intervention, although lasting longer than the American Civil War, was insufficient in scale and impact to achieve success and was cut short by French concern about Prussian schemes in Europe. In 1867, the French withdrew, and the Conservatives were totally defeated, a defeat enforced by the execution of their leaders, notably Emperor Maximilian I, Napoleon's protégé and the brother of the ruler of Austria. Had France, however, been more successful in Mexico, it would still probably have found itself committed, as Marshal Bazaine admitted, to resisting long-term guerrilla activity.

As with other episodes of foreign intervention, for example in Central America, there was the need to consider opposing intervention. Having defeated the Confederacy in 1865, American military pressure included provocative maneuvers on the Rio Grande border, as well as providing ammunition and arms to the Republicans. The belief that Napoleon had to increase his commitment to Maximilian in order to counteract the possibility of American action, Bazaine mentioning fifty thousand more troops if necessary, placed considerable pressure on him.[16]

Chapter 2
WARS OF GERMAN UNIFICATION

Explanations for military outcomes, notably at the strategic level, benefit from the avoidance of monocausal accounts. The French withdrawal from Mexico provides a good example. The intractability of the struggle was a factor, as was the threat of American intervention. However, French withdrawal also reflected the speed of the Prussian success over Austria in 1866. Indeed, compared to the conflicts in the Americas, the Prussians were able to deliver rapid victories. Scale was a factor but should not be pushed too far: the distance between Washington and Richmond is not great, and both the Austrian Empire and France were large territories.

Sweeping Prussian victories over Denmark in 1864, Austria in 1866, and France in 1870–71 gripped the attention of contemporaries. This ensured that Western and Japanese planning for land war thereafter, especially down to 1914, but even until 1944, took place in part under the shadow of Prussian (German) models and strength, whereas France had earlier been the dominant model. The Prussians sought to apply rigorous and comprehensive analysis and planning in order to reduce the element of risk and, instead, to control conflict as a process in which the systematized application of planned pressure led to predicted results. Furthermore, this planning interacted with attempts to take advantage of specific changes in the nature of war at different levels. Helmuth von Moltke, the chief of the Prussian General Staff from 1857 until 1887, adapted Napoleonic ideas of the continuous offensive to the practicalities and potential of the industrial age, including deployment by railway and telegraphed instructions.

At the tactical level, in place of frontal attack, Moltke tried to envelop opposing forces and oblige them to mount such risky frontal attacks themselves in an effort to regain their freedom of maneuver. He thereby sought, using the operational and tactical advantage, to work with the major benefits that rifled weapons, both handheld and artillery, and the scale of conflict had given the defense. The Prussians also benefited from the adaptability with which they responded to new weaponry. The Dreyse "needle" rifle could be fired four to seven times a minute, and its accuracy rate helped cause disproportionately heavy Austrian casualties in 1866.

Alongside tactical flexibility came operational skill, reflecting effective staff work. Prussia developed a system of General Staff work, and the training of staff officers gave the Prussian army a coherence that its opponents lacked. Prussian staff officers were given an assured place in a coordinated command system. Officers from the General Staff were expected to advise commanders, and the latter were expected to heed their own chiefs of staff. This system of joint responsibility contributed to a high level of planning.

Whereas Napoleon I had used separately operating corps within his army, notably in his offensives in 1805–6 (against Austria and Prussia) and 1809 (against Austria), Moltke employed independently operating armies. Furthermore, unlike Napoleon I, who concentrated his forces prior to the battle, Moltke aimed for a concentration of his armies in the battle itself.

AUSTRO-PRUSSIAN WAR, 1866

Prussian advantages were accentuated and aided by Austrian disadvantages. Thus, Moltke's skill was accentuated by the incompetence of Ludwig Benedek, the Austrian commander. Moreover, Prussian advantages in equipment and training were strengthened by Austrian disadvantages in both, including a shortage of artillery horses and a lack of understanding of ballistics. Although much was spent on the Austrian military, it was poorly spent, not least because of the emphasis in expenditure on the top-heavy bureaucracy. There was a shortage of training by means of large-scale maneuvers.[17]

Each side deployed a quarter of a million troops at Sadowa/Königgrätz, the decisive battle, fought on July 3, 1866. Benedek was in a reasonable defensive position, had better artillery, and had the possibility of using interior lines to defeat the separate Prussian armies in detail. This, however, was not easy, as Napoleon had discovered at Leipzig in 1813 when successfully attacked by Prussian, Russian, and Austrian forces. No Napoleon, Benedek was affected by an irresolution encouraged by the speed and range of the Prussian advance. In the battle, Moltke showed himself superior in maneuver, while, in combat, Prussian units possessed a flexibility their opponents lacked, ensuring that the Austrian positions were caught in the flank and hit by cross fire. Massed Austrian attacks led to heavy losses. The Prussian tactic of concentrating strength on the skirmishing line and adapting more extended formations that were less dense than columns or lines, and thus less exposed to fire, commanded attention. Cavalry played no significant role in the battle, confirming what was becoming a pattern in recent European battles.

Heavily defeated at Sadowa/Königgrätz, Austrian morale collapsed, and, without the need to conquer Austria, peace was conceded with Prussia (hereafter called Germany in this book), now dominant in Germany where Austria's allies had been overcome. There, the Prussians had again benefited from the speed of their operations. For example, at Langensalza, the Hanoverians defeated a smaller Prussian force, only for the Prussians to be able to bring up a larger force and surround them before the Hanoverians could unite with their Bavarian allies. The Hanoverians then surrendered. The conflicts in Germany were significant as the Prussian success deprived Austria of allies that could have provided over one hundred thousand troops. The war with Austria, in contrast, was won on the "frontiers," unlike the American and Mexican civil wars or the Paraguayan War.

FRANCO-GERMAN WAR, 1870–71

War with the now-outnumbered French followed in 1870–71. Unable, unlike in 1859 at the expense of Austria in northern Italy, to use the initiative offered by declaring war and initially advancing, Napoleon III had to respond to the rapid German advance. This advance had the benefit of operational and tactical strengths, while victory over Austria's allies in 1866 meant that Prussia could now draw on the whole of Germany for manpower, resources, and space.

On campaign, the German use of dispersed forces had the advantage over the more concentrated and slower-moving French armies. In part, this advantage reflected German superiority in command and control, but a fixity in purpose, and a clearly planned and ably executed strategy, was as important. Whereas the French essentially sought to muddle through, the Germans operated a coordinated command system to ensure coherence and to manage and respond to risk. There was also an emphasis on trained decision making at all levels, indeed on training so as to deliver a capacity for skilled decision making. A dynamic interaction between hierarchy and devolved decision making meant that small-unit operations supported and harmonized with those of large forces; not that this idea and practice were new. At the tactical level, the more dispersed formations favored by the Germans were less dense than columns or lines, reducing the target for French firepower. This deployment reflected a tactical adaptation to new technology that represented an end to Napoleonic warfare with its emphasis on advancing and fighting in dense columns.

Rapid German victories near the French frontier, especially the envelopment of French forces that surrendered with Napoleon III at Sedan in the spectacular debacle of a regular army, were followed in late 1870 by a

German advance on Paris and across much of northern France. The French fought on, and the new republic, ordering a *levée en masse* (universal conscription), raised a number of armies. However, the success of these largely ad hoc forces was limited. For example, the Army of the North under Louis Faidherbe, although able to win small-scale clashes, was a scratch force facing major logistical difficulties, with the Germans dominating the dynamic of the war and occupying the central place around Paris. Faidherbe's attempt to relieve Paris was defeated at Saint Quentin on January 19, 1871. With French forces engaged elsewhere in northern France, Paris was besieged and subjected to a heavy bombardment. Defeated and divided, the French accepted an armistice and then terms that left most of Alsace and much of Lorraine, a key center of French coal and iron production, annexed by Germany, which declared itself an empire.

The war ended with France divided as a result of the seizure of power in Paris by a revolutionary commune that resisted the new national republican government. The result was the subsequent storming of the city, with heavy casualties and much brutality. Few prisoners were taken, and about twelve to fifteen thousand Communards were executed, while about 4,500 were deported to the tropical death of the French penal colony of New Caledonia. Paris remained under martial law until 1876.[18]

GERMAN WAR MAKING

The perceptive Moltke himself warned of the hazards of extrapolating a general principle of war from German successes, and he was increasingly skeptical about the potential of the offensive. German skill, at the operational and tactical levels, had not prevented many difficulties from arising, not least at the hands of Austrian artillery and French rifles. In practice, as in 1914 and 1940, the Germans faced major problems, notably, in 1870–71, with logistics. Moreover, the difficulties, for Germany and its opponents, of coordinating units and also arms (infantry, cavalry, and artillery) looked forward to the practical issues that were to be encountered in the two world wars.

Furthermore, in 1866 and 1870–71, deficiencies in leadership and strategy on the part of Austria and France had played into German hands, enabling them to outmaneuver their opponents. Napoleon III proved an especially poor leader for the French, while, despite their experience against Austria in 1859, most of his generals were not up to the task, and certainly not in a fast-moving conflict. They were not accustomed to being forced onto the defensive, nor to the high tempo of conflict seen in 1870–71; whereas the French eventually managed both in 1914.

These factors prefigured German success in 1914 against the Russians and initially against the French, and, more generally, in 1939–41, especially in 1940 against France. As with these cases, so in 1864–71, it is necessary to focus on relative capability and on the extent to which offensives were (or were not) countered by defensive skills, not least by the availability and use of reserves.

German victories in 1866 and 1870–71 also anticipated eventual failure in the two world wars, as the German military was better prepared for quick victory than for long struggle. In particular, the lack of a quick victory in 1870–71 put the Germans in serious logistical difficulties. Moreover, in the closing stages of the Franco-Prussian war, *francs-tireurs* (civilian irregulars) disrupted German operations far more than their numbers might suggest. Their presence, and the very harsh German response, triggered a debate on the identity and status of combatants. It also led some German military commentators to suggest that future warfare might become intractable as a consequence of this aspect of the *Volkskriege* (nation in arms).

The Germans emerged from 1870–71 with a high reputation, notably for methodical effectiveness,[19] a reputation all the greater for being won at the expense of the French who had hitherto appeared the most impressive power. This reputation encouraged a focus elsewhere on German ideas and campaigns in the teaching process now increasingly seen in German military professionalism. German campaigns were studied in staff colleges, such as those in the United States, another state whose armies wanted short wars. An ethos of professional, intellectual analysis, based on calculations of benefit and outcome, was widely applied both to change institutional practice and to prepare for conflict.[20]

VARIETY

Many key developments in this period were continuations of earlier processes, as in the Egyptian expansion southward and that of the Russians in Central Asia. Yet outcomes differed. The Egyptian forces under Sir Samuel Baker confronted the Omukama Kabaléga, the ruler of Bunyoro, at Masindi in modern Uganda in 1872 but then had to retreat in the face of continued opposition. In contrast, in Central Asia, the Russians captured Tashkent in 1865, overran the khanate of Bukhara in 1868, defeated that of Khiva in

1873, and overran that of Khokand in 1876. These were major successes over tracts of territory greater and more difficult than those that had faced the Prussians/Germans in 1864–71. More generally, far from learning from the latter, the Russians largely drew on their established operational practice. Continuity, as much as change, was a feature of the period.

Although also looking back to previous conflicts between the two powers, the Russo-Turkish War of 1877–78 provided a classic example of the attempt to repeat a verdict, with the Russians seeking a speedy victory on the model of their previous conflicts with the Turks as much as any model offered by German victories. Despite being delayed by the effective resistance of a Turkish force in the besieged fortress of Plevna in modern Bulgaria, the Russians indeed delivered a verdict. Having crossed the Danube at Svishtov in June 1877, by early 1878 they had inflicted heavy losses and pressed on to threaten Constantinople (Istanbul). This threat led Britain to threaten war in order to restrain Russian gains, which served to underline the extent to which the Balkans might trigger a wider conflict, as indeed was to happen in 1914.

As a related aspect of the wider crisis, Austrian forces in 1878 occupied Bosnia, until then part of the Turkish Empire. This campaign involved a range of types of conflict including battles, street fighting in the city of Sarajevo, and guerrilla resistance in the hills. The Bosnian population was divided, with the Catholic Croats sympathetic to the Austrians and the Muslims and Orthodox Serbs far more hostile. The Austrians deployed 82,000 troops initially but, in the face of guerrilla opposition, eventually sent 153,000 troops. They treated their opponents with great brutality, including summary executions. This looked toward later hostility between the Austrians and the Serbs.

WARS OF ITALIAN UNIFICATION

The full range of conflict was seen in the Wars of Italian Unification, as was the role of great-power commitments. Neither the kingdom of Piedmont nor revolutions within individual states had managed to overthrow Austrian control of Lombardy and Venetia or Austrian-supported conservative regimes elsewhere in Italy. In 1859, however, France came to the assistance of Piedmont and, in a conventional conflict, defeated Austria, leading it to cede Lombardy to Piedmont. France, however, did not pursue a wider agenda of change. Instead, radical irregulars under Giuseppe Garibaldi sailed to Sicily to join a rebellion against the Bourbon-ruled Kingdom of the Two Sicilies

(Sicily and Naples). This campaign involved battles, street fighting, and sieges and culminated in total success. Piedmontese forces, meanwhile, had intervened to overthrow the old order in much of Italy, with the exception of Venetia, where the Austrians maintained control, and the area round Rome where French intervention backed the maintenance of Papal rule. The Piedmontese occupation of Parma, Tuscany, and the Papal States east of the Alps, as well as the handing over of the South by Garibaldi to Victor Emmanuel of Piedmont, indicated the key political dimension of force. As with the Prussian takeover of most of Germany in 1866, notably the conquests of Hanover, Hesse-Cassel, and Saxony, this was militarily secondary to the great-power dimension of the conflict but, nevertheless, highly significant politically and also instructive militarily.

In 1866, in a renewed episode of great-power decision making, Italy backed Prussia against Austria, being rewarded with Venetia. The key battle, that at Custoza on June 24, was actually an Austrian victory. The Austrians had had the advantage of interior lines, but the battle was an encounter one. After hard fighting, including bayonet attacks, both sides thought they had lost, only for the Austrians to win by exploiting a gap in the Italian lines. The Italians were driven back from Venetia, which they had invaded, but the Austrians failed to exploit their success. The transfer of troops to cover Vienna from the Prussians provided the Italians with an opportunity to advance again and then to conquer the bulk of Venetia. In 1870, Italy remained neutral in the Franco-German War. France withdrew its units from Rome, and Italian forces took control.

An element of continuity was provided by the continuation of the struggle over unification. The kingdom of Italy was declared on March 17, 1861, but widespread armed resistance against the "Piedmontese" continued in southern Italy in 1861–64. Prefiguring the situation in Iraq from 2003, the mistake of dismissing former soldiers from the Kingdom of the Two Sicilies, leaving them without wages, fed the brigandage. The populace found itself between the brigands and the army and suffered from both. Civilians were shot by the army for using their weapons against the troops, but also as retaliation, or because they had been found with weapons, or by mistake. From 1864, due to the extension of police activity based on new police stations and to the use of army flying columns, the populace started to react against the brigands, who became weaker and lost their political side. However, thanks to the harsh terrain that they could exploit for shelter, the brigands remained active across the entire South as well as in central Italy until the end of the century.

WESTERN EXPANSIONISM

Russian advances, both in Central Asia and in the Balkans, were an aspect of a more general pattern in which Western forces displayed great effectiveness, albeit not to the degree that was to be seen in the 1880s. Indeed, there were to be important checks in this period, notably for the British in the initial stages of the Anglo-Zulu War of 1879[21] and in Afghanistan during the war of 1878–80.[22] Western forces benefited greatly from enhanced power projection and the use of better weaponry, but the ability to win local support also continued to be an enabler. For example, in 1872, San Carlos, the battle in which Argentine troops defeated the Indian (native) leader Juan Calfucurá, was also a struggle between Indians as the government was helped by Indian allies under Cipriano Catriel. In 1879, General Julio Roca, the Argentinean war minister, commanded advancing columns equipped with repeating rifles, which rapidly conquered the Rio Negro area. Land was seized and distributed to the officers, while Chilean expansion was thwarted. The consequences in terms of the boundaries of Argentina have remained to the present. In Mexico, the government suppressed Maya opposition.[23]

More generally, the interactions of technology, politics, and the environment were highly significant. Alongside Western activity, that of others was important.[24] Thus, in North America, it is important to emphasize Native American "agency" and expansionism. Native Americans had rapidly appreciated the advantage brought by guns, and their dependence on the technology of the West did not translate into political subservience to particular Western powers. Native Americans allied with Euro-Americans against other Native Americans, not only to deal intertribal rivals a blow, but also to secure guns and ammunition through gifts and trade.[25] Most Native American nations remained well armed up to the period of collapse. This collapse can be attributed not to better Euro-American firearms, important as they were, but to war starvation and war weariness stemming from the enemy's scorched-earth tactics and the killing of women, children, and the elderly.

The demographic imbalance was also highly significant. The combination of demographic and economic factors led Adam Smith to suggest, in *The Wealth of Nations* (1776), that, although the Native Americans "may plague them [European settlers] and hurt some of the back settlements, they could never injure the body of the people." He was much more impressed by the "Tartars" in Asia.[26]

The lack of Native unity and the ability of the United States to win allies were crucial. For example, in the Sioux Wars in the late nineteenth century, of which the most significant was in 1876–77, most of the other tribes from the Plains joined the United States, as they saw the Sioux as a far more immediate threat to their safety. The Sioux, in turn, viewed the Americans as merely one more tribal enemy for much of the time and alternated attacks on Euro-American units and forts with raids against Crows and Shoshones. The same was true of the Comanche.

Firearms were not the sole military factor. The Sioux adapted their traditional style, one of individual fighting that stressed bravery yet also the avoidance of casualties, but there were major limits to the process of change. The Sioux did not adequately alter the seasonal nature of their warfare nor, it could be argued, did they ensure the introduction of necessary coercive leadership and military discipline.[27]

CONCLUSION

Many of the themes of this book as a whole can be readily seen in this chapter. The variety of conflict and context is most readily apparent. Allowing for a major degree of overlap, a crude threefold typology of wars within the West, those between Western and non-Western powers, and those within the non-West is valid. At the same time, it is misleading to suggest that this means there was any essential character to any of these particular categories.

The military history of the period also demonstrated that war could deliver results. In 1860–80, these included the continued unity of China and the United States in the face of large-scale revolutions, the ability of Prussia to force itself into the ranks of the major powers, and the continued process of Western expansionism across the world, the latter demonstrated when British forces took Beijing in 1860.

There was also a more general success in incorporating new weaponry and adapting to new technology, although, understandably, the potential on offer could not be readily applied. So also with the consequences of industrial growth and sophistication. The basis for the military developments of the following decades was laid, a truism, as that is always the case, but, nevertheless, one that was to be apparent once the First World War had broken out.

On the other hand, the systematic analysis of military operations was still in its infancy. Indeed, that was a major reason why the lesson of the devastating effect of the rifle had to be learned several times in the 1860s and 1870s.

So also with the quick-firing artillery developed later in the century. However, defense analysis became more significant than hitherto in military science and planning.

Chapter Three

Different Types of Conflict, 1880–1913

The crucial counterpointing here is of the Russo-Japanese War (1904–5) and the conflicts of imperial conquest, notably the inexorable British conquest of Sudan in 1895–99. Each was of significance within wider patterns of imperial warfare, while also showing that one type of conflict had many variations. The Russo-Japanese War brought two rapidly expanding and recently successful imperial powers into conflict and was very much a high-specifications conventional war, fought with the cutting-edge technology of the period. In contrast, the British in Sudan, notably at the Battle of Omdurman in 1898, confronted the Mahdists, opponents who fought in a different fashion and with weaponry that in large part was not modern, for example, spears. This was a contrast to the British conquest of Egypt in 1882.

Repeatedly victorious, Western forces, if understood to include Japan, made impressive territorial gains around the world, gains that brought tens of millions of people under their control. They benefited from resource availability and allocation, as well as technological enhancement in force projection, communications, firepower, mobility, food preservation, water treatment, and health. As before, support from local people and forces was also important, for example (very much) for the British in India and the French in West Africa, and (less prominently) for the Americans in the West and the Germans in Africa.

There were defeats, however, notably for British-led Egyptian forces in Sudan in 1883–85 and for the Italians at Adwa at Ethiopian hands in 1896, a battle that settled the issue of regional dominance until the Italians attacked Ethiopia anew in 1935–36. Adwa was the fault of poor political direction leading to an unwise advance. The daily pressure from Rome by telegraph for an attack ensured that the generals did not wait until reinforcements arrived. The Italians had 17,700 troops, Menelik II of Ethiopia, 100,000, and, thanks in large part to support from other European powers, particularly France and Russia, more than half of the latter had modern weapons, although he faced serious logistical problems. The Italians had no good maps, just drawings, and did not know the terrain well. The Italians advanced in separate brigade columns, but each into a different canyon so that they were engaged separately and could not support each other. The exposed Italians were vulnerable to Ethiopian firepower. The Italians suffered about 11,500 casualties and lost all their artillery. The defeat led to the fall of the Italian government and to Italy's recognition of Ethiopia as an independent state.

Nevertheless, despite defeats, it was the change in control across the world as a whole that was notable. This was not only true with well-known episodes such as the British conquest of Sudan in 1895–98;[1] their successful advance on Lhasa, the capital of Tibet, in 1904; and the international force that advanced on Beijing in 1900, defeating the Boxers. It was also the case with expansion by Latin American states, notably by Argentina and Chile southward, but also, for example, by the Nicaraguan government when resisting the War of the Comuneros in 1881—an Indian rebellion against the takeover of ancestral lands for coffee production—and in 1894 when taking over the Mosquito Coast, long an autonomous, native-controlled area in the jungles along the Caribbean.

Imperial expansion and consolidation took many forms, but it was the dominant trend of these years. As such, expansion and the expectation of success became normative. Western forces relied on speed, especially with column advances and the use of bombardment, and sought to force their opponents to battle or to resistance from a fortress that could be seized. This seizure of the initiative and dictation of a dynamic became the key elements in success. Technology, in the shape of firepower, was very important, but it was subordinate to this achievement.

There were a number of conflicts in the West, each important to the fate of individual regions. The most prominent were the War of the Pacific (1879–83), the Spanish-American War (1898), the Anglo-Boer War (1899–1902), and the Russo-Japanese War (1904–5). All, bar the Boer War, involved conflict at sea, although the leading naval power, Britain, was not directly involved in such conflict. Thanks to the oceanic steam transport of troops and to landings in contested territories, naval strength, activity, and conflict to a degree "placed" the land warfare, and vice versa. Indeed, power projection and logistics ensured that land and sea were closely linked at the strategic and operational levels. Alongside these conflicts, and in part explaining the last, it is necessary to turn first to developments in East Asia.

JAPAN AND CHINA

Japan had begun a serious effort to remodel its army from 1867, and this effort was pushed forward as a result of the strengthening of the emperor in the Meijī Restoration in 1868. The domestic conflicts of the period had demonstrated the superiority of Western weaponry, and it was now easier to introduce a new military order. The privileged, caste nature of military service, monopolized for centuries by the samurai, was replaced by conscription, a universal (albeit male-only) and thus inclusive practice, which was introduced in 1872. Conscription enhanced and demonstrated the power of the government.[2] A Japanese military university for the army was founded in 1868.

Moreover, in 1874, the Sambōkyoku, an office to develop plans and operations, was created within the Army Ministry. This office became, first, the Staff Bureau and, subsequently, the General Staff Headquarters. The German model was readily apparent. After French influence on the development of the Japanese army in the 1870s and early 1880s, German norms came to the fore. The organizational transformation of the army was linked to an institutional professionalization and, also, to the creation of a capacity for overseas operations. In the 1880s, not least owing to the creation of a system of divisions, the army was transformed from a heavily armed internal security force, reliant on static garrison units, into a mobile force. The Japanese were readily able to defeat China in 1894–95. The two powers had competed for influence in Korea from 1882 and, in 1894, the Japanese capture of the Korean king led to war. The Chinese held the city of Pyongyang, but a Japanese assault from a number of directions led to its capture in September 1894. The Chinese then abandoned northern Korea and adopted defensive positions along the Yalu River, only for the Japanese to cross undetected by building a pontoon bridge on October 24, following which they drove in the defenses and invaded southern Manchuria. The Japanese operations, in both Korea and Manchuria, indicated an ability to operate effectively across a large expanse of territory. The use of maps at different scales can be misleading, as Korea appears small in comparison to the area in contention during the Wars of German Unification or the Eastern Theater of the American Civil War. However, in practice, not least when terrain and communications were taken into account, the Japanese displayed an ability to advance and attack rapidly over contested territory and difficult terrain. In the Treaty of Shimonosekei (1895), China ceded Taiwan and the Liaodong Peninsula to Japan and recognized Korean independence, but in the "Triple Intervention," Russia, Germany, and France forced Japan to give up the Liaodong Peninsula. Popular resistance in Taiwan to the Japanese takeover was treated with great brutality, and many civilians were slaughtered.

Chinese developments were important but more limited in their impact than those in Japan. Under the Qing (Manchu) dynasty, which ruled from 1644 to 1911, the main military formations were the banners, which had been formed before the mid-seventeenth-century Qing invasion, at first consisting of Manchu and Mongol banners and later also Chinese banners. After the invasion, these units were garrisoned around the country. They were supported by the Chinese army, known as the Army of the Green Standard, which was used for internal security. These forces were unable to deal with the military challenge of the Opium Wars with Britain in 1840–42 and 1856–60, although some banner troops fought very bravely. In 1860, British artillery played a major role in defeating Mongol cavalry at Baliqiao. The Chinese guns had been silenced in an artillery exchange. The British had benefited from sequential campaigning, focusing on China in 1860 after crushing the Indian Mutiny. The Chinese banner forces were also ineffective against the great wave of rebellions that convulsed China between 1850 and 1873, the greatest of which was the Taiping Rebellion, on which see chapter 2.

The first response to these events was the emergence, in part in response to the foreign-led forces used to help suppress the Taiping, of what are known as regional armies, raised by leading officials, notably Zeng Guofan and Li Hongzhang. Their armies adopted Western drill and more modern weapons, and Li established the first arsenals. These forces played a major role in the suppression of rebellion. However, they were defeated catastrophically on land, and also on sea, by the Japanese in the Sino-Japanese War of 1894–95.[3]

These events led to a second phase in military modernization, which gathered pace after the Boxer Uprising of 1900 in the reform program adopted by the Qing in the last decade of the empire—in other words, later than Japanese modernization. The leading figure in this development was

Yuan Shikai, commander of the Beiyang army. A key feature of these new forces was a strong nationalist commitment. Military modernization became the goal, modern weaponry was adopted, and Western military advisers were employed.

WAR OF THE PACIFIC

The War of the Pacific (1879–84) was waged over the rich deposits of nitrates in the Atacama Desert, deposits important as agricultural fertilizers as well as for war, as nitrates were of great value for explosives. Bolivia's demand for more revenue from an Anglo-Chilean company working the deposits triggered the crisis. Peru backed Bolivia, but in 1879, despite being poorly prepared for war, Chile overran the Bolivian Pacific coastline and invaded southern Peru. Amphibious operations were exploited by the Chileans, but this exploitation required both battles and the storming of positions. This was a war of many battles that are neglected today, such as San Francisco, Pisagua, and Tarapacá in 1879; Los Ángeles and Tacna in 1880; Chorrillos and Miraflores in 1881; and Huamachuco in 1883. As with colonial operations in Africa, this was a war of rapid advances. Sometimes these led to failure, as when a foolish Chilean attack on a larger Peruvian force at Tarapacá was defeated with heavy costs. Logistical difficulties encouraged the high-risk tactic of frontal assaults. Casualties could be heavy. Out of the seventy thousand troops involved in Chorrillos and Miraflores, about eleven thousand to fourteen thousand were killed. The Peruvian defenses were overcome in these battles. Defensive firepower was less concentrated and less strong than in the Wars of German Unification. Chile benefited from educated officers, modern weapons, both rifles and artillery, and a better navy than that of Peru.

Yet, although Chile captured Lima in 1881, the Peruvians fought on, leading to a guerrilla war against Chilean forces and their supply routes. A series of successful and brutal Chilean counterinsurgency campaigns led Peru to agree to terms in 1883. In the peace settlement, victorious Chile annexed Bolivia's Pacific coastline and three Peruvian provinces. The prestige of the Chilean army rose significantly.

SPANISH-AMERICAN WAR, 1898

Spain's colonial position in Cuba was greatly affected by a major insurgency from 1895, which had shaken Spanish rule and hit the army there. More generally, the Spanish military was in difficulties, due in particular to the politicization of the officer corps and the army's lack of training and experience.

Nevertheless, the American invasion of Cuba faced significant problems. Although enthusiastic, the army was small, untrained for such operations, and seriously outnumbered, and the state militias proved weak in many respects.[4] Furthermore, the climate and terrain in Cuba created problems for the Americans. However, the Spaniards fought badly at the operational level, failing to dispute the American landing near Santiago. Instead, the Spanish forces retired into a poor defensive perimeter round Santiago and did not attack American communications. The initiative was thereby left to the Americans. The fighting indicated the importance of entrenchments and the firepower provided by magazine rifles firing steel-jacket, high-velocity, smokeless bullets. The German Mauser rifle used by the Spaniards proved particularly effective, and their artillery was also superior as a result of the use of smokeless powder, which kept their position secret. Tactical Spanish strengths, however, could not counteract a vulnerability that resulted in the overwhelming victory of the American fleet over the Spanish squadron in Cuba. Having lost crucial positions to frontal attack, Santiago surrendered.

The subsequent peace saw Spain cede to the United States the Philippines, Puerto Rico, and Guam, while Cuba became an independent state very much under American influence. However, in the Philippines, the Americans then had to suppress a local nationalist movement in what became a bitter counterinsurgency struggle that lasted for three years. This struggle was very different in kind to the fighting against the Spaniards in Cuba, although, in both, the Americans depended on naval strength and the resulting amphibious power projection. In 1899 in the Philippines, the Americans won a conventional campaign despite the difficulties posed by the climate, but the subsequent antiguerrilla war that lasted until 1902 posed major problems in imposing control. Intelligence proved significant alongside a balance of coercion and conciliation.[5]

The Americans were more generally active in extending their power and influence in the Caribbean, the Pacific, and Central America. Thus, in 1909–10, the Americans supported the overthrow by the Conservatives of the

Liberal government of Nicaragua, and in 1912 and 1926, they maintained the new order against Liberal rebellions, leading to the deployment of American forces from 1912 to 1935 and from 1926 to 1933.

SECOND BOER WAR, 1899–1902

The British had already experienced the lethal skill of defensive Boer firepower at the Battle of Majuba Hill of 1881 in the First Boer War, a battle in which British defeat had led them to abandon their attempt to impose control. This contrasted, both militarily and in terms of the political outcome, with British successes against local African polities in the late 1870s and early 1880s.

Fought with the Afrikaner republics of Transvaal and the Orange Free State, the Second Boer War proved more difficult than the British had anticipated, because the Boers launched the war and thus initially took the initiative, and they were also more tactically adept. Superior Boer marksmanship benefited from Mauser rifles. Similarly, the British in the Tirah campaign of the North-West Frontier of India in 1898–99 suffered from a combination of their opponents' use of breech-loading rifles and British inexperience.[6]

Moreover, as with the Prussians in 1866 and 1870, the effective use by the Boers of the strategic and operational offensive, combined with the successful employment of the tactical defensive, inflicted heavy casualties. In December 1899, the British were defeated at Stormberg, Magersfontein, and Colenso. Moreover, their positions at Kimberley, Ladysmith, and Mafeking were besieged. However, these sieges led to a loss of Boer momentum that threw away the initiative gained by beginning the conflict and invading the British colony of Natal.

British fighting methods proved inadequate. Artillery was still sited in the open, as it was thought the best way to establish the range. This practice, which was used in other imperial campaigns, ignored Boer rifle capability, and the gunners were shot down. Moreover, the Boer use of trenches, as at Magersfontein, limited the impact of British artillery.

As with the Crimean War (1854–56), the First World War, and the Soviet army during the Winter War with Finland in 1939–40, there was an improvement in British fighting capability that tends to be ignored as a result of the focus on initial failures. In practice, the capacity to improve during conflict, by analyzing problems, identifying solutions, and implementing them, was very important.

In 1900–1902, the British developed a better tactical grasp with an appropriate use of cover, creeping barrages of continuous artillery fire, and infantry advances in rushes that were coordinated with the artillery. The British proved adept at improvisation, even adapting naval guns for use as artillery. These innovations were combined with a seizure of the initiative, at both the strategic and operational levels, under more effective generals, especially Roberts and Kitchener. The Boer field army proved less effective than the Boer commanders, and, trapped, it was forced to surrender at Paardenberg on February 27, 1900. All the Boer sieges were raised. The British pressed on that spring and summer to capture the major Boer towns and overrun the Transvaal. This success brought strategic-political advantages, notably exacerbating Boer divisions.

Once the Transvaal had been overrun, Boer forces focused on dispersed operations in which their mounted infantry challenged British control. British counterinsurgency practices developed accordingly, with blockhouses, barbed-wire fences, column advances, and reprisals. Albeit at the cost of a major effort, the British forced the Boers to surrender.

RUSSO-JAPANESE WAR, 1904–5

Of the wars of the period, the greatest in scale was the Russo-Japanese, notably at the Battle of Mukden in 1905, in which each side deployed about three hundred thousand troops along a nearly fifty-mile front. In terms of weaponry and tactics, there was much similarity with the First World War, but there were also major differences, notably the brevity of the conflict and its restricted geographical scope. The war was fought in Manchuria, the northernmost part of China, as part of a struggle to control not only the province but also northern China as a whole and to pursue regional hegemony. The decline of Chinese power and authority created opportunities as well as problems. More specifically, Russia wanted to expand its naval position on the Pacific by acquiring warm-water ports.

Unlike the American and Mexican civil wars of the 1860s, the War of the Triple Alliance, and the War of the Pacific, this was a frontier war, rather as the Austro-Prussian War had been in 1866. The Russians lacked the capability to invade Japan, Korea, or Taiwan. In turn, the Japanese were able to defeat the Russians in part of Manchuria and to establish control over Korea. The Japanese could not afford to sustain the war by pursuing the Russians further, and their war goals were formulated accordingly.[7] There was no attempt to match Japanese war making in China in 1937–41 or the German invasion of the Soviet Union in 1941. In 1904, the Japanese were able to gain the central position between the Russian garrison in the port of Port Arthur and the main Russian army in Manchuria. This enabled them to move their forces between the fronts until the costly siege of Port Arthur ended with its surrender in January 1905.

The war showed the strength of entrenched positions supported by quick-firing artillery and machine guns. In the American Civil War, masonry works, the staple of fortifications, had proved vulnerable to rifled artillery, but earthworks were more resilient, a situation which looked toward twentieth-century trench warfare. The Japanese made use of entrenchments in assaults on Russian positions, using them to get closer before launching the main attack.

In the Russo-Japanese War, the diffusion of technology was significant. The Russians employed British-made Maxim machine guns, the Japanese the French-made Hotchkiss. Field telephones increased the adaptable use of artillery by improving coordination with infantry and aiding the resort to indirect fire. The course of operations was carefully followed by Western observers, who came away from the war convinced that the Japanese had won because they had taken the initiative, and that frontal assaults and a war of maneuver were still feasible. These lessons influenced planning for what was to become the First World War. The improvisation of hand grenades and light mortars was noted by observers and led to development work in Britain (grenades) and Germany (grenades and mortars) in particular. However, the power of quick-firing artillery to break up attacks, which had earlier been seen with the suppression of the Boxer Rising in China, was not adequately heeded. Moreover, the significance of trench warfare was not appreciated. The effect of machine guns was unclear. The British were not overly impressed with the Hotchkiss, while the Russians did not use the Maxim to good effect to sweep ground.

In practice, as so often, a range of factors were pertinent to victory. Operating at the end of very long and limited supply lines, the Russians, who were not ready for war in the Far East, and certainly not for large-scale war, weakened first. Moreover, the cautious generalship of Aleksey Kuropatkin, which affected the rest of the Russian officer corps, ensured that the Japanese dominated the tempo of operations despite the serious problems they faced in sustaining the struggle. The Russians had more resources than the Japanese, but revolution in European Russia in 1905, revolution encouraged by Japanese military intelligence (as that in 1917 was to be by the Germans), pushed the standard issue of military prioritization into a more serious choice. In contrast, the Soviets were not only able to deploy more troops to fight Japan in Manchuria in 1945, but they also had more active commanders then, as well as a far better supply structure.

ASSESSING CONFLICT

All the conflicts of the period saw clashes and trade-offs in which firepower and movement were key issues. This was within a pre-mechanized context, as the tank and armored car were not available, although the Italian invasion of Libya in 1911 saw a number of important innovations, notably the use of aircraft. Troops could be moved long distance by train and ship, but they approached and operated on the battlefield by foot. This ensured their exposure to a defensive firepower that was far more effective than it had been in the mid-nineteenth century when the number of shooters was often the key element, as in the American Civil War.

By the 1900s, the technology available provided significant force multipliers, notably machine guns and quick-firing field artillery, and in 1901 Jean de Bloch (1836–1902) argued in public lectures in London that technology had made the old offensive tactics impossible.[8] Troops were not able to outrun or redeploy to avoid machine guns and, especially, artillery. The technology to transport troops was slower than the technology to increase the range of the troops' firepower. In a combination of machine with manpower, higher casualty rates in the attack encouraged the use of even more troops to do so, a tendency that linked the Russo-Japanese War to the First World War. The sustained growth in world population and in the world economy made this practice possible, as did a relative lack of necessary training for soldiers in order for them to advance in formation and use rifles.

The wars of the period did not always demonstrate the value of attacking, as the Bulgarians discovered at the hands of the Turks at the Çatalca Line near Constantinople in 1912. Nevertheless, a willingness to attack brought victory to Chile in 1879–83, the United States in 1898, Britain in 1900–1902 at the expense of the Boers, Japan in 1905, Turkey's opponents in 1912, and Bulgaria's in 1913.

The value of mass for land warfare appeared clear. The Americans suffered from the absence of troops in the Philippines when the Spanish fleet was totally defeated in 1898. Moreover, the harsh treatment later of the resistance to American occupation arose in part from racism, but in part from a sense of being outnumbered. The legacies last to the present. In 1901, when forty-eight American troops were killed on the island of Samar in an ambush, the American general Jacob Smith ordered his troops to "kill and burn" across the island, and they did. In 2017, President Duterte, in his State of the Nation address, called for the return of the three church bells of Balangiga, used to give the signal for the ambush, two of which are now part of a memorial in Wyoming to the US troops who died.

As far as the relationships of mass and the offensive were concerned, the First Balkan War (1912–13) showed that Turkey's strategic dispersal enabled its opponents to achieve crucial superiorities on specific axes of attack. The Turkish situation indeed reflected the dominance of strategy over operational considerations or, rather, the heavily political character of strategy. As with Poland in 1939 and Yugoslavia in 1941, Turkey in 1912 sought to prevent territorial loss in the face of attack from a number of directions, notably from Bulgaria, Greece, and Serbia, dispersing forces to protect a long perimeter in the Balkans. In a sense, Paraguay had to do the same in the War of the Triple Alliance, while both Peru, in the War of the Pacific, and Spain, in the War of 1898, were forced into this situation because of the range their opponents enjoyed due to amphibious capability. This point exemplified the potential significance of naval considerations for land warfare. In contrast, Russia in 1904–5 was at war on land on only one front, that in Manchuria. This was very different from Russia's situation in the First World War, when Russia fought Germany, Austria, and Turkey, deploying substantial land forces against all three.

Alongside the dominance of strategy or, rather, strategic culture, there was that of other forms of military culture. In particular, the continued cult of the advance, including the use of cold steel in the shape of the bayonet, indicated the conviction that the ability thus to close with the enemy was crucial to a struggle for will, instilling and displaying confidence and overthrowing that of the enemy. Morale was regarded as crucial, indeed as the means to negate similarities in weaponry or even a superiority on the part of opponents. This was a vestige of the preindustrial world in which the elite still dreamed of the glorious knights who charged the "barbarians" that endangered the Western world.

At the same time, as a reminder of the need for caution in deciding what was anachronistic, the use of cold steel is still taught in armies. As a shock tactic, the bayonet charge delivered with conviction can indeed unnerve an enemy. It was used by British troops in Afghanistan in 2011 to good effect. The bayonet was also seen as an element in infantry morale in close-quarter fighting. In contrast, the use of cavalry is anachronistic, not least due to their vulnerability to fire as well as their restricted capability in contrast with armor.

Related to ideas about the bayonet, there was a linked, vitalist belief that troops had to be blooded in order to understand war and to participate properly. In part, this was an aspect of an "anti-intellectualism" in which Courage beats the Brain. These cultural factors were all to be important in the conduct of the First World War. They tend to be criticized, but in practice they were, are, and will be important to success, although not if substituted for training and weaponry.

These notions were similar to those of many non-Western forces, for example those of the Mahdists in Sudan, the Boxers in China, and the Zulus in Natal who unsuccessfully rebelled in 1908. An emphasis on will also appeared especially appropriate in civil warfare, as force was then clearly intended to dominate the will of opponents. This was very much the case with the use of the military in Latin America, as in Brazil, Colombia, and Venezuela, although there were major differences between the military revolts in the first, in 1889, 1891, and 1893, and the civil wars in the last in 1898–99 and 1902–3. To complicate the matter, civil wars could be linked to international intervention at least by neighboring states, as repeatedly occurred in Central America.

Land warfare in 1880–1913 was therefore varied in its setting. However, there was a general emphasis on the attack, for tactical, operational, strategic, cultural, and political reasons. This emphasis took precedence over equations linked to the lethality and quantity of weaponry.

PREPARING FOR WAR

Prior to the outbreak of the First World War in 1914, the General Staffs of all the European belligerents had preplanned and executed maneuvers on a massive scale in war games and staff rides. Fears of invasion, in Britain in 1889 "the probability of our finding the French army on our breakfast tables with the *Times* tomorrow morning,"[9] encouraged a search for responses, both defensive and preventive, the latter involving offensives.

Across Europe, annual summer maneuvers saw the deployment of reservists as well as regular troops. With these numbers, staff officers convinced themselves that they could knock out their opponents before their own resources ran out. The defensive advantages resulting from the new breech-loading, smokeless, quick-firing firearms were understood. More modern rifles that came into service in the late nineteenth century had ranges of more than one thousand yards and could certainly kill at that range, but again battle ranges were usually far shorter. Efforts were made to counter the defensive advantages. The Germans emphasized infantry-artillery coordination and also advancing in dispersed formations that coalesced for a final assault. A British observer at the German maneuvers in 1896 commented, "It is impossible not to be deeply impressed by the smoothness and ease with which the German military machine works . . . a well-trained and thoroughly practical staff. . . . The German army corps is no collection of units hurriedly collected for a time."[10]

Cavalry became less important, both proportionately and in doctrine. In 1906, Emperor Wilhelm II of Germany was told by Helmuth von Moltke, Moltke the Younger, the new Chief of the General Staff, and the nephew of the Moltke who had taken that role during the Wars of German Unification, not to command a cavalry charge on the final day of the annual maneuvers as he had done hitherto. On staff rides, Wilhelm was apt to dismiss anything that contradicted his views on how the event was supposed to play out, and that included the effectiveness of machine guns. Prior to the First World War, the British army had more machine guns than the Imperial German Army.

Field artillery operating in support of the attacking force was regarded as a way to challenge defensive fire, and Germany doubled the complement of field guns to 144 per corps between 1866 and 1905. The advent of quick-firing systems made artillery more deadly. There was a firm conviction within the General Staffs that, sooner or later, the supply of artillery firing high-explosive shells, combined with the élan of (their) infantry advances, would overcome trenches, barbed wire, and automatic weaponry. Indeed, the trench lines seen prior to 1914, and in that year as well, did not anticipate what was to happen in terms of the greater sophistication of trench systems. And the Russo-Japanese War did not suggest that such an evolution in trench systems might occur.

Earlier, the use of trenches in the last stage of the American Civil War had not sufficiently engaged European observers. They did not consider America to be significant in ways of making war and put down the advent of trench warfare to poor military skill, which the martial states of Europe would inevitably avoid. This view persisted with the Russo-Japanese War. This lack of willingness to treat America or even Japan seriously was a cultural and military snobbery that was significant for the tactics adopted in 1914. However, European observers in Manchuria appeared to favor the Japanese, partly because Russia had been an enemy (for Britain and France) or rival (for Germany and Austria), whereas Japan had not. Japanese command and control impressed them, whereas the Russian structure was dismissed as unworkable and corrupt.

Observers saw the Balkan Wars of 1912–13 as confirming their faith in massed infantry assaults. This lesson was taken in particular from the Bulgarian victories over the Turks in 1912, such as Kirkkilese and Lyule Burgas, which appeared to show the effectiveness of high morale and of infantry charging into the attack. For example, the French army, which generally ignored experiences that did not conform to its thinking, deployed the wars to support their offensive doctrine. German observers confirmed the insight gained in the Russo-Japanese War that combined-arms combat was crucial, notably open-order infantry advances after adequate artillery preparations. In practice, the unsuccessful Bulgarian attack on the Çatalca Line in 1912 demonstrated the power of entrenched positions supported by artillery when neither had been suppressed by superior offensive gunfire. This was an aspect of a more general use of field fortifications in the half century before the First World War.[11]

Continuing earlier ethnic and religious hostility, for example that relating to the Austrian conquest of Bosnia in 1878, the Balkan Wars of 1912–13 also anticipated the ethnic conflicts and violence that occurred later in the century. As a consequence of massacres and expulsions in the Balkans, the relationship between Christians and Muslims was strained at all levels. From the political elites to the ordinary people, polarization sharpened. Making nations out of a multinational space was a brutal process. The opportunities the Balkan states seized to assert their national claims transformed the international situation and thus accentuated the complexities of threat assessments and the linked encouragement to military action. The domestic consequences were also significant, as in the ruthless mobilization of the armed forces and society as a whole, especially in Bulgaria, Serbia, and Montenegro.[12]

There was a parallel in the Turkish Empire, with the seizure of power by the Young Turks movement in the revolution of 1908, followed by the use of force for political reasons, indeed as politics itself, both at the center and in the provinces. Due to its multiethnic character, the empire could not readily be a national Turkish project, and the attempt to transform it involved conflict. Moreover, the violence seen in wars, which, for Turkey, began as a near-continuous process in 1911, was linked to violence within states.[13] Similarly, in Afghanistan, Abdur Rahman, the "Iron Amir" (r. 1880–1901), built up a better-armed national army that he used against those he regarded as "internal enemies," including the Hazaras, who were unorthodox from his religious perspective.

At every level, there was a determination to make the human or moral forces involved in war equal to those of the newly more powerful material factors. The spirit of the offensive was seen as a necessary response. A union of man and machine was sought, but, although the casualties likely were understood, the thoroughness of planning and preparation necessary and the length of the likely struggle were not appreciated.[14]

Chapter Four

The First World War, 1914–18

The range of conflict in the 1910s, from China to Mexico, provides a way to contextualize the First World War in terms of a global variety of warfare. This is also the case for the First World War itself. The dominant image of that cataclysmic conflict is the apparent bloody stasis and senseless slaughter of trench warfare. That view is endlessly repeated and became the leitmotif of public commemoration during the anniversary occasions from 2014 to 2018. Indeed, many public myths invest in this account of the First World War. In particular, it serves as a way to discredit the ancien régimes of Europe, to provide a counterpoint to military conduct subsequently, notably in the Second World War, and as an allegedly key background to the foundation in 1958 of what became the European Union. The last was symbolized in 1984 by President Mitterrand of France and Chancellor Kohl of West Germany holding hands when visiting the deadly battlefield of Verdun, the site of a major and sustained Franco-German clash in 1916. The ceremonies in 1984 were preceded by joint military exercises. Family narratives, and influential literary constructions of the novels and poems deemed worthy of attention, also look back to these views of the war. Explanations of the Russian Revolution, the development of Fascism, the rise of the United States to great-power status, the origins of instability in the Middle East, the foundation of Israel, and much else all focus on this conflict.

So it should surprise no one that the situation was in fact far more complex. To take the most basic points, those of tactical stasis, operational failure, strategic nullity, and indecisive conflict, none in fact is well founded if the war as a whole is considered, as opposed to many individual offensives, while certain offensives were indeed successful, decisive, and effective. This is a contrast more generally true of warfare. From the perspectives of Eastern Europe, the Balkans, the Middle East, and Germany's overseas colonies, the war saw much movement. Moreover, Serbia and Romania were in effect knocked out of the war in 1915 and 1916, respectively, while in 1917 Russia was knocked out, and Italy nearly was. In 1918, Bulgaria, Turkey, Austria, and Germany were all defeated to the point of surrender.

Even if attention is shifted solely to the Western Front, that in France and Belgium, the concentration of so much force and resources did not prevent near victories for Germany in 1914 and 1918, and victory for its opponents (principally Britain, France, and the United States) in 1918. Moreover, as part of this process, the major tactical problems posed by trench warfare were overcome, at the tactical, operational, and strategic levels. The Western Front was never in stasis, although it did appear to be static. The Allies worked out how to direct unprecedented firepower with effect, German trench systems were broken into and through, fresh advances were made, and it proved possible in 1918 for the Allies (although not earlier for the Germans) to coincide and sustain attacks along a broad front in order to prevent the sealing of any breakthrough by means of concentrating reserves.

Problems that had confronted perceptive commentators in the prewar decades were overcome, but so were longer-lasting command issues, notably that of the combination of firepower and mobility. Technology played a role, not so much with the tank, as its potential, at once undoubted and problematic, was not yet brought to fruition, but rather with the use of effective aerial reconnaissance in order to map opposing trench systems so that artillery fire could be accurately directed and monitored. The net effect was a conflict that, despite its being between advanced economies deploying unprecedented resources, was, nevertheless, able to deliver a decisive military and political result, and in fewer campaigning seasons than in the Second World War.

CHINA AND MEXICO

These points offer a perspective in which to consider some of the other conflicts of the decade. Comparisons (and contrasts) are generally with those that immediately preceded the war, notably the two Balkan wars of 1912–13 and, further back, the Russo-Japanese War of 1904–5. While valuable, that approach does not consider the range of the use of force in the 1910s, which included the Chinese Revolution of 1911; the Mexican Revolution, notably a civil war after a coup in 1913; and American interventions in Nicaragua, Haiti, the Dominican Republic, and Mexico.[1] All delivered results and all involved equations of firepower and mobility, and therefore the contrasts with the First World War are instructive. The most significant are that, in each case, resource availability was lower than in the First World War, and also that civil conflicts had a different dynamic, with a much more important focus on swiftly ensuring a political outcome. To that extent, the obvious comparison in the First World War was with the two Russian revolutions of 1917, both events that require consideration in terms of the contexts of conflict and the use of force.

On October 10, 1911, in China, an army mutiny in Wuhan sparked a nationwide republican revolt. This, however, rapidly fractured. On January 1, 1912, Sun Yat-sen declared a republican constitution in Nanjing. Eleven days later, the emperor abdicated in Beijing in favor of Yuan Shikai, a general who presented himself as provisional president. This created a divided situation that Yuan, thanks to his military power, dominated, only for his death in 1916 to cut short his desire to become emperor. A warlord period then developed, with the strength of local military figures dictating political outcomes.

So also in Mexico. In 1913, a military coup led to the murder of the president and to revolts against the new order. In contrast to the First World War on the Western Front, force-space ratios in Mexico, as well as logistical limitations, encouraged a style of campaigning focused on rapid advances, short battles, the storming of towns, and a determination to secure political outcomes. The willingness of troops to resist was a key factor in the fighting. Civil war in Mexico in 1913–14 led the militaristic president, Victoriano Huerta, having seized power by force and murder, to increase greatly the size of the military, although his decrees for conscripting large numbers were countered by large-scale desertion. By early 1914, Huerta had about three hundred thousand men under arms, about 4 percent of the population. The *leva* was used for forcible recruitment, including from prisons, but, as a result, the Federal Army was largely kept in garrison to prevent it from deserting. The army of the rival Constitutionalists (the rebels), who pressed for land reform, had better morale. The overlap of military with political power in the provinces ensured that state militias were political forces. Defeats led Huerta to resign the presidency in July 1914.

The key defeat occurred at Zacatecas, a railway town important for the protection of Mexico City. The rebels under Pancho Villa benefited from superior numbers and better artillery to drive Federal troops from the hills around the town, and, with the town then exposed, the defenders' morale collapsed and, with their retreat cut off, many were killed by the advancing rebels.[2] Railroad junctions had also been important to the American Civil War, and were again to be so for the Russian and Chinese civil wars after the First World War.

It is instructive to reconsider the First World War in light of these other conflicts, because the key element that emerges is that the campaigns of movement in that war were not, as it were, falling away from the "true state" of the conflict, that on the Western Front, but instead were more consistent with campaigns elsewhere. The major contrast is that of the political dimension, in that the conflicts in Mexico and China were civil wars, whereas the different aspect of the First World War was that it did not involve much civil warfare. This contrast serves to remind us of the different strands of war in terms of their political context. Wars between states necessarily focused on frontier zones, unless there was a collapse of one state and occupation became a key means through which the continuing conflict was pursued. In contrast, the capture of the capital and of other major cities was the central means in civil warfare of any scale, as opposed simply to regional insurrections. As a result, capitals were the crucial settings for the Irish rising in 1916, the Bolshevik takeover of Russia in 1917, and the nationalist movements in the Austro-Hungarian Empire at the close of the war.

STRATEGIES

The First World War was intended by each of its participants as a short and manageable, albeit costly, war, indeed as a reprise of the Franco-Prussian and Russo-Japanese Wars. It was understood that there would be heavy casualties due to the nature of military technology, but it was believed that a speedy victory could be delivered by the side that attacked. Speedy victory, the ideas of Nietzsche calling on what were understood as those of Clausewitz in the case of Germany, was what was attempted by all the major powers in 1914 once war had begun.

That did not mean that all the powers were equally to blame for the war. The centennial anniversary in 2014 of the opening of the war led to even more division among scholars than might have been anticipated. This division related not only to discussion about the nature of the conflict, but also to the responsibility for the war. This debate, often contentious in character, was not always terribly helpful. Indeed, much of it repeated themes already seen in the 1920s in the discussion over war guilt. There was also a widespread failure adequately to integrate into the discussion of diplomacy the often excellent scholarly work on the military preparations for the conflict. In particular, the nature of Austrian and German planning scarcely accords with the unconvincing argument that Europe somehow slid or sleepwalked into war, an approach that turns perpetrators into victims.[3] Instead, a degree of preparedness encourages support for the argument that war was intended. In Austria, the army leadership, which believed that war would be socially rejuvenating, failed to inform civilian ministers about the reality of the military situation.[4]

This approach suggests that the war was not so much a failure of statecraft, as some have argued, but, instead, a breakdown of deterrence. If the latter was combined with strategic confusion at the heart of the decision making, the combination was deadly. Alongside this came the extent to which the dynamic of the crisis meant that constructive ambiguity was no longer credible. While planning for a war is not simple proof of intent, pressure from the military was highly significant. The decision makers had lost the sense of fragility of peace and order. The politicians used the threat of war to put the other side at a disadvantage with the aim of increasing their own leverage, and, in doing so, they miscalculated. Everyone made mistakes.[5]

There was long a complaint among British military historians that there was a major disjuncture between their work, notably on the learning curve of the British army during the First World War, and, on the other hand, the understanding of the war in contemporary popular culture. Now as an example of differing tramlines, we can add much of the recent work on the diplomatic background to the war. The military dimension was sidelined. Thus, Gordon Martel has argued, "premeditation is not to be proven by the existence of war plans or by the warlike pronouncements of military men. Strategists are expected to plan for the next war: the politicians and diplomats decide when that war is most likely to occur."[6]

That, however, is a highly unconvincing account of the role of military planning, procurement, and preparations in the situation in 1914, let alone of military influences in the decision-making process, and of cultural bellicosity. These factors were present for all powers—even the Swiss mobilized—but they were crucially different in character, context, and consequences. Moreover, this difference is underplayed by the historians of diplomacy. At one level, the obvious contrast is between France and Britain, on one side, and Austria, Germany, and Russia on the other, with the difference linked to the nature of the individual states. It is instructive to note, for example, that prewar, the French government had decided not to pursue the military option of advancing against Germany via neutral Belgium, while Germany took a very different view of conflict with France and made its attacking military operational plan central to its war strategy. Yet this point about political systems is insufficient, for, even in the case of Austria, Germany, and Russia, there were important contrasts. In particular, what mobilization meant for Germany was very different from what it entailed for Russia, a point widely neglected in much of the discussion in 2014. For the former, mobilization was a move to immediate conflict that was not the same as for Russia.[7]

Such distinctions are important because they counter a widespread intellectual tendency to focus on the supposed faults of "the system," rather than of particular actors and groups within it. The consequence is a form of transferred responsibility, so that, to take another prominent example, appeasement by Britain and France in the 1930s is somehow made responsible for Hitler's expansionism and for Stalin's decision to join in himself in this expansionism. This approach takes responsibility from where it truly lies, with Hitler and Stalin.

In 1914, the British sought to rely on the traditional means for addressing an international crisis, that of the Concert of Europe, which indeed had succeeded in the case of the First Balkan War (1912–13). However, operating to different purposes and on other timetables, Austria and Germany were unwilling to do so. Their policies and attitudes caused the war, not the varied errors of the statesmen struggling with the developing crisis, the latter the theme of diplomatic historians. It is also of course necessary to locate this German preference in the political and cultural bellicosity that was so strong in Germany, in particular in the early 1910s. A fervent national patriotism was linked to a strong fear of falling behind and a sense that the opportunity that existed to attack might not continue.

With respect to the British government, criticisms fail to take into account simple parliamentary arithmetic. Any attempts to issue a warning to Germany before the invasion of Belgium that such an invasion would bring Britain into the war were likely to be hollow because of the makeup of Asquith's cabinet and because the governing Liberals were dependent on Labour and Irish support for a majority in the House of Commons.

British participation in the war helped to ensure that Germany would not win. This participation was not itself responsible for the serious failures to achieve victory in 1914 at the operational level, notably that of Germany, but was of strategic significance from the outset. That the attempt for victory was continued, with a degree of success against weaker states, until finally it resulted in the defeat of all the German-led Central Powers in 1918 is a dimension that deserves attention. There is an obvious contrast with the Franco-Prussian (1870–71) and Russo-Japanese (1904–5) Wars, but this was due not to a change in weapons technology but to the scale of conflict. The key scale was strategic, not operational, notably the extent to which alliance systems made it difficult to isolate a conflict and, instead, ensured that a military-political outcome involved the overthrow of an entire alliance. But for that, it was possible that the 1914 German campaign might have led to the overthrow of France, rather as the 1870 one had done. The involvement of an alliance made the First World War, and indeed the Second, very different from any major war since the Napoleonic Wars; and in the latter, the alliance system had essentially been one sided, in that it was composed of Napoleon's opponents.

The primacy of politics was demonstrated by the failure of the German alternative of dictating victory by means of pushing military factors to the fore. Germany subordinated political to military considerations in bringing Britain and the United States into the war against her respectively in 1914 and 1917. In each case, although policies were justified on military grounds, those of advancing more easily via Belgium and knocking out British trade by submarine attack respectively, this was a serious strategic mistake, and one that contributed greatly to Germany's eventual failure, a key point.

The German campaign had failed already in 1914 before the Allied counterattack in the Battle of the Marne and the subsequent stabilization of what became a Western Front in France and Belgium. This failure was because Britain's entry into the war promised that what was already, due to Russian involvement, a two-front war would become a longer and more difficult struggle. This was so as long as France did not collapse, as it was to do in 1940 when Germany faced only a one-front war. In 1864–71, there had been no two-front wars for Prussia/Germany.

By late 1914, Germany's carefully prepared prewar strategic planning[8] appeared precarious and overly optimistic. A dangerous overconfidence was apparent. The Germans were apt to consider the enemy a "constant" instead of an "opposing variable." Germany had envisaged a repeat of the Franco-

Prussian War, with France collapsing, having suffered similar command failures to those in 1870. Austria similarly believed that a war would be quick and decisive. Nothing really played out according to the script, as their opponents proved to be tougher to break than anticipated, which led to exhaustion as well as very high casualties. Austria failed badly in an attempt to conquer Serbia, whose army was less well resourced but much better commanded,[9] and Austria was also put under heavy pressure by Russia. The 1914 campaign showed, moreover, that German war making, with its emphasis on surprise, speed, and overwhelming and dynamic force at the chosen point of contact, was not effective against a French defense that retained the capacity to use reserves by redeploying troops by rail during the course of operations.

German troops were well trained, and their morale may have been better than that of the French and British, although that is both far from clear and, anyway, something that is difficult to assess in aggregate. Nevertheless, aside from serious faults in German planning and execution, notably the lack of coordination between the moves on the German left flank and overall German strategy, as well as serious operational incoherence on the right flank, there were also problems with German equipment and discipline that qualify the usual picture of German competence.[10] This is a point that is also valid for the Second World War, and one that, because it is widely underrated, raises questions about how armies are assessed, both in scholarly terms and by the public.[11]

The Germans had also failed to appreciate the exhaustion their troops would experience on their rapid and lengthy advance. This was an aspect of the German failure to understand the weakness of their plans and that Germany, as well as France, would suffer from "friction." This was a key to the failure of the German plan in 1914. It required faultless execution and little friction. So also for the other powers, such that it was a question of which among the armies, all of whom had grave structural, logistical, and leadership problems, would manage most successfully.

The "fog of war" discerned by Clausewitz—the distorting impact of circumstances and events on plans—was much in evidence, as it was again to be with the German offensives in the West in 1916 and 1918. In the Battle of the Marne in 1914, the overextended, exhausted, badly commanded, and poorly deployed Germans were stopped and driven to pull back. The absence of a German plan B became a readily apparent issue as the Germans did not know how to deal with the check, either operationally or strategically. Helmuth von Moltke, the chief of the General Staff, was then replaced.

German strategy was also affected by the extent to which the rate of change in military technology outstripped strategy because the tactics employed did not match with the power of the technology. This was a problem more particularly in the stalemate following the opening battles of the war. The tactics simply did not take account of the capabilities of the technology, largely because no one fully appreciated what those capabilities were. The shortness of European wars from the 1860s did not help. Easy victories against less able opponents were misleading.

In late 1914, after the Battle of the Marne, both sides, in the "Race to the Sea," then sought, but without success, to turn their opponent's flank toward the English Channel in a new version of envelopment. The result left a front line, now extending from the Alps to the Channel—the Western Front. Initially not continuous and poorly fortified, this line was soon consolidated. That bland remark scarcely gives due weight to the nature of the fighting. On November 12, 1914, Lieutenant John Dimmer of the British army, in command of four machine guns at Klein Zillebeke, Belgium, was exposed to heavy German attack, subsequently writing to his mother,

> They shelled us unmercifully, and poured in a perfect hail of bullets at a range of about 100 yards. I got my guns going, but they smashed one up almost immediately, and then turned all their attention on the gun I was with, and succeeded in smashing that too, but before they completed the job I had been twice grounded, and was finally knocked out with the gun. My face is spattered with pieces of my gun and pieces of shell, and I have a bullet in my face and four small holes in my right shoulder. It made rather a nasty mess of me at first, but now that I am washed and my wounds dressed I look quite all right.[12]

Dimmer was to be killed in action in 1918. His account is instructive for the fortitude he displayed, a factor that does not tend to be emphasized in the modern treatment of the contemporary British literature of the war selected for consideration, which instead focuses on criticism of the conduct of the war and the despair of the writers.

Strategically, the Germans were now committed to the two-front war they had launched. Fixed in the West, they could not switch all their forces eastward to knock Russia out of the war, as had been initially planned for the aftermath of a rapid victory in the West. However, in 1914, the German defeat of invading Russian forces in East Prussia, as well as of the French offensive in Lorraine, ensured that Germany's problems were not those of having to defend itself from sustained major land offensives, as was to be the case in the Second World War in 1944–45.

The failure of the 1914 plans led not to a strategic impasse, but to a struggle with a different timescale than the anticipated one. What has been presented as the tactical impasse of the trenches was in reality subordinate to this situation. Indeed, the strategic situation was inherently volatile, as each side made major efforts to alter the equations of alliance strength, either by bringing down the alliance structure of the other side or by increasing their own system. Thus, the entry of Italy (1915) and the United States (1917), and the loss of Russia (1917), in the system of the Allies, were all crucial events for land warfare as they affected the number of fronts and the forces available, sometimes greatly so. Won by promises of territorial gain, Italy's entry put pressure on Germany's leading ally, Austria, although less than the British and French had hoped. The entry of the United States greatly enlarged the Allied forces available for the Western Front, although, unlike in the Second World War, it did not mean an increase in the number of fronts on which the war was contested. The loss of Russia gave Germany the prospect of a one-front war, albeit against far worse odds than in 1870–71: Britain, the United States, and Italy were now allied to France. Japan's participation in the war on the Allied side was most significant at sea, but it also lessened the number of strategic challenges the Allies had to face.

Returning strategic considerations to their due place, and within a conflict characterized, like other wide-ranging ones, by simultaneity and interactions,[13] particular offensives should be seen in the light of these issues and opportunities. The Allied Gallipoli expedition of 1915 would, it was hoped, knock Turkey out of the war, help keep Serbia in it, and maybe also lead to Greek entry. Romania's entry on the Allied side in 1916 did not produce the hoped-for results, for an invasion by Austria, Bulgaria, and Germany rapidly defeated Romania. Nevertheless, this was another instance of strategic enhancement by alliance building and one that tied down some German forces that year.

THE WESTERN FRONT AND STRATEGY

On the Western Front, the stalemate, threatened by the turn to trench warfare in late 1914 arising from the failure of Germany's war plan, was eventually overcome by France, Britain, and their allies, particularly the United States. However, this success, which was necessary in order to regain territory conquered by the Germans, gains they were not willing to negotiate away, was achieved only after a very costly learning curve. In contradiction to what might appear today to be the obvious danger of advancing against defensive positions, both sides believed that they would be more successful if they took the initiative. By doing so, they would be able to choose the terrain for attack, as well as a battlefield where they had amassed artillery and, if possible, undermined some of the opponent's defenses, and the timing of the attack, the last calculated for time of day and also likely weather conditions. These factors, it was assumed, would lead to success by countering the advantages the defenders enjoyed.

In practice, however, repeated attacks revealed the difficulties of breaking through an opposing front line, as opposed to breaking into it, costly as the latter was. The scale of operations, even early in the war, and its linkage to the struggle to produce goods on the "home front" were apparent in the account by journalist Philip Gibbs, published in the *Daily Telegraph* of September 29, 1915, about the major British assault on German lines at Loos five days before, an assault that was poorly conceived.[14] Of the preliminary bombardment, he wrote,

> All the batteries from the Yser to the Somme seemed to fire together, as though at some signal in the heavens, in one great salvo. The earth and the air shook with it in a great trembling, which never ceased for a single minute during many hours. A vast tumult of explosive force pounded through the night with sledge-hammer strokes, thundering through the deeper monotone of the continual reverberation. . . . This was the work of all those thousands of men in the factories at home who have been toiling through the months at furnace and forge. They had sent us guns, and there seemed to be shells enough to blast the enemy out of his trenches.

The physicality of the combat was described by Gibbs: "The battalions disappeared into a fog of smoke from shells and bombs of every kind . . . our soldiers, digging themselves into the ground they had gained, were clogged with mud and soddened with water, red with German blood." In practice, the German lines were breached at Loos, but, as on other occasions, the exploitation of this success was mishandled, a situation made easier to understand by the parlous nature of the communications available. The British reserves were fed in too late, and they could make no impact on the German second position, which provided a crucial defense in depth. The British suffered sixty-two thousand casualties at Loos and Germany twenty-six thousand.

From Loos, the British took the lesson of the need to increase the intensity and duration of preparatory bombardment, which led to the massive (although inadequate) preparatory bombardment at the Somme in 1916. The British had adopted a policy of destruction, but the Germans had already abandoned such an approach in their attack at Verdun in 1916 where they went for neutralization with a hurricane bombardment of great intensity but short duration. They had realized that a bigger *and* longer bombardment was repaid by diminishing returns. The British and French had yet to reach the same conclusion.

The Germans took the lesson from Loos of the value of defenses in greater depth in order to contain any break-in and to prevent the breakthrough that nearly happened there. This helped to ensure that, on a greater scale than at Loos and with far heavier casualties, the British failed in their Somme offensive in 1916, although they also inflicted heavy losses on the Germans.

In early 1915, having failed on the Western Front in 1914, the Germans, under Moltke's replacement, Erich von Falkenhayn, had sought to attack again, breaking through and driving Britain or France, or both, out of the war. However, instead, the serious problems facing Austria led in April 1915 to a shift to the Eastern Front, where the Germans sought, and succeeded, to turn to their advantage victories won over Russia in 1914. Nevertheless, although a significant amount of territory was gained by repeated attacks in Russian Poland in 1915, they did not lead to any decisive military or political breakthrough. In practice, this conclusion underplayed the success that had been obtained by the Germans and, as a key strategic point, the serious strains already present in Russia and in the Russian war effort. Indeed, these strains encouraged the Western Allies to launch attacks in an attempt to take pressure off Russia. This helped explain both the Gallipoli offensive against Turkey in 1915 and the Anglo-French attack on the Somme on the Western Front in 1916.

Having failed to force the Russians into a separate peace, the Germans in 1916 sought in effect to do so to the French by inflicting a serious defeat in the Verdun offensive. This was at once operational, strategic, and political. Falkenhayn felt that a breakthrough attack was not easy given the nature of warfare on the Western Front. On the pattern of Moltke the Elder in 1866 and 1870, Falkenhayn planned to gain the advantages of the strategic and operational offensives and the tactical defensive. He aimed to do this by advancing rapidly, on the front of his choice, to capture territory, which the French would then suffer heavy losses seeking to regain.

More generally, this approach represented an attempt to get within the French strategy by causing losses, of territory and manpower, that would sap the French will to persist, let alone win. The approach, which was similar to that of Japan toward the United States in 1941–42, was flawed in its understanding of French willpower and political cohesion, and it also rested on an assumption that the opposing alliance could readily be disassembled. In practice, there were operational as well as strategic flaws in the plan: Falkenhayn attacked on too narrow a front and initially with too few troops. He also exposed the German troops to French artillery fire from the other bank of the Meuse River. As the offensive developed, it served no strategic purpose and cost the Germans, as well as the French, very heavily.

Falkenhayn also hoped to make the British attack before they were ready and thus prepare the ground for a successful German counterattack.[15] The Verdun offensive certainly ensured that the British would take a bigger role in the Somme offensive later that year: a campaign originally planned in order to take German pressure off the Russians instead became one designed to help France. In that, the strategy succeeded, with the Germans having to deploy reserves accordingly and therefore losing the initiative, or at least the ability to apply significant pressure, on the Verdun front. This point is lost sight of due to the focus on the heavy British casualties in the Somme offensive, and notably in its first day.

This focus also detracts from the learning curve seen with British attacking techniques in 1915–16 and during the 1916 campaign. The experience of war on the Western Front was very different from that on the Eastern. In the former, defenders fought in fixed positions and were heavily exposed to the power of artillery. Whereas in 1915, France and Germany focused on the production of field artillery, the British concentrated on adding heavy guns, which were designed to destroy the opponent, a contrast that prefigured that in the Second World War when the Germans deployed a tactical rather than a strategic air force. Although the British were unable to produce sufficient artillery by the summer of 1916, their attack put the Germans under great pressure that year.[16] In response, the German High Command pressed for an increase in the production of guns and shells. Moreover, the Allies sought to produce the numbers of troops and artillery necessary to win on the Western Front.

Alongside criticism of the Allied attacks, there is a tendency to underplay the heavy casualties inflicted on the Germans and the psychological impact of the Allied offensives. The German line did not break, but, as with the naval battle of Jutland in 1916, German confidence in existing arrangements was hit hard. Heavy casualties, and the strains resulting from the Somme offensive, helped ensure that the Germans did not mount a major attack on the Western Front in 1917, while their 1918 offensives there were dependent on troops transferred from Russia and on the prospect of more transfers.

Indeed, in 1917, the Germans fell back to a stronger line in the West, the newly constructed Hindenburg Line, which was a zonal defense system. This was a way to resist the Allies, but not one with which to impose a settlement on them. Indeed, apart from Russia's collapse, which gave Germany an opportunity in 1918 to try again for a military verdict, the Germans had lost in the West but were unwilling to accept this, a situation that was to recur in 1944–45. In 1917, the Germans beat off the Allied attacks in the West, but the Germans were pressed hard at Third Ypres (Passchendaele). Moreover, Germany's decision to attack in 1918 reflected America's entry into the war, because it suggested the closure of any window of opportunity the Germans might enjoy. The Americans had already made a great contribution to the Allies in the shape of industrial production and credit, but the prospect of a major addition in manpower was important.

As so often with warfare, the hypotheticals of conflict come into play when assessing power. The Americans were constrained by the small size of their prewar army and were affected by inadequate and inappropriate doctrine, by their lack of training for trench warfare, and by an overconfident failure to appreciate the nature of the conflict and to learn from British and French experience, one seen in particular with General Pershing. This led to outdated tactics and heavy American casualties on the Western Front in 1918 when the Americans still played a significant part in Allied operations, notably in the Meuse-Argonne offensive,[17] although this role was not instrumental to victory.

Yet the American role would have been more important had the war continued into 1919, as was widely anticipated. Large numbers of trained American troops would have provided the Allies with an important advantage in manpower. Moreover, such an advantage was necessary given the reliance of both sides on infantry in large quantities and the prospect of Germany redeploying more troops from Eastern Europe. Thanks to the Americans, the German superiority of three hundred thousand troops on the

Western Front in March 1918 was transformed into an Allied superiority of two hundred thousand troops four months later. Nearly two million American troops were in Europe by the armistice in November 1918. Their arrival greatly affected German resolve. It was more significant in terms of relative power than the impact of American support at sea. Had the war continued, American productive capability would have offered the Allies an avalanche of heavy equipment in the shape of tanks and heavy artillery.

THE FACE OF BATTLE

Placing the strategic dimension first offers a way to provide meaning to the nature of the fighting. This is necessary because the costly trench warfare that most characterizes the First World War on land, both for public discussion and for the academic approach described as "face of battle," can make the struggle seem not only worthless but also pointless. Neither is a fair view unless it is assumed that aggression should not be resisted and that international agreements, notably the German guarantee of Belgian neutrality, should be ignored, a point that pacifists appear to forget. That strategies failed, or only succeeded after very many problems, did not make them pointless.

Tactics were in many respects a response to the opportunities offered by artillery and the problems it correspondingly caused. The greatest killer on the battlefield was artillery, followed by machine guns and rifles. In the opening battles of 1914, artillery firing by line of sight was more than capable of breaking up an attack. Thanks to the French invention in 1897 of a reliable hydraulic recoil system, the French 75 mm field gun could fire over fifteen rounds a minute,[18] while German 150 mm field howitzers could fire five rounds per minute. Air-burst shrapnel shells increased the deadly nature of artillery fire and encouraged the use of steel helmets to reduce head injuries. Fifty-nine percent of the casualties of the British Expeditionary Force (BEF) on the Western Front were caused by high explosives, which included trench mortars, while 39 percent were caused by small-arms fire, including machine guns that could scythe through attacking waves like no other weapon and could do so in minutes. As a reminder of the problems posed by statistical analysis, however, notably the assumption that a single classification is possible, grenades might be used to force the enemy out of cover and into the killing zone of a light mortar or a rifle. The static nature of defenses increased the lethality of artillery, while the close ranges in trench warfare led to the development of the submachine gun.

Italian attacks in 1915–17 were greatly hit by shortages of artillery. Successive Italian attacks on the Austrians in the harsh, rocky terrain on the Isonzo front, designed to open the way to Gorizia, Trieste, and Istria, were unsuccessful. On a concentrated front, where there was no way to outflank the Austrians and few opportunities to vary the axis of attack, Austrian defensive firepower prevailed, and, advancing uphill, the Italians in 1915 suffered about 250,000 casualties (compared to about 160,000 for the Austrians) for very few gains. Thanks in large part to the advantages of the terrain, Austrian defensive positions were strong. In 1914, the Italian chief of staff had notified the government that the army was not ready for war, and it entered the conflict in 1915 with only 618 machine guns and 132 pieces of heavy artillery. The Italians were unable to open up the battlefield and gain mobility.

In May 1916, in turn, the Austrians attacked from the Trentino, making significant gains and inflicting heavy casualties, before the Italians, using Fiat lorries and railways to bring up reserves, held the offensive. In August, the Italians captured the city of Gorizia in yet another Isonzo offensive, but again there was no breakthrough. The unimaginative emphasis by Luigi Cardona, the chief of the General Staff, on successive attacks represented an instance of the more general failure to rethink goals and methods.

Poison gas was first used in this war by the Germans in the Second Battle of Ypres in 1915, and to considerable effect.[19] However, it was the British, in the form of the Special Brigade, who became the biggest user and indeed the most effective user of gas, developing new techniques such as the hundreds of Livens projectors fired simultaneously on a small area (although the Germans learned about the projector as a piece of equipment and even copied it, they never caught on to the fact that its success lay in simultaneous firing) and the successful use, late in the war, of specially built railway tracks, in an arc, for goods trucks carrying gas cylinders.

The stress in much discussion of the war is on impasse and indecisiveness. There are frequent complaints about incompetent commanders and foolish command cultures, and the abiding image is of machine guns sweeping away lines of attackers. Battles such as Verdun (1916), the Somme (1916), and, in particular, Passchendaele (1917) are presented as indictments of a particular way of war.

On September 21, 1917, the *Times* of London, writing about the British offensive at Third Ypres (Passchendaele), captured the reduction of campaigning to fighting over small areas at great cost, as well as the horrors of the battleground:

> The extreme depth to which we sought to penetrate [today] was about one mile, but that mile we have overrun, and grasped, and hold. Already the enemy has been counter-attacking. . . . We in these last seven weeks have made no, or very little, progress. . . . All shell-holes are full of water. Every man I saw was coated with mud, some only to the knees, but many to their very throats, and it is to be feared that some wounded must slip into the holes and never get out again.

There was, indeed, an attritional character to particular battles as they developed without breakthroughs, but that does not mean that combatants simply set out to wear down their opponents. Instead, there were attempts to develop the handling necessary for offensives carried out by very large forces taking part in theater-wide campaigns and with combined-arms methods.[20] Like the Confederates in the American Civil War and the Germans in the Second World War, the Germans in 1918 were eventually outfought and defeated, both in offensive and defensive warfare.

In terms of casualty rates, the war was one of a number of conflicts in which rates were very heavy, as notably on the Eastern Front and in the Normandy campaign in the Second World War. To give an example, Canada, which provided important sections of the British (i.e., British Empire) army on the Western Front, had sixty-five thousand dead and over one hundred thousand wounded out of a population of just over eight million, of whom 620,000 enrolled. The modern tendency to regard casualties as avoidable does not match the reality of the consequences of engagements between large forces, a point readily apparent from the Iran-Iraq War of 1980–88.

The heavy casualties of the First World War, for example, 1.4 million dead in the French army and nearly three million Germans with permanent disabilities, owed much to its being waged by well-armed and populous industrial powers that were willing and able to deploy much of their young male populations. It is reasonable to focus on the repeated failures and heavy costs of operations, but it is also necessary to note the adaptability of militaries, economies, and governments so that they were able to sustain a large-scale, long-term war and to increase their effectiveness.

TRENCH WARFARE

Trench warfare is frequently held up for much of the blame, but, had the campaigns been waged in a different manner, for example, had they been more maneuverist and less static, which was implausible given the limited mobility of the infantry, there is no reason to assume that casualties would have been lower. Instead, in the open, troops would have been more exposed to both offensive and defensive fire. Indeed, trenches served to protect troops as well as to stabilize the line.[21]

However, once the trenches had been constructed, it proved difficult to regain mobility, despite the combatants seeking to launch attacks that would enable them to do so. These attacks were both a measured response to the political and military issues posed by the war and a reflection of the aggressive spirit and attacking ideas inculcated prewar.[22]

The problem was not so much posed by the inherent strength of trench systems, significant as they became, because these could be broken in and even through as with the German Hindenburg Line in 1918. Instead, problems were posed by the force-space ratios of the war, notably, but not only, on the Western Front. The available manpower made it possible to hold the front line with strength, and to provide reserves. Moreover, although front-line trenches were not held in strength by the Germans from 1916 onward, this was part of the defense in depth around strongholds that was designed to counter artillery bombardments and break-ins and facilitate counterattacks.

The scale of warfare was matched by grim determination[23] and organizational sophistication. General Monash of the Australian army wrote to his wife in 1915,

> We have got our battle procedure now thoroughly well organized. To a stranger it would probably look like a disturbed anti-heap with everybody running a different way, but the thing is really a triumph of organization. There are orderlies carrying messages, staff officers with orders, lines of ammunition carriers, water carriers, bomb carriers, stretcher bearers, burial parties, first-aid men, reserves, supports, signalers, telephonists, engineers, digging parties, sandbag parties, periscope hands, pioneers, quartermaster's parties, and reinforcing troops, running about all over the place, apparently in confusion, but yet everything works as smoothly as on a peace parade, although the air is thick with clamour and bullets and bursting shells, and bombs and flares.[24]

Although generals planning attacks had plentiful troops, and the supplies to sustain them, they faced the difficulties of handling large formations in battle and of devising an effective tactical system that would not only achieve a breakthrough of the opposing trench line but then be able to sustain and develop it. This problem was greatly accentuated by facing defenses in depth, such as those developed by the Germans in 1917. This task was far from easy, not least because of the problem of advancing across terrain badly damaged by shell fire, as well as the difficulties of providing reserves in the correct place. It was difficult to maintain the availability of shells for the all-crucial artillery, and to provide adequate information to commanders about developments. Deficiencies in communications fed directly into command: the potential of radio was inadequately grasped, although that is a view that reflects the strength of hindsight.

In the major British offensive of 1917, which subsequently became known as Passchendaele (Third Ypres), the planned breakthrough-battle did not occur, in part due to the inherent difficulties of the task and to appalling and unseasonal wet weather. The British commander, Douglas Haig, subsequently justified the heavy casualties in the very different terms of attritional calculations. The Germans, indeed, also suffered debilitating casualties, but Haig seriously underrated the strategic problems arising from manpower shortages caused by British losses.[25] Moreover, the long term appeared increasingly precarious in late 1917 as Russia slipped away.

THE EASTERN FRONT

Where, in contrast, the force-space ratio was lower, weaker defenses, notably less developed defenses in depth, ensured that it proved possible to achieve breakthroughs, make major gains, and obtain decisive results. This was particularly the case on the Eastern and Balkan Fronts, on which, in 1915–17, the Germans, Austrians, and Bulgarians captured large swathes of territory and defeated enemy armies in impressive campaigns of maneuver that were frequently aided by a geography that was easier for such advances than the Western or Italian fronts. Serbia was conquered by overwhelming Bulgarian, German, and Austrian forces in 1915,[26] while Romania was largely overrun in 1916.[27] Russian Poland was conquered by the Germans in 1915, countering multiple failures[28] by the badly commanded Austrians. The Germans proved particularly successful in employing heavy artillery barrages against the primitive Russian trench systems.[29]

In 1917 in Russia, a crisis in support for Tsar Nicholas II, due to failure in the war and its management, led to his abdication. The new Russian government continued the war, but without success, and was overthrown in a Bolshevik coup in November 1917. The new leadership, under Lenin, negotiated the Peace of Brest-Litovsk with Germany the following spring, accepting major territorial cessions. This hardly demonstrated the indecisiveness of conflict in this war, and it contrasted with Russian resilience during the Napoleonic Wars and the Second World War.

ITALY

Nor did the fate of Italy, nearly knocked out of the war by the surprise Austro-German Caporetto offensive of October 1917, demonstrate indecisiveness in campaigning. Launched on October 24, 1917, the rapid Austro-German advance greatly disrupted Italian communications and cohesion, leading to an enforced withdrawal. Withdrawing eighty miles, the Italians lost 20,000 dead, 40,000 wounded, and 350,000 prisoners, as well as 3,152 pieces of artillery, one-third of their firearms, ordnance and supply depots, and airfields. Nevertheless, in December the Italians were able to return to the front line most of the troops that had lost cohesion in the retreat. Meanwhile, the Austrians and Germans were able to advance to the Piave River, but their exhaustion, combined with the stiffening of the Italian line, led to the stabilization of that line.

In June 1918, the Austrians attempted to resume their offensive but totally failed. On June 12, Italian artillery silenced the Austrians with counterbattery fire, and on June 13 the attack by the Austrian infantry was wrecked by Italian artillery.[30]

THE MIDDLE EAST

In far more difficult circumstances, notably in terms of terrain, climate, infrastructure, logistics, and disease, Britain and the Turks fought in the Middle East, with Palestine and Mesopotamia, to use the contemporary British terms, the major areas of operation. The British hoped that they would cause the Turkish Empire to collapse, providing opportunities for pressure on the opposing coalition and for postwar territorial gains.

The deployment and sustaining of forces were key elements.[31] Although their army had been improved by German advisers, the Turks faced major problems, not least because they were deploying larger numbers of troops in these areas than hitherto and were obliged to move resources for a period of time greater than in recent wars. Moreover, the heavy costs in manpower to the Turks, even in victorious campaigns, notably Gallipoli (1915), Kut (1915–16), and Gaza (1917), exacerbated these problems,[32] while helping to ensure that the Turks derived scant strategic success from operational victories.

As on other fronts, the British faced problems of developing capabilities and pursuing learning curves, but in harsh circumstances, notably of logistics, and with the additional problems created by a tendency to disparage their opponents. Failure in Mesopotamia in 1916 was followed by modernization, and the British were able as a result to capture Baghdad (1917) and Mosul (1918). The Turkish collapse in 1918 proved the precursor to postwar instability.[33]

1917–18 ON THE WESTERN FRONT

Germany was not just fighting on. It had a strategy. In 1917, this entailed going on the defensive on the Western Front, indeed retreating to the straighter and better-fortified Hindenburg Line, thus freeing up some forces; knocking out Russia; using unrestricted submarine warfare, as well as bombing, to weaken Britain; and testing new infantry tactics of surprise attack and infiltration of opposing defenses against Italy. Having beaten Russia, the Germans planned to transfer forces to the Western Front so as to defeat Britain and France before the United States could make a key contribution. It also hoped to use submarine attacks to limit the number of American troops crossing the Atlantic.

By 1917–18, the nature of fighting on the Western Front was very different from 1915, let alone 1914. What were to be called storm-trooper techniques or infiltration tactics had been developed by the Germans, notably so in raids against the French from October 1915. These storm-trooper techniques, for which the Germans get the credit because of the term *Stosstruppen* (storm troops), relied on carefully planned surprise assaults employing infiltration and focusing on opponents' strong points in order to destroy the cohesion of their defense. The Germans used these techniques on a wider scale at Verdun and in Romania in 1916, and at the operational level in 1917 and 1918. For the Germans, these tactics were those of specialists. They helped ensure the defeat of the Italian army at Caporetto. Gas was also significant there. In the winter of 1917–18, an attempt was made to train

German units so as to inculcate the need for appropriate action at the level of individual soldiers.

The British and the French developed similar tactics at much the same time, with Captain André Laffargue of the French army possibly launching the idea in print in August 1915 with his pamphlet *Étude sur l'attaque dans la période actuelle de la guerre* (*Study of the Attack in the Current Period of the War*), which called for mobile firepower and infiltration. An English version was published that December.[34] The British made the tactics widespread across the BEF on a pattern also to be seen in the Second World War. As a result, the "ordinary" German infantry was not necessarily better trained in the latter stages of the war compared to their British or French counterparts. Training took place near the front line as a way to incorporate field experience. The British gained a lot of tactical experience from raids, which often encouraged infiltration and artillery box barrages, as well as mortars and machine guns operating in fire-suppression roles, before these tactics became widespread among the infantry during larger-scale operations. The Canadians developed raid-like tactics for major operations in 1916–17.

Thus, the idea that the Germans alone invented so-called storm-trooper tactics is misleading. More generally, tactics evolved continuously, often in response to what the enemy was doing. Generals approved tactics, rather than devising them, and these tactics evolved from experience. For example, British grenade and mortar tactics came from experience, which was taught in infantry schools set up from mid-1915 onward. With both grenades and mortars, inventors exceeded what had existed hitherto. Their inventiveness led to the proliferation of grenades and light mortars. Without these inventions in 1914 and 1915, the fighting on the Western Front would have been very different.

The Germans used their techniques with considerable success in their spring 1918 offensives. However, the Germans won tactical breakthrough, only to lose the advantage because, owing to very poor military leadership, they had not thought out how to exploit success militarily or politically. Instead, focused on the tactical level and with no adequate operational or strategic understanding, the Germans assumed they could use shock to force an Allied collapse. In practice, Allied defenses in depth and the use of reserves helped thwart the Germans, who failed to persist on any individual axis of attack or to capture the key rail junctions, while the offensive also led to heavy German losses that could not be replaced and to a new extended front line that left them vulnerable to attack.[35]

The British, in contrast, successfully focused in 1917–18 on improving artillery firepower and accuracy, so that they could dominate the three-dimensional battlefield and apply firepower more effectively than in earlier attacks. The number of heavy guns increased greatly. For example, in preparation for the Canadian attack on Vimy Ridge in 1917, more than 125,000 shells were fired by the Canadians, who engaged in successful counterbattery work.[36] In addition, a better scientific approach to gunnery and ranging calculations had a major impact as it changed how artillery was, and still is, used. By late 1917, gunners could calibrate their guns for every shot and take account of air temperature, barrel wear, and propellant power. This did not so much need new technology, but new devices were invented to help, ensuring that what had not been feasible in 1914 was now practical. The more scientific approach saw meteorology become increasingly important and led to advance weather forecasting. Wind speed and air temperature were given to artillery batteries several times daily.[37]

With these advances, more sophisticated barrages could be fired, which was not possible earlier in the war. A creeping barrage that could match the trace of the enemy trenches meant that the entire length was hit at the same time, which was not possible if each gun was not calibrated according to its own requirements. Artillery-infantry coordination was also significant. In place of generalized firepower, there was systematic coordination, reflecting precise control of both infantry and massive artillery support, plus improved communications. Creeping barrages were developed as was effective counterbattery fire. The key to converting a break-in into a breakthrough was artillery neutralizing the German ability to mount counterattacks. And the key to breaking in was infiltration rather than wave assaults. This neutralized the German defenses in depth, whereas sheer firepower alone could not do that.

The Allies' 1918 campaign on the Western Front, a counterattack to the recent German offensives, was eventually a great success in the shape of the "Hundred Days Offensive." The German defenses were breached, and German military morale faced a crisis at every level.[38] In contrast to poor German leadership, the Allies were ably led by Ferdinand Foch, who provided effective coordination of the often bickering coalition. In fighting quality and combat effectiveness, the Allies benefited from their marked capacity for improvement.[39] Under the pressure of defeat, the German delegates signed the Allied armistice terms on November 11, 1918.

The resolution of stalemate on the Western Front might appear to be a vindication of the prewar belief in the triumph of attack over defense, but it was not on the timetable envisaged. Moreover, the scale of the conflict proved very different. This led to a vocabulary of total war. The French minister Georges Clemenceau pressed for "La guerre intégrale" when he took office in 1917, and the German general Erich Ludendorff used the term in his postwar memoirs, eventually writing a book on *Der Totale Krieg* (1935). In pursuit of higher morale and in response to concerns raised about the impact of the Somme offensive, Ludendorff in 1917 had instituted political instruction for the German army in order to explain to the soldiers what they were fighting for. The British did the same. There is little evidence of this method proving successful. Many soldiers slept in the classes. Nevertheless, the effort was instructive as, more generally, was the greater concern with morale in 1917–18 as a consequence of the problems that had faced the French, Italian, and Russian armies in 1917. This was one of the many ways in which the war was different in its last section from the opening campaigns. British morale held up well, and the soldiers continued resilient and confident that success would be soon.[40]

TANKS

The unexpectedly early end to the war left unclear the consequences of the development of the tank. Plans for armored land vehicles were pushed forward as a result of the outbreak of the war and the helter-skelter of inventiveness it encouraged. This inventiveness was furthered by the existence of well-developed social and industrial bases for innovation and manufacture. Invented independently by Britain and France in 1915, tanks were used in combat from September 1916. In contrast, in the case of the tank, German inventiveness and application proved deficient, and few were built. The German A7V tank was huge and required a lot of armor plate, but Germany was affected by metal shortages and had other priorities for metal use.

From the perspective of just over a century later, the invention and deployment of tanks provides a development that looks to the modern situation and, moreover, one that helps structure this book, coming as it does roughly a third of the way through chronologically. Furthermore, the tank acts as an exemplar of the more general point that the armies went into the First World War looking backward and ended looking forward. The plentiful presence of cavalry and bright (and uncamouflaged) infantry uniforms (notably those of the French) in 1914 is held to encapsulate the former, while mechanization in 1918 apparently represents the latter. This interpretation, however, faces problems, not least an overly pat, even rigid, notion of modernization and a teleology of development. More significantly, there is a misleading tendency to primitivize the situation leading up to (and including) the first campaign and, correspondingly, a misreading of the situation in 1918.

The usage of tanks provides a good instance of this misreading. The war did see a development from fluid to static warfare, such that the idea of a front line took hold. As the means of, and to, maneuverability, tanks were to be seen as the antithesis of the front line. That, however, underplayed the problems involved in sustaining mobility in the late 1910s. Indeed, tanks, essentially a tool for operating on the front line, were suited in 1918 more for assisting in transforming static into maneuver warfare than for the latter itself. Like light mortars, in providing moving firepower, tanks helped overcome the problems that trenches posed to attackers. They offered precise tactical fire to exploit the consequences of the massed bombardments that preceded attacks. A memorandum of June 1918 from the British Tank Corps Headquarters claimed, "Trench warfare has given way to field and semi-open fighting . . . the more the mobility of tanks is increased, the greater must be the elasticity of the co-operation between them and the other arms."[41]

In practice, however, durability, firepower, protection, speed, range, mobility, command and control, and reliability were all major problems with tanks. These problems were accentuated by the rapid development by the Germans of antitank techniques and weaponry, a process already seen in countering airships and aircraft. There was also the problem posed by the use of tanks in small numbers in order to help the infantry, instead of in large formations, that were better able to achieve their goals.[42]

ENHANCED CAPABILITIES

Tanks were most successful if part of a combined-arms force, a point that directs attention to the more general value of the Allied development of effective artillery-infantry tactics and the provision of necessary equipment. In particular, well-aimed, heavy indirect fire, ably coordinated with rushes by infantry who did not move forward in vulnerable lines, were important in 1918 in overcoming the German defense in depth. Some commentators have seen this as ushering in the "modern system," one requiring initiative and leadership way down the command hierarchy, so that technology and tactics are brought into appropriate harmony.[43] In specific terms, this is a questionable definition, however, as, in practice, it describes most combat. Instead, 1917–18 saw an effective response to the particular tactical and operational issues of the moment. As such, it demonstrated the continual process of assessing and implementing fitness-for-purpose, rather than establishing a more general condition of industrial warfare or, indeed, modernity.

Fitness-for-purpose was part of a more general process of learning, one in which training and improved staff work played a major role.[44] For example, before the war, French artillery officers relied for aiming their artillery on independent local grids based on Bonne's projection (a nonconformal polyconic variant) and centered on strongholds from which fixed guns might conveniently bombard targets in the region. However, after the angular distortions and awkward discontinuities of the Bonne grids became apparent early in the war, French officials devised a single military grid based on a Lambert conformal conic projection. Directionally accurate long-range artillery and "map firing" also established a need for military surveyors, who relied on conformal projections in helping gun crews get a fix on true north by tying the gun's position into a precisely measured triangulation network.[45] This made it easier to coordinate artillery fire by means of telephone links.

MAPS

This was a particular instance of the more general way in which the demands of land warfare drove forward associated techniques and technologies such as cartography (mapmaking). The unprecedented range, scale, and intensity of the First World War ensured that this war proved particularly significant in the military use of cartography. Again, the reaction to existing and new problems was crucial. There were deficiencies with existing maps and with the use of these maps for military operations. This proved especially so for the British and French attacking the German colonies in Africa, as Africa was poorly mapped, and notably so at a large or medium scale, while a lack of adequate maps made it difficult to predict terrain and watercourses.

Serious problems with maps also faced Turkish operations in the Caucasus in 1914 and German planning for a Turkish invasion of Egypt in 1915. More generally, the mapping of the Turkish Empire in Asia, as opposed to its former empire in the Balkans, was poor. That posed problems when campaigning began in Mesopotamia and Palestine, both of which the British eventually conquered. As a result, the British devoted much attention to the cartography of the Middle East. They used the survey systems they had already established in Egypt and India; thus, the empire provided a basis for the mapping for a war that was far more intense than anything faced hitherto. Fortunately, the British had already encountered serious deficiencies, in mapping and much else, at the time of the Boer War. These had led to a measure of postwar reform in surveying, which was part of a more general process in postwar reform, and, as earlier with the response to the Crimean War (1854–56), this reform improved subsequent British effectiveness.

Alongside the serious issues faced in having adequate maps of regions outside Europe, and in producing new ones, there were the major problems posed by interpreting existing maps of Europe. This was crucially seen with the German invasion of Belgium and France in 1914. Maps had to be read in light of how swiftly the opposing forces would be able to move depending on terrain, and how difficult they would find it to mount an offensive. The French, for example, could readily use their rail system to move troops from eastern France to support the defense of Paris, whereas the Germans faced the problems of taking over the rail systems of conquered areas, including different gauges of track. The use of maps did not necessarily cover such issues, and, moreover, maps did not always ensure that commanders could locate their units as accurately as might be anticipated.

In turn, from the First Battle of Ypres in the autumn of 1914, the particular needs of trench warfare created new demands. These needs had not been anticipated by military cartographers. The French, for example, had concentrated their prewar military mapping on major fortified positions near the border with Germany, such as Belfort (the site of a major and unsuccessful German siege during the Franco-Prussian War of 1870–71), only to discover that most of the fighting took place nowhere near these and that they were not prepared for the mobile warfare within France that occurred in 1914. Nor were they prepared for the subsequent trench warfare. Instead, it became necessary to respond to the need for detailed trench maps in order to be able to plan both effective defenses and successful assaults on the trenches. Reliable infantry-artillery coordination was important to success in attack and defense. Accurate surveying and mapping reduced the need for the registration of targets by guns prior to attack and thereby allowed an element of surprise, a crucial element due to the strength offered by defensive firepower.

When the BEF was sent to France in 1914, one officer and one clerk were responsible for mapping, and the maps were unreliable. By 1918, in contrast, the survey organization of the BEF had risen to about five thousand men and had been responsible for more than thirty-five million map sheets. No fewer than four hundred thousand impressions were produced in just ten days in August 1918. Ordnance Survey military topographic sections and field survey battalions surveyed and mapped different sectors of the front from mid-1915 and were coordinated in France through the Ordnance Survey Overseas Branch from late 1917. The overwhelming majority of the thirty-two million maps produced by the Ordnance Survey during the war were large-scale battlefield sheets. This was not all. Many commercial businesses also played a major role in producing maps.

Due to the nature of trench warfare, maps were produced for the military at a far larger scale than those with which they had been equipped for mobile campaigning. These maps required a high degree of accuracy in order to permit indirect fire, as opposed to artillery firing over open sights. This accuracy came in part from better guns and from improvements in photogrammetry, but aerial information was very important. Indeed, the breakthrough in surveillance resulted from manned flights, which began in aircraft (as opposed to balloons) in 1903. Cameras, mounted first on balloons and then on aircraft, were able to record details and to scrutinize the landscape from different heights and angles. Instruments for mechanically plotting from aerial photography were developed in 1908, while a flight over part of Italy by Wilbur Wright in 1909 appears to have been the first on which photographs were taken. The range, speed, and maneuverability of aircraft gave them a great advantage over balloons.

With the First World War came air-artillery coordination, which greatly enhanced the potential of the latter. At first, maps did not play much of a role. Thus, a report in the *Times* of London on December 27, 1914, noted of the Western Front in France and Belgium,

> The chief use of aeroplanes is to direct the fire of the artillery. Sometimes they "circle and dive" just over the position of the place which they want shelled. The observers with the artillery then inform the battery commanders—and a few seconds later shells come hurtling on to, or jolly near to, the spot indicated. They also observe for the gunners and signal back to them to tell whether their shots are going to, whether over or short, or to right or left.

However, with time came more static positions, as well as a need for heavier and more precise artillery fire in order to inflict damage on better-prepared trench systems in an attempt to renew mobility. Both led to the use of maps as the key means for, and of, precision and planning.

The invention of cameras able to take photographs with constant overlap proved a technique that was very important for aerial reconnaissance, and thus surveying, notably with the development of three-dimensional photographic interpretation. Maps worked to record positions as well as to permit the dissemination of this information. The ability to build up accurate models of opposing trench lines was but part of the equation. It was also necessary to locate the position of artillery in a precisely measured triangulation network. This network and location permitted directionally accurate long-range artillery by means of firing on particular coordinates. Responding to a German attack, Lieutenant Colonel Percy Worrall noted of the Western Front in April 1918, "The artillery and machine-gun corps did excellent work in close cooperation . . . it was seldom longer than 2 minutes after I have 'X-2 minutes intense' when one gunner responded with a crash on the right spot."[46] In turn, the intensity of reconnaissance photography was such that the Germans were able to produce a new image of the entire Western Front every two weeks and thus rapidly produce maps that responded to changes on the ground.

More generally, there was a recruitment of geography for the cause of war. In May 1916, the General Staff urgently demanded from the Royal Geographical Society (RGS) special thematic maps of the British sector of the Western Front colored to show different relief and drainage features. Knowledge of these features was crucial in planning attacks. In 1914, the RGS urgently addressed the tasks of producing an index of the place-names on the large-scale maps of Belgium and France issued to the British officers sent there. A four-sheet 1:500,000 wall map of Britain was also produced in order to help the War Office plan home defense strategies in the event of a German invasion. The RGS then pressed on to produce a map of Europe at the scale of 1:1 million. By the end of the war, over ninety sheets had been prepared, covering most of Europe and the Middle East. The RGS also played a significant role as a cartographic agency closely linked to the British intelligence services.

The war greatly increased public interest in maps, and newspaper readers expected news coverage to be accompanied by them, a process that had already been greatly encouraged by the wars of 1898–1905. Maps were used both to provide what were intended as objective accounts and for what was consciously provided as propaganda, although the distinction between the two was not always easy to see. In the first case, large numbers of maps were printed in newspapers in order to locate areas of conflict. They provided a more valuable addition to text than photographs and were especially useful for distant areas that were not well covered in conventional atlases, notably in Africa, as well as because of the detail necessary to follow trench warfare in Europe. The color photography that was to come later in the century was not yet an established part of newspaper publishing and, as a result, black-and-white maps were not overshadowed. Providing helpful newspaper maps, however, was not easy. The simple black-and-white maps generally included little, if any, guidance to the terrain or to the difficulties of communications.

There was also a rapid production of atlases to satisfy consumer interest. These included the *Atlas of the European Conflict* (Chicago, 1914), the *Daily Telegraph Pocket Atlas of the War* (London, 1917), *Géographie de la Guerre* (Paris, 1917), *From the Western Front at a Glance* (London, 1917), *Petit Atlas de la Guerre et de la Paix* (Paris, 1918), and *Brentano's Record Atlas* (New York, 1918). The value of geography during the war helped ensure that it developed as a university subject. In Britain, honors schools in geography were established during or immediately after the war, including at Liverpool University in 1917, at the London School of Economics and Aberystwyth in 1918, and at University College, London, Cambridge, and Leeds, in 1919.

CONCLUSION

During the war, there was a need to rethink combined-arms operations in order to suppress defenses that were stronger than those generally anticipated prior to the conflict. This need gave urgent point to widespread interest in new technology and new tactics, each drawing on a mobilization of resources, both human and economic. The costs of this mobilization were formidable. In 1917, the British public was informed that the daily cost of the war to Britain was nearly £7 million.[47] Eventually on all fronts in 1918, the Allies developed the mechanisms necessary to sustain their advance and offensive in the face of continued opposition, thus acquiring an operational dynamic that gave effect to their strategy. The large numbers of troops involved posed particular problems of logistical support. Filling the many gaps created by heavy casualties meant that there was a continual need for the mobilization of manpower, and this need posed organizational, political, and social challenges, in addition to meaning that training proved a continuing demand.

The effort of war, a conflict waged on land in Africa[48] as well as in Europe and the Middle East, entailed a mobilization of resources and a militarization of societies. The latter was especially apparent in countries that hither had not had conscription, such as Britain and Canada. There was some opposition, as in Quebec City in April 1918, when four rioters were shot dead, but surprisingly little. So also with the general pattern of loyal service among the military despite harsh and unprecedented circumstances. The situation varied by individual and state but was generally more positive than later critical literary accounts would suggest.[49]

The political issues involved in raising support overlapped with another aspect of the war that tends to be underplayed, that of the war as an imposition of control in the domestic sphere. This was more frequently a matter of force than tends to be appreciated. Force played a role in the maintenance of control in occupied areas, and also in controlling discontent, notably in multinational empires such as, very differently, those of Turkey, Russia, and Britain. Britain suppressed an Irish nationalist rising in Dublin in 1916, and Russia a larger-scale rebellion in Central Asia.

The war also saw considerable novelty, notably in the use of new weaponry, particularly tanks, submarines, gas, and aircraft, but also in the industrial scale of production. Vast and unprecedented quantities of munitions were produced. Combined with improvements in fighting quality and skill, these helped deliver the military decisiveness that swept aside or dislocated the old order across much of the world.

In 1917, the Romanov dynasty was overthrown in Russia,[50] followed in 1918 by the Habsburg, Hohenzollern, and Ottoman Empires of Austria, Germany, and Turkey, respectively. The earlier failure of the powers to negotiate a peaceful end to the conflict was a key feature of the war, as it also was to be of the Second World War. This failure ensured that the destructiveness of the conflict did not lead to its end but, instead, to a determination to devote even more effort to it. This effort proved politically traumatic but militarily conclusive.

Chapter Five

Between the Wars, 1918–39

The interwar period is generally presented in terms of digesting the lessons of the First World War and preparing for the Second. This, traditionally, is a tale of tanks, aircraft, and new military doctrine, with this doctrine being tested out, notably, by the Germans in the Spanish Civil War (1936–39). The assessment of this period was conventionally presented in terms of the varied degree to which militaries responded to the possibilities of the new, notably mechanization and, in particular, the development of doctrine, operations, and tactics, such that tanks were used en masse and for bold attacking maneuvers, rather than being split up among the infantry and employed as a form of mobile artillery.[1]

The potential for air warfare also appeared immense, with only the sky apparently as the limit. The Allied generalissimo on the Western Front in 1918, Marshal Ferdinand Foch, wrote two years later,

> Today, the ability for aviation to carry increasing weight furnishes a new method for abundantly spreading poison gases with the aid of stronger and stronger bombs, and to reach armies, the centres of population in the rear, or to render regions uninhabitable.

That his remarks appeared in a book, *The Riddle of the Rhine: Chemical Strategy in Peace and War*, by Victor Lefebure, a wartime gas officer, indicated the extent to which military issues were presented to the public. The book's introduction was by Field Marshal Sir Henry Wilson, the chief of the [British] Imperial General Staff. False assumptions about the future after the First World War included the likelihood of gas warfare.[2]

Also in 1920, in a memorandum titled "Explanations of the Theory of the Application of the Essential Principles of Strategy to Infantry Tactics," Basil Liddell Hart (1895–1970), a British army officer turned commentator, sought to turn his perspectives into rules given credence by recent history:

> The improvements in weapons and the wide extensions enforced by them have created new conditions in the infantry fight. It has developed into what may be termed group combats; the defenders realising that a self-contained group based on a tactical point is more effective than a trench line, the breaking of which results in the whole line falling back; the attackers countering this method of defence by endeavouring to penetrate between the centres of resistance and turn their flanks.[3]

The focus on preparing for great-power war, however, led, and leads, as in the 1980s, to an underrating of other political and military tasks, particularly the defense of imperial possessions, authority, and claims from insurrections and disturbances, as against British rule in Egypt, Iraq, and India; French rule in Morocco and Syria; and Spanish rule in Spanish Morocco. In particular, the overthrow of the Ottoman Empire (Turkey) in 1918, especially due to British pressure, had resulted in an unprecedented advance of the Western empires into the Islamic world, but this, alongside the new volatility in the Middle East, led to a number of conflicts that tested new imperial pretensions and patterns of control. In response, the imperial powers, as well as regional states struggling to enforce their rule, notably Persia (Iran) and Saudi Arabia, used established means of operations, especially rapidly advancing columns of infantry and also cavalry, and new means, notably aircraft and lorries with mounted machine guns. The latter were a predecessor of the recent use of jeeps and other vehicles with a machine gun or an antiaircraft gun in the back, as in Chad in the 1980s and Libya, Iraq, and, to a lesser extent, Syria in the 2010s. By the end of the 1930s, a series of revolts had been suppressed in Persia (Iran), Iraq, Saudi Arabia, and Turkey.

The pursuit of advantage in civil wars was also very important in the interwar period. Indeed, the biggest wars of the period from 1919 to 1936 were the civil wars in Russia and then China. As with the struggles over imperial control, these conflicts brought together traditional and new elements, and they did so in states made volatile by the end of monarchical rule and by the related introduction of new governmental systems and ideologies. Control over troops played a major role, as it also did in Mexico, which was convulsed by revolution. However, whereas in China and Mexico the resulting dominance of generals or warlords remained significant in the governmental structures that were established, in Russia, the Soviet Union after the First World War, the warlord generals, who were indeed fundamental to the counterrevolutionary "White" side, were rapidly defeated. Thus, they were unable to ground themselves in regional power bases and, crucially, were not brought over to the new ruling system.

In turn, the Soviet army abandoned and avoided many of the regime's initial revolutionary ideas about military organization, but it was under civilian control. This control was brutally demonstrated in the purges of the late 1930s carried out by the order of the suspicious dictator Josef Stalin. Begun in 1937, these purges led to the slaughter of most of the leadership, notably Marshal Tukhachevskii, and part of the officer corps.[4] The result was a loss of experience, cohesion, and operational skill and a marked degree of caution on the part of most of the survivors. This led to an avoidance of risk and an obedience to orders that helped result in devastating losses at German hands in 1941, although overly rapid expansion and a crucial weakness in junior officers and NCOs may well have been more significant.[5]

Moreover, as another instance of the variety of warfare, there was significant civil conflict elsewhere in 1919–36, for example in Brazil. It was only from the early to mid-1930s that the military and political agenda focused on impending conflict with other major powers, which began with the Japanese invasion of China in 1937.

DIFFERING GOALS AND MEANS

It is understandable that, if a period is delimited in terms of the end of one world war and the start of another and is defined as an interwar period, there is a tendency to look for the consequences of the former war and the anticipation of the latter one. These indeed are part of the story, and, in the public eye, there was a focus on the Western Front and thus on the possibility of another such war.

However, land warfare in these years also included much else. Moreover, the combination of the two provided an opportunity not only for different narratives at the time (and subsequently), but also for some major powers to decide how best to prioritize between clashing commitments and the differing requirements they posed.

The immediacy of the conflicts that occurred after the First World War will take precedence here, to be followed by the working through of the supposed lessons of the war. This distinction can be complicated by pointing out that one lesson was that war could cause the total overthrow of a political system, as happened with the Russian, Austro-Hungarian, German, and Turkish Empires. Moreover, the significance of conflict within China and Mexico in the 1910s provides a way to assess similar patterns of civil warfare in the 1920s and 1930s.

The interactions of politics, ideology, and warfare frequently encouraged antisocietal practices, notably the determination to isolate and destroy what were presented as internal enemies. This was very much seen in the warfare in Europe that followed the First World War, and notably so in the Russian Civil War. In part, this situation can be treated as a simple product of civil wars and also of the projection into Europe of the small-wars techniques hitherto employed as an aspect of imperial conquest. However, there was an added element of political terror directed against those presented as social enemies. This was not new and had been clearly seen with wars of religion in the past, but it certainly contrasted with the situation during the First World War. In Europe, there was relatively little deliberate slaughter of civilians by armies during that conflict, and certainly not as compared with German military conduct on the Eastern Front during the Second World War.

After the First World War, however, military necessity contributed to the internal violence, because the mobilization of society had to operate in an inchoate political context. Tensions were not only ethnic-nationalist, but also ideological, with the Bolsheviks (a Communist faction), notably but not only in Russia, seeking to use class identity to bridge ethnic divides and, instead, in a warfare they actively wanted,[6] to isolate and destroy what were seen, and presented, as internal enemies. The consequences were brutal, with the mass killing of those regarded as social enemies and, therefore, political traitors. Soviet attempts to build support ultimately relied on violence, and this violence was social warfare. This violence and warfare were on a massive scale, for example the killing of up to one hundred thousand in Crimea in 1920–21 after the fighting had ended, with over twenty thousand executed in the city of Simferopol alone.

Moreover, the conflict continued. Although the Russian Civil War is conventionally dated 1918–21, it can be extended to 1926, when the Red Army finally suppressed active resistance on the Turkestan Front in Central Asia.[7] In addition, opposition then, and later, to the Soviet regime, and to its brutal and uncompromising policy of farm collectivization, can be regarded as part of the continuance, or at least aftermath, of the extremely violent civil wars and of the inability of the Bolsheviks to treat opposition as anything less than a foe.[8]

The fighting, both in the Russian Civil War and in other conflicts of the period, was far more confused than that during the First World War. In place of clear-cut adversaries came shifting alignments and uncertain interventions, both international and domestic. The coalitions that had waged the First World War were more coherent.

Also, instead of regular forces, readily apparent command structures, and clearly demarcated front lines, there were irregulars, complex relations between civil and military agencies and goals, and fluid spheres of operations. Guerrilla groups played a significant role.[9] The emphasis was on activity (albeit small scale compared with the world war), raids, and the seizure of key political centers, rather than on sieges or on staging battles from prepared positions. The difficulty of sustaining operations, a difficulty that stemmed from the lack of an organized logistical support system, encouraged this emphasis. As a result, the focus was very much on the offensive, not least in order to seize resources, as in 1918, when the newly established Communist government in Tashkent sent a small force that rapidly seized Khokand, overthrowing the Muslim government that had been established there.

The wars of the period indicated the difficulties both of sustaining a revolutionary struggle and, conversely, of mounting effective counterinsurgency action. The force-space ratios of conflict in Eastern Europe were different from those in Western Europe during the recent world war; but, far more, the problems of political and, to a lesser degree, military control were greater. The need that both revolutionaries and their opponents faced to create new armies put a premium on overcoming problems in recruitment and in resisting desertion. The creation and implementation of government structures were important in providing the context for harnessing resources.

Remedies were often brutal. Recruitment was enforced with violence and the threat of violence, and desertion, a major problem, was punished savagely, often with executions. Faced with major logistical problems, armies raised supplies through force. There was much destruction, both in order to deny resources to opponents and to punish those judged disloyal.

The defensive remained important at the tactical level, and in some respects more so than in the First World War, in part because the artillery necessary to suppress fire was in limited supply and not really useful for fast-moving operations over large areas. At the same time, defensive positions could be stormed, while the absence of continuous fronts made it easier to outflank defensive positions. This encouraged a stress on maneuver, one very much seen in the Russian Civil War, in which large-scale battles were few, as opposed to small-scale clashes.

The stress on maneuver was also encouraged by the need to establish control rapidly in contested areas in order to present peacemakers and other powers with faits accomplis. This was a response to such action by others, and also to the international context. The latter included both the failure of peacemakers to accept the complexity of situations on the ground and a rejection, in the latter, of the attempt by outside bodies to dictate developments. Moreover, the presence of German forces in the western parts of the former Russian Empire, and their active role in political struggles, notably in Latvia, ensured that there was no clear divide between the First World War and postwar struggles.

Internal conflict in Europe began in Russia in 1917, with the Bolsheviks successfully imposing their order, but spread as the Austro-Hungarian Empire collapsed in 1918, leading to struggles over the existence, boundaries, and government of states. By the end of the year, Germans and Czechs were clashing in the Sudetenland, as were Carinthians and Slovenes in what became the Austrian-Yugoslav border area. Prewar disputes became postwar clashes. Civil war ensured that the number of sides and participants in conflict rose, and, with this, notions of a clear-cut definition of military forces, and of war as the prerogative of the state, were both put under severe strain. As a result, regular armies, some newly formed as states were created, were obliged to confront situations in which goals and opponents were far from clear, and atrocities, terrorism, and terror became more than the small change of war. Paramilitary forces took a significant part.[10] In November 1918, Foch only permitted the Germans one modification to the armistice terms: they were allowed to keep some of their machine guns in order to help against a Bolshevik rising.[11]

Ideology and nationalism both played a role. In the former case, Romanians and Czechs suppressed a Communist regime in Hungary in 1919, a conflict that involved relatively large forces. Nationalism was to the fore in the occupation of the town of Fiume by an Italian volunteer force in 1919, the Polish seizure of Vilnius from Lithuania in 1920, and the Lithuanian seizure of Memel (Klaipeda) in 1923. There was also considerable overlap between ideology and nationalism.

While this wave of conflict was largely over by 1923,[12] there was no guarantee that it would not revive. Territorial claims, for example by Hungary on Romanian-held Transylvania, remained an issue. The shadow of the First World War, although powerful at the political level, was less pronounced in terms of military lessons than is generally believed, and certainly if the focus for the latter is on a small number of commentators. In part, this was because the postwar concerns for most states were not those of large-scale conflict. Moreover, the First World War, although different in scale from what had gone before, was part of a sequence of conflicts for many states and areas. It was less novel, for example, for Bulgaria, Romania, and Greece than it was for Britain.

Similarly, in Latin America, the years after the First World War saw a continuation of earlier patterns of conflict. In Mexico, the Constitutionalists had fallen out after the overthrow of Victoriano Huerta in 1914. Venustiano Carranza, one of the key political figures, who had a base as governor of Coahuila and who was the *primer jefe* (first chief) of the Constitutional Army, seized power, running Mexico from 1915 until 1920. Essentially, he was a conservative unwilling to accept the social reforms demanded by Pancho Villa and Emiliano Zapata, key figures in the opposition to Huerta. As in China, the provinces splintered under the control of various generals in 1914, but Carranza benefited from control over the major ports and oil production and enjoyed more revenue. In 1915, Villa was defeated by Carranza's follower General Álvaro Obregón, and Carranza was in control of much of the country from 1915, including, crucially, Mexico City. That year, he had cooperated with the Casa del Obrero Mundial (House of the World Worker), a labor union that raised troops, but in 1916 this relationship collapsed and the Red Battalions raised in 1915 were dissolved, while the army suppressed striking workers, prefiguring the situation in China in 1927 when Jiang Jieshi turned on the Communists. In Mexico, Zapata, who led opposition from the mountains of Morelos, was assassinated in 1919 as a result of a bounty on his head. Several provinces, however, remained under the control of opponents of Carranza.

In 1920, Obregón and allied generals turned against Carranza. They drove him from Mexico City, and the former president was killed soon after. Obregón was president until 1924, overcoming a rebellion in 1923–24 by Adolfo de la Huerta, a former supporter. Obregón won the 1928 election but was assassinated soon after by a Catholic radical.

Much of the warfare in Latin America was insurrectionary in character—for example, the failed invasion of Costa Rica in 1919 by exiles based in Nicaragua, the Liberal revolt in Nicaragua in 1925, and the Cristero rebellion in central-western Mexico in 1926–29, a Catholic rising against the secularizing policies of the government. Estimates of the dead in the last focused on the figure of ninety thousand. The rebels were effective against the local militia but found the well-armed federal forces more difficult. A conciliatory governmental approach led to a settlement in 1929.[13]

In the Western colonial empires, policies designed to ensure control did not change in the 1920s, with the major exception of the addition of air power.[14] In China, the atomization of power seen in the 1910s and notably later in that decade continued in the early 1920s. Japan (in China) and the United States (in the Caribbean and Central America[15]) continued their power projection in what they sought to define as their areas of control. These elements of continuity provide an important aspect of the military history of these years, and one that should not be treated as eccentric to the legacy of the First World War.

Another element of continuity was provided by the struggle against banditry. By 1931, most of Corsica was under the effective control of bandits who charged for transit through their zones of control. In 1931, France deployed troops, armored cars, and aircraft from the French mainland under General Fournier, the commander in chief in Corsica, in order to provide mobile columns to advance into the mountains and seize bandit leaders. Benito Mussolini, the Fascist dictator of Italy, used force to try to suppress the Mafia in Sicily and also against banditry in Sardinia.

Novelty was not simply a matter of the response to new technology. The ideological dimension focusing on Communism and the Russian Revolution was significant. So also, in the colonial context, as mentioned earlier, was the transfer of control over much of the Arab world to Western colonial control at the expense of the former Turkish Empire. This transfer led to resistance in Egypt, Iraq, and Syria[16] and was related to a wider problem for Western power in Islamic lands, notably in Morocco, Turkey, Persia, and Afghanistan. Warfare was a result in the years immediately after the First World War, as in the Third Anglo-Afghan War (1919),[17] and remained a possibility thereafter. Indeed, it was seen on the North-West Frontier of British India, in Waziristan, in the late 1930s.

These conflicts entailed a range of military environments, including the classic mountain redoubts of resistance, as in Waziristan and, for opposition to Spain, in the Rif Mountains in Morocco. At Annual, in these mountains in 1921, Spain suffered at least twelve thousand casualties as an army disintegrated rather than staging a fighting retreat. At the same time, the urban spaces, both old and new, of cities in the Muslim world became more challenging, a situation that looked to the present. In 1925–26, in overcoming the Great Syrian Revolt, the French shelled and bombed Damascus, causing great destruction. The rebels were also overcome in the cities of Homs and Hama, where their concentrations of strength provided a target for French firepower.

The complex interrelationships of ethnic and religious rivalries and the interaction of ideologies were such that it could be very difficult for outsiders to understand the dynamics of any situation. Force proved one way to seek to contain and control the situation, but force was generally only a panacea. Indeed, the most successful policy, one that overlapped with force, was the alliance with local groups. This was a process facilitated by the extent to which the military strength of Western empires relied on local forces, as with the French in Lebanon, and notably so if policing was concerned. The British sought to lessen this issue by using Indian units in the Middle East, as in Iraq in 1919, but it was still a factor of consequence, and notably as policing was essentially paramilitary.[18]

The analysis in terms of resistance to imperialism is common, but that was not the sole issue. For example, in the case of the conflict between Greece and Turkey in 1919 and 1922, the war was a struggle between two independent states. Although not on the scale of the Russian Civil War, this was a major conflict, and one that in 1921—when the Greeks were checked at the Battle of Sakarya—and, far more, 1922 delivered a clear verdict, that of total Greek defeat. The fighting had elements of the First World War, with commanders and troops experienced from that conflict and using similar weaponry and tactics. The contrast with the Western Front was apparent in the maneuverability shown by the forces and in the search for open flanks and encirclement. This entailed considerable overlap with the campaigning in Eastern Europe and, more particularly, the Balkans during the First World War.

The Greek-Turkish War was also significant for features notable in current conflicts, especially the antisocietal elements of ethnic brutalization seen with the Turkish treatment of those of Greek origin living in Turkey, notably at Smyrna/Izmir when it was captured in 1922. This was a long-standing and large group, but it was treated as unacceptable by the Turks, who sought a monoglot definition of nationalism, one that took forward pre–First World War ethnic violence and the mass murder of Armenians during that conflict.

Secondly, the Greek-Turkish War very much involved international tensions. It was the key element of the Turkish attempt to reverse the treaty settlement that had followed the First World War, notably the establishment of British, French, Greek and Italian spheres of influence. This came to be intertwined with the Cold War between the Soviet Union and its opponents. The Soviets backed the Turks as part of a more general and successful process of encouraging anti-Western nationalism, one also seen in China, Persia (Iran), and Afghanistan. At the same time, the alliance against the Turks disintegrated, with the Italians helping the Turks against the French, and the Greeks, who followed their own course, making themselves the focus of Turkish attack.

The war in Turkey, like the Russian Civil War, showed the difficulty of ensuring international cooperation against a determined adversary, a conclusion that is still valid today. In each case, the international coalition suffered from a lack of strong support within the country in which it was intervening. This was far more the case in Turkey, where nationalism was a greater factor than in Russia. Kemal Atatürk, in practice, overthrew local opponents, notably those who had agreed to accept the Allied terms, but this element was not one that the Allies could turn to their advantage.

The Russian Civil War also entailed efforts by the Bolshevik government, thwarted in its hopes of world revolution, to regain control by force of regions where non-Russian ethnic groups had sought to win independence. Russian control was reimposed in the Caucasus, Central Asia, and Ukraine, but not in the Baltic states (Estonia, Latvia, and Lithuania), Finland, or Poland. The Russo-Polish War in 1920 demonstrated the characteristics of the warfare of the period. It was very mobile, both militarily and politically. This type of warfare, which was typical of many of the conflicts after 1945, was also important earlier. Attacking in April–May 1920, the Poles overran western Ukraine, capturing Kiev. In turn, a Soviet counterattack in late May led to an advance approaching close to Warsaw, only for a well-executed Polish counterattack to drive the Soviets back in August. The advancing Soviet forces were poorly coordinated and overextended, and they failed to understand Polish intentions. The Red Army lost about 150,000 troops.

Lenin had had a clear strategy, one in which military operations sat within a political prospectus. He hoped that the Polish working class would support the cause of the working class in the shape of the Red Army and lead to an advance of the latter that would secure revolution in Germany. However, this proved as much wishful thinking as the hopes of the French Revolutionaries in the 1790s.[19]

Nationalism as an opponent of Western control was seen not only in Turkey but also in Persia (Iran), China, Iraq, and Arabia and, less successfully, Afghanistan. In Turkey, Persia, China, and Iraq, the nationalist movement, having overthrown local rivals, established a militarized regime, for example the Jiang Jieshi government in China. The conflicts that led to these outcomes, and that stemmed from them, were an important part of the military history of the 1920s and, to a degree, 1930s. Moreover, much of this warfare was sustained because the sole means of registering opposition and securing control was through violence or through a politics of patronage that was negotiated by means of violence. In Afghanistan, the British backed tribal revolts that led to the abdication of Amanullah (r. 1919–29). He failed to devote the attention to the army shown by Kemal Atatürk in Turkey and by Reza Khan in Persia.[20]

Again, when space is at a premium, such conflicts tend to be downplayed or ignored in the rush to get from one world war to another. This is mistaken, not least as the military verdicts of the period were often lasting, and more so than some of those of the world wars. Moreover, the experience of the period remained significant in the subsequent and current attitudes of governing groups, notably with the ruling House of Saud in Arabia. These conflicts are again resonant of those at present, in that nationalism was frequently imposed with brutal force at the expense of ethnic and religious groups, whose difference and autonomy appeared unwelcome, as with Assyrian Christians in Iraq and Arabs in southwest Persia.[21] These issues provided a continuity that has lasted to the present. In the fighting, battle was less significant than the "small war" methods of raids and small-scale clashes. This was a warfare of rapid advances, not of front lines, and the tactics used in fighting accorded with this dynamic.

IRELAND

In contrast to the determination shown in Iraq (although not in Iran, Afghanistan, or Russia), the British made only a modest effort to maintain control in Ireland. This provided an instructive instance of the difficulties of suppressing an insurrection, and in the part of the empire longest under British control, the sole part, moreover, that was represented in the London Parliament. The Irish Republican Army (IRA), a violent nationalist force, drawing its support from much (but by no means all) of the Catholic majority, organized its active-service units into flying columns that staged raids and ambushes in order to undermine the stability of the British government. Assassinations and sabotage were also employed. The IRA was short of arms and gained many by raids on the British. The Thompson submachine gun came from the United States. The IRA was outnumbered by the army and the police but was able to take the initiative, to profit from its willingness to use murder and intimidation, and to benefit from the limited options available to those trying to restore control. The murder of about one hundred Protestants in the south helped terrorize the bulk of the Protestant community, many of whom fled.[22] British reprisals against Catholic civilians, though limited, sapped support for British rule within Ireland among the Catholic majority.

Nevertheless, the British were not clearly failing, and it is worth noting that earlier Irish rebellions, from the sixteenth century to 1916, had failed, as did later IRA campaigns, including in 1939, 1956–62, and 1969–98. Indeed, the IRA, in the summer of 1921, was under severe pressure from the British army. Over the previous two years, the government and army had developed a series of responses, including internment (detention without trials), the employment of active-service platoons, wireless telegraphy, and air power. The introduction of these measures meant that the IRA had ceased to provide a significant military threat, and by 1921, as in 1971 in Northern Ireland, their operations had been reduced to a terrorist, rather than a military, threat. The ability of the British army to respond flexibly is clear.[23]

Crucially, however, the British government, in part because of the range of its international commitments, was unwilling to take the firm steps advised by military leaders and instead favored negotiation. Most of the island was then granted independence in the Anglo-Irish Treaty of December 1921, although the Protestant-dominated region in the north, most of the historic province of Ulster, remained with Britain.

Ironically, the IRA then divided, leading to a civil war in the new Irish Free State. This was won by the pro-Treaty forces, in part because the government was willing to take a firmer line than the British had done, not least with the trial and execution of prisoners. To critics, British influence in the new state was being maintained by the forces of local allies. A key contrast was provided between the new National Army, which had an effective logistical system, with all the subsequent advantages for morale and capability, and the anti-Treaty IRA. The latter could not provide the supplies to support a large force in the field or to resupply smaller groups. These groups turned to guerrilla warfare but also commandeered supplies, which hit their local backing.[24]

CHINA

In China, the key form of conflict in the early 1920s was that between warlords, but, from the mid-1920s, that between the Guomindang (Nationalists) and the warlords became more important, while a rift developed between the Communists and the Guomindang and came to lead to significant conflict. There were elements similar to the Russian Civil War in terms of a conflict of maneuver and presence, rather than of battle or siege. At the same time, the recent reevaluation of the major role of fighting in the Chinese Civil War of 1946–49 suggests that greater attention to the situation in the late 1910s and 1920s will throw more light on the extent to which the warfare then involved fighting as well as the securing of consent by means of the demonstration of strength.

The warlords who ruled much of China were aligned by means of leagues. This was scarcely a stable system, as there were serious personal rivalries, no experience of making the new system work, and no institutional context to provide cohesion. The similar difficulties of getting the "White" generals in Russia to cooperate were also notable, as was the situation in Mexico. The 1920s in China are characterized as the warlord era. However, this was a judgmental, indeed polemical, term, one introduced from the Japanese *gunbatsu*, meaning the militarist interest. Those referred to were generals, mostly members of a fissiparous, but internationally recognized, government in Beijing. As an instructive instance to a more general situation in military history, the vote for the winner, the warlords are treated as anachronistic and in a pejorative fashion. This is because they lost to the Guomindang, which, in practice, was an insurgent movement. In contrast, in the 1920s alone, as Kemal Atatürk showed in Turkey, Ibn Saud in Arabia, and Reza Khan in Persia, success can provide a very different gloss.

There is also the problem of semantics, a problem that is more significant in military history than many readers appreciate. The term *warlord* suggests that warlord warfare was somehow qualitatively different from the other warfare waged before and after. This is incorrect. So also with the teleologies that assert a certain course of military as well as political and economic modernization.[25]

In the case of China, long-standing regionalism, including strong historical tensions between north and south, as well as political and military developments prior to, during, and after the 1911 revolution, were all of significance. The collapse in 1916 of the presidency of Yuan Shikai, commander of the Beiyang Army, helped discredit the central government based there. Subsequent rivalries among the now leaderless northern generals were a key element in the breakdown of order. Large-scale conflict began in 1920 with the overthrow of General Duan Qirui, the prime minister, by the forces of two leading generals, Wu Peifu and Zhang Zuolin. This step brought the power of the warlords to fruition.

The local commanders were essentially regional figures, but the leading generals used territorial bases to contend for power over all of China. Anti-Republican Zhang Zuolin (1875–1928), the Manchurian warlord from 1916 and head of the Fengtian Clique, was the leading figure in northern China, and in 1928 he and his allies were able to deploy four hundred thousand troops. In Central China, the major figure, Wu Peifu, was head of the Zhili Clique. In 1922, in the First Zhili-Fengtian War, Wu defeated Zhang in a struggle for control of Beijing, whereupon Zhang declared Manchurian autonomy. The pressure of conflict caused a military modernization in China that was fit-for-purpose as far as circumstances permitted, a situation seen more generally in the 1920s. In contrast, this process was less apparent in states that were not involved in large-scale conflict. Reorganizing and retraining his army, Zhang brought forward younger officers.[26] In the Second Zhili-Fengtian War, Zhang moved south. He occupied Beijing in 1926–28.

Large infantry armies were the situation in China, with scant mechanization. This lack of mechanization was the norm across much of the world, although trucks in Arabia demonstrated the place for variety. In the Spanish Civil War (1936–39), the competing Nationalist generals were to be brought to cooperate, and one, Franco, from late 1936, ruled a regime that lasted until his death in 1975. In China, the Guomindang offered the same because, under Jiang Jieshi, they came in part to operate as a military faction of their own, indeed as the faction that came, with the Northern Expedition of 1926–28, to dominate most of China, with the significant exception of Manchuria. Jiang succeeded by fighting his opponents sequentially[27] and by an aggressive, attacking fighting style, notably using columns, as in the Battle of Longtan in 1927.

The result of this cohesion was to be challenged in the 1930s by Japanese expansion, and overthrown in 1946–49 by eventual Communist success. On another timescale, however, this result was to be lasting as it left China as a coherent state and not as, in effect, a series of states. The latter had been the pattern during periods of Chinese history, for example the eleventh and early twelfth centuries, and there was no reason to believe that it would not recur. The Turkish and Austro-Hungarian Empires had totally collapsed. That China did not is part of the military history of the period that does not attract attention because, however significant, Chinese military history tends to be underplayed in Western military history, and there is generally a lack of attention to what would have been important outcomes had they occurred, and notably so at the political level.

At the Gutian Conference in December 1929, the Chinese Communists decided that the Red Army was both a "mass propaganda" organ as well as a fighting force, under the total control of the Communist Party. In China, the nature of military struggle changed in the 1930s, first with the rise of large-scale hostilities between the Guomindang and the Communists in the early 1930s, which led to the deployment of significant forces in search-and-destroy operations in marginal areas, and second, from 1937, with full-scale Japanese invasion.

Initially very successful with the capture of Beijing, Shanghai, and Nanjing in 1937, and of Guangzhou and Wuhan in 1938, the Japanese invasion of China did not bring Japan the victorious closure it had anticipated. The Japanese invasion at first saw Japanese forces attack Chinese regular units in the major settled areas of the country, notably in the difficult and lengthy battle for control of Shanghai in 1937. The Japanese had better air support and artillery, profited from amphibious capability, and faced poor command by Jiang Jieshi. The military methods the Guomindang had used so successfully in 1925–30 no longer proved appropriate. Thus, it suffered from continuity in what was a changing context.[28]

Despite inflicting many casualties, however, including the destruction of the best-trained Chinese divisions,[29] as well as numerous civilian casualties, the Japanese could not drive the Chinese to surrender. This situation prefigured the later German invasion of the Soviet Union. Instead, by late 1938, they found that much of their effort was tied up in a fruitless attempt to enforce control in occupied areas, while it proved impossible to maintain the dynamic of advance. The resulting sense of frustration affected Japan's response to the international situation in 1939–41, particularly with the developing conviction that supply routes to China had to be cut, notably via Vietnam and Burma, respectively French and British colonies.[30]

Each type of military struggle indicates the range of land warfare in the period, but they also captured the dependence of this warfare on the ability to persuade defeated opponents that they had lost. Because this did not occur, the ability to win success in the field did not lead to an outcome. In contrast, but crucially for other reasons, both the Japanese and the Guomindang had failed totally in China by the end of 1949, although, in the former case, this was not a result of the fighting there.

THE PURPOSES OF FORCE

A similar point could be made about much of the warfare of the period, which demonstrates the importance of considering significance in a range of contexts. That process was apparent in the aftermath of the First World War, as commentators sought to assess both how to win war and how to avoid it. In the aftermath of what was termed "the war to end all wars," the understanding of victory varied greatly. One purpose of military capability was to create a deterrent that would ensure that no future wars were attempted. This was seen in particular with ideas of air warfare, the probable extreme destructiveness of which was regarded as a deterrent to future hostilities or as likely to cause a rapid outcome to any war.

International cooperation, even agreements, appeared as other means of deterrence. If the former had not led to success in overthrowing Russian Communism, it had better fortune in blocking Communist/Russian expansion in Hungary and Poland and in confining Russia. Indeed, in the 1920s, there were not, as there were to be from the late 1940s to the end of the 1980s, two competing alliance systems with the military strength of both affecting the equations of deterrence.

This situation changed in the 1930s, helping to cause the outbreak of the Second World War in 1939. That shifting international context centered on the rise, expansionism, and aggressiveness of Germany under Adolf Hitler, its ruler from 1933, notably at the expense of Czechoslovakia in 1938 and Poland in 1939. This process became more important because of Hitler's ability to align with other powers, notably Italy, Japan, and, eventually in 1939, the Soviet Union, and, more specifically, to prompt the backing of lesser states, such as Hungary, Bulgaria, Romania, and Finland.

THE MEANS OF WAGING WAR

Changes in the means of waging war were less significant than political developments. The period is generally seen in terms of the rise of mechanization, more specifically the development of armored warfare, and the bringing forward of ideas that were subsequently to be labeled (and simplified) as blitzkrieg, the term that is applied to the methods employed in German offensives in 1939–41. In practice, that was not the obvious narrative in the 1920s and 1930s. Even if attention is restricted to Europe, the emphasis on infantry, artillery, and fortifications is readily apparent. This was the case with doctrine, force structure, procurement, training, and command patterns. Indeed, the "froth" created by some of the protagonists for armored warfare reflected their desire for attention in what they felt was a largely indifferent, even hostile, environment. More positively, there was an engagement with armor on the part of military leadership, but as part of a process of devising a range of capabilities in response to a variety of commitments.

Debates over capabilities and procurement were an aspect of the analysis of the First World War during the 1920s, and of the linkage of what became the 1930s' arms race to the distinctive strategic culture of particular states. This arms race was unprecedented as it involved not only what had been conventional weaponry prior to the First World War, but also a novel race in air power over both land and sea. The arms race was not a case of matching like for like, for much of the race involved trying to develop particular capabilities or deploying antiweaponry to cope with such capabilities on the part of others. As a result, there were major contrasts between militaries.

Equipment was obtained from other states by means of purchase and gift, as with the important arms relationship between Germany and the Soviet Union that helped each to rearm. In 1921, Spain purchased tanks, aircraft, and artillery from France, with which it had shared interests in Morocco. In 1922, twelve Renault FT-17s, each armed with machine guns and supported by tank transport trucks and tanker trucks, were deployed by Spain. In their initial use at Ambar in Morocco, three of the tanks were disabled while many of the machine guns jammed due to faulty equipment. However, in turn, improved mechanical reliability and better ammunition led to enhanced performance.[31] As so often, it is necessary to note both aspects of the situation.

At the same time, the large size of most militaries made the cost of improving them especially high. Indeed, the burden of sustaining forces that were so numerous, in particular, feeding, clothing, housing, and arming such numbers, was a serious problem. This problem accentuated the tendency to focus on key sectors, which in turn helped encourage debate about their identity. In contrast, the bulk of the military lacked comparable investment and improvement. This bulk provided the mass that appeared necessary to many, notably most army commanders. In 1936, Sir Archibald Montgomery-Massingberd, chief of the [British] Imperial General Staff from 1933 and a general, like many, from an artillery background, wrote at the end of his period in post,

> I feel that the biggest battle that I have had to fight in the last three years is against the idea that on account of the arrival of air forces as a new arm, the Low Countries are of little value to us and that, therefore, we need not maintain a military force to assist in holding them.... The elimination of any army commitment on the Continent sounds such a comfortable and cheap policy... especially among the air mad.[32]

However, in 1934, Stanley Baldwin, the leading British politician, told the House of Commons that Britain would not accept inferiority in air power and, soon after, a large majority voted in the Commons for a major increase in the size of the air force by 1939. By 1940, Britain had a numerical superiority over Germany in single-engined fighters. The Munich crisis with Germany in 1938 had further encouraged an emphasis on air power in British rearmament. Moreover, no other state had a capability matching the integrated air defense system founded on a chain of early-warning radar stations that Britain had built from 1936. Air power, which was also much used in policing the empire, was seen as the necessary way to defend the country and the best way to hit at opponents. In the Anglo-Italian crisis of 1935–36 over Ethiopia, the Royal Air Force (RAF) proposed to bomb the industrial centers of northern Italy from bases in southern France.[33]

The emphasis by many on the leading sectors of mass militaries, including air power, was an attempt to reconcile the need for both quality and mass in modern warfare, and the apparent requirements of individual states in each case. This was seen in the French army, where the development of mechanized and motorized divisions was intended to provide a mobility capable of countering the German advance in Belgium, as a prelude to an engagement by the mass army with its infantry and artillery. The British army committee that in 1938 recommended the merger of the Royal Tank Corps and the newly mechanized cavalry (an achievement for which Montgomery-Massingberd deserved much of the credit) pressed for the need for centralized training "at a depot equipped with suitable vehicles and staffed by technically qualified instructors."[34]

The taskings related to strategy and the politics of prioritization had implications for industry capacity and policy, and for politics. In the Soviet Union, Josef Stalin, the dictator from 1924 to 1953, moved to support a major military buildup because of the emerging threat of war with Japan from 1931.[35] However, Marshal Tukhachevskii, who was purged in June 1937, was a danger to Stalin because he had displayed an unhealthy habit of elevating military necessity to the point of demanding the subordination of the whole economy to the army. The Soviet Terror overlapped with, and was related to, the acceleration of the arms race.[36] Tukhachevskii was associated with an emphasis on armor designed to give force to doctrines of "deep battle" focused on taking and sustaining the offensive. The Soviet Union, which was investing heavily in equipment, had as many as seven thousand tanks in 1935, but the 1936 maneuvers revealed serious tactical and operational problems in their use.[37] Thus, even before the 1937 purges, there were major problems with the Soviet army.

In hindsight, as with the protagonists of aircraft carriers as opposed to battleships, the pattern of finding good and bad, progress and reactionary failure, in the discussion of force structure, doctrine, and procurement is seriously misguided; and anyway it requires a measured assessment of conflict in the Second World War. Turning, instead, to the situation prior to the war, it is readily understandable that powers confronted with a range of commitments did not invest heavily in unproven technologies, such as large tank forces, that could not fulfill all their needs. This point helps ensure that doctrinal arguments have to be put in the context of the greater urgencies of current concerns. At the same time, the reliance of rearmament on economic strength was readily understood.[38]

THE CHACO WAR OF 1932–35 AND SPANISH CIVIL WAR OF 1936–39

Resources were significant, but they did not determine the outcome of conflicts. In the Chaco War, Paraguay defeated Bolivia despite the greater wealth and population of the latter. In part, this was due to the quality of Paraguay's military leadership. President Salamanca of Bolivia anticipated a rapid victory that would consolidate his domestic position, and he launched a surprise attack with his larger and more modern army. Initial gains, however, were followed by severe logistical problems and a successful Paraguayan counterattack. Fortified positions linked to wells and their supply of water were the key points in the desolate Chaco, and in 1933 the defeat of Bolivian frontal assaults on the fort of Nanawa proved important.[39]

As part of the discussion over capability, effectiveness, and thus best practice, the Spanish Civil War suggested that artillery would be more significant than armor and that the ability of tanks to provide mobile artillery was limited, although the environment in Spain lacked the flat open plains of Poland and the western Soviet Union. That war also demonstrated the continued centrality of political factors, not only in the cause of the conflict, but also to the goals of both sides. The length of time it took the Nationalists, the insurgents, to win in Spain in part reflected the use of attritional means to grind down the Republicans, the government side, but also the degree to which, as with the Chaco War between Bolivia and Paraguay and the Japanese intervention in China, it was actually difficult to deliver a verdict. There was more movement in Spain, the Chaco War, and China than might have been appreciated had the model been that of the Western Front in 1915–17, but not enough to ensure a speedy end to the conflict.

The practice of military violence in domestic politics was well established in nineteenth-century Spain, as in Portugal and Latin America. In part, this was a baleful consequence of the destabilization wrought by the Napoleonic conflict in 1808. The twentieth century offered a new iteration of old themes and methods, a situation also familiar with the Balkans. For example, the successful Spanish military coup of 1923 was a conservative response to the challenge of mass politics in an age of rapid modernization. In turn, the Nationalist uprising in 1936 was a military coup against political change. It was accompanied by extreme violence, as in Seville, that was employed irrespective of the degree of violence required to achieve particular goals. Both sides were guilty of terrible crimes and policies, not least because violence to those judged opponents was a means of establishing control. The victors had more of an opportunity to enforce their new order in, and through, blood. Repression employing disproportionate force continued after the conquest of particular areas and after the war. Indeed, the brutality of civilian life in Spain in the 1940s reflected an extended state of war.[40]

Unlike the Chaco War and conflicts in China (a far larger area), that in Spain was the only one in which the entire area in dispute was conquered by one power. Sequential campaigning by the Nationalists proved the means to do so, and that in part depended on preventing the opponents from countering with an equal effectiveness. To take the pressure off the north in 1937, the Republicans counterattacked in the center, especially in the Battle of Brunete, west of Madrid, on July 6. The Republicans broke through the weak Nationalist line, but Franco sent reinforcements including German and Italian aircraft. The Republicans proved unable to maintain their impetus, a general problem in military operations, and their troops lost more heavily. Brunete revealed their deficiencies, not least poor coordination between the arms and, related to this, an inexpert use of the available artillery and tanks. The Republicans also lacked sufficient air power.[41] The Soviet decision in July 1937 to dispatch aid to the Guomindang in China against Japanese attack greatly reduced the amount available to help Spain, while Stalin was increasingly uninterested in the Spanish struggle.

Defeated at Brunete, the Republicans were unable to prevent the Nationalists from capturing the port of Santander on the northern coast on August 26, while San Sebastián fell on September 13. The loss of ports reduced the possibility of obtaining foreign supplies and, indeed, of counting internationally. Similarly, a Republican offensive near Zaragoza in late August revealed the same problems as Brunete and failed to prevent the Nationalists from overrunning the region of Asturias in October. This success gave the Nationalists an important industrial zone and freed up their troops and warships to operate elsewhere against the divided Republicans. As in the Russian Civil War, the relationship between the fronts was readily apparent for both sides. So also was the cumulative nature of success, in terms of military success, military and civilian morale and resolve, and international support and recognition.

The desire to gain the initiative was understandable, but repeated offensives had already weakened the Republicans and the next, launched on December 15, 1937, only did the same. The Republicans captured the city of Teruel. However, instead of this success leading to hoped-for peace negotiations, an effective Nationalist counteroffensive regained the town on February 22, 1938, and inflicted heavy casualties in fighting during the bitter winter.

Contemporaries looking at the war in Spain for guidance to the nature of a likely future conflict focused on the use of bombing by Franco's German and Italian allies, notably of Guernica and Barcelona. Ground warfare in Spain did not attract the same interest. In large part, this was because of the pejorative views held about both sides and, as with the Balkan Wars of 1912–13, the sense that they were not at the cutting edge of conflict. This attitude was similar to that toward the Chaco War. In practice, aside from the extent to which the war was settled in ground warfare, principally by Spanish forces, foreign support could be significant for ground offensives. This was the case more for the Nationalists than for the Republicans, despite the attention devoted to the International Brigades of volunteers, mostly Communists, who fought for the latter. Thus, the Italians provided Franco with the experienced and talented maneuvering mass he required. The Italian forces were moved according to the urgent needs of Franco's strategy.

The slighting of the ground warfare of the Spanish Civil War might appear vindicated in terms of the campaigns of rapid victory repeatedly seen during the Second World War, notably in 1939–41. However, the slighting ignored the lessons that 1930s conflicts offered for civil wars after the Second World War and even, as with Yugoslavia in 1941–44, during it. Moreover, the fate of the newly created German and Japanese Empires in 1942–45 suggested the need to consider all teleological views with caution.

Chapter Six

The Second World War, 1939–45

The image of land warfare over the last 160 years is very much dominated by the two world wars. The First World War is particularly important for the Europeans, but it is less dominant an issue and image for the United States, China, and Japan. As the latter became the world's leading powers, so this ensured that images changed. The views, indeed images, held in the United States were particularly prominent, notably as a consequence of Hollywood. However, the Second World War also supplanted the First because it was more recent, it defined experiences that were more strongly present, and it left more, and more varied, photographic images.

The Second World War was a global one from 1939 because it was then that Britain and France went to war with Germany, mobilizing their global empires, the largest in the world, in doing so. Moreover, war between these powers and Germany added a far-flung naval dimension that was missing in the case of that already started between Japan and China, which had broken out in 1937. Rapidly conquering France in 1940, and defeating British forces in France (and Norway) at the same time, the Germans brought to a final end the interwar period, both militarily and politically, as well as the final end of the revived First World War that had broken out in 1939: Germany and Russia had produced a de facto alignment in 1918 that prefigured their alliance in 1939.

The defeat in 1940 of the imperial systems of France and, to a lesser extent, Britain in their European heartland ensured that Germany would only be stopped as a superpower if the Soviet Union and America came into the war. This factor also meant that a major American role would be necessary to defeat Japan once it entered the war in December 1941: Britain and China would be able to deny Japan victory—which the British did by holding on to India, and the Chinese by continuing the war begun in 1937—but not defeat it.

The fall of France in June 1940 also marked the end of limited war because the new British government under Winston Churchill was not interested in a compromise peace dictated by a victorious Germany. Churchill's decision, and the inability of Germany to invade Britain or bomb it into submission, meant that the conflict would continue until the actions of the Soviet Union and the United States could play a decisive role.

In contrast to the systemic flaws in German war making that were readily apparent from late 1941, Allied improvements in fighting effectiveness by 1944 reflected the general Allied success in directing resources, in appreciating the interdependence of weapons and operations, and in improving training. In particular, the Soviets, having recovered from the purges of the late 1930s, showed that they had mastered the capabilities of their weaponry and fighting systems, learned how to outfight their opponents, and developed not only a "Deep War" doctrine but also the ability to maintain the pace of a rapid fighting advance.

POLAND AND SCANDINAVIA, 1939–40

The Germans conquered Poland in 1939 in a rapid campaign of maneuver launched from several directions against an opponent that had a long perimeter to protect. The major individual battle, that of the Bzura, saw an initially successful Polish attack on exposed German forces but ended with a German victory that benefited from air and artillery superiority. Largely reliant on railways and draft animals, the Germans also benefited from Soviet intervention against the Poles.

The Germans switched between opponents in 1940 in a fashion they had not been able to do in 1914. First, they expanded their Western Front, hitherto only on a largely inactive French frontier, by attacking neutrals. In Denmark and Norway, the Germans proved highly successful, in part due to their use of air power. This was of great significance for land warfare. General Auchinleck, who commanded the Anglo-French expeditionary force to Narvik, attributed the German victory primarily to air power:

The predominant factor in the recent operations has been the effect of air power.... The actual casualties caused to troops on the ground by low-flying attacks were few, but the moral effect of continuous machine-gunning from the air was considerable. Further, the enemy made repeated use of low-flying attacks with machine guns in replacement of artillery to cover the movement of his troops. Troops in forward positions subjected to this form of attack are forced to ground, and until they have learned by experience its comparative innocuousness, are apt not to keep constant watch on the enemy. Thus, the enemy was enabled on many occasions to carry out forward and outflanking movements with impunity.... The first general lesson to be drawn is that to commit troops to a campaign in which they cannot be provided with adequate air support is to court disaster.[1]

Far more was in fact involved in Allied failure, not least the inability to implement strategic decisions at an effective operational level and to appreciate the need to make these decisions in the light of tactical and operational circumstances. These included the dynamic of German operations, which was seriously underestimated.[2] Yet the problems of inadequate training, organization, preparation, and intelligence of particular environments were revealed throughout the war, for example in the fighting between Japan and the Americans on the Pacific island of Guadalcanal in 1942, which became the first Japanese defeat on land at American hands.[3]

Alongside German expansionism, there was its Soviet counterpart, as Stalin sought to gain control over neighboring territories in order to provide defensive buffers.[4] This policy led to an invasion of eastern Poland in 1939 in agreement with the Germans, as well as to an attack on Finland in 1939–40 and, in 1940, to the occupation of Estonia, Latvia, and Lithuania, and the extortion of territory from Romania. These operations, notably the most violent, the "Winter War" with Finland, revealed serious limitations with the Soviet army, particularly its unfamiliarity with operating in the snow in extensive forests, but ultimately it prevailed. The key campaign, that on the Karelian Isthmus, saw Soviet artillery provide the means to break through the Finnish Mannerheim Line of fortifications, which was far weaker than the French Maginot Line.

COLLAPSE OF THE WESTERN FRONT, 1940

Before Norway finally fell, the Germans, on May 10, also attacked Belgium and the Netherlands, both hitherto neutral, and also invaded France. Belgium and the Netherlands had been unwilling to make the necessary prewar defensive arrangements with Britain and France, and this left them all in a strategically vulnerable position.[5] The rapid defeat of the Dutch, who surrendered on May 14, indicated the success of German methods. Swiftly gaining and employing air superiority, the Germans advanced rapidly, using paratroopers, glider-borne forces, and tanks to weaken the cohesion of the defenders. Heavy civilian casualties caused by the bombing of the undefended city of Rotterdam sped the surrender. To use a term applied (and misapplied) at the time of the American-led attack on Iraq in 2003, this was a case of "Shock and Awe."

The crucial victory occurred further south: poor Allied strategy had led the Allies to move their strategic reserve on their far left into Belgium, in order to protect northern Belgium and the southern Netherlands, before they were aware of the main direction of the German attack. As a result, these forces were not available in a reserve capacity. Thus, taking the initiative did not do the French much good.

The German attack came through the supposedly impenetrable hilly woodland of the Ardennes, bisecting the Allied line, outflanking the fortifications of the French Maginot Line and their defensive forces, and exposing the Allies' failure to prepare for fluid defense in depth. The French attention to a continuous front greatly limited their ability to respond to the German breakthrough. They did not maneuver well for, or in, defense. The French also lacked an effective doctrine for their armor and tended to see it in terms of infantry support. Helped by air superiority, the German panzer (tank) divisions proved operationally effective as formations, maximizing the combat characteristics of tanks. German signaling capacity was also superior. When tank conflict occurred with the British or French, the Germans tended to control its pace. French failures, which included a lack of peacetime training for reserve units, magnified German efforts at innovation, efforts that were later in the war to be revealed as inadequate against defense in depth.

Serving as a reminder that conflict was given significance by strategy, notably due to its geopolitical context, the world was provided with its greatest geopolitical crisis over the last century, one that was even graver than that in 1917–18, serious as that was. In 1918, the Treaty of Brest-Litovsk between Germany and Russia posed the threat of a new alignment, one that would enable Germany to turn all its efforts on the Western Allies (Britain, France, and the United States), while Bolshevism was able to establish itself with German help. In January 1918, Arthur Balfour, the British foreign secretary, suggested that the Allies help anti-Bolshevik movements in Russia that "might do something to prevent Russia from falling immediately and completely under the control of Germany.... While the war continues a Germanised Russia would provide a source of supply which would go far to neutralise the effects of the Allied blockade. When the war is over, a Germanised Russia would be a peril to the world."[6] The challenge was not ended by the close of the war. Indeed, in July 1919, the British General Staff argued, "taking the long view, it is unquestionable that what the British Empire has most reason to fear in the future is a Russo-German combination."[7]

In 1940, the threat returned, but in a more acute form. By the end of 1939, Germany was allied with Japan, Italy, and the Soviet Union and had cooperated with the last in conquering Poland and determining spheres of influence in Eastern Europe, which left the independent states there with few options. The United States was neutral. Britain and France, while supported by their mighty empires, were reduced to somewhat dubious hopes of long-term success, in particular through a blockade that was in practice not going to work due to the Russo-German alignment.

German successes in early 1940, first against Denmark and Norway and then against the Netherlands, Belgium, France, and Britain, were a product of the existing geopolitical situation, because Germany was able to fight a one-front war and thus maximize its strength. In short, Stalin was the root cause of the German triumph in the West in 1940. In 1939, by allying with Hitler, Stalin had followed Lenin in 1918 by joining the cause of international Communism to that of Russian state advancement in concert with Germany.

This process was greatly facilitated by a shared hostility on the part of Communist and Nazi leaders to Britain and its liberalism. This hostility stemmed from a rejection of liberal capitalism as a domestic agenda for liberty and freedom, but also hostility to it as an international agenda focused on opposition to dictatorial expansionism. Just as Britain had fought to protect Belgium in 1914 and had intervened in favor of Estonia and Latvia in 1919–20, so it went to war in 1939 in response to the invasion of another weak power, Poland, although failing to act then with sufficient energy to help the Poles.

The past rarely repeats itself, as comparisons between the German offensives in 1870 and 1914, and in 1918 and 1940, indicate, or, indeed, between the Russo-German combination in 1939–41 and more recent relations between the two powers. German success in the field in 1940 owed much to the serious deficiencies of Allied strategy and planning.

The problem with war is ultimately that of forcing opponents to accept your will. That is the outcome sought. Output, the "boys and toys" of killing and conquest, is important to the process, but only if linked to a political strategy that will deliver the outcome. That strategy involves maximizing international advantages, as the Germans did in 1939 and continued to do in 1940 with Italy's entry into the war, and dominating the political agenda of your opponent's society.

There is no inevitability about either process. In particular, in 1940, Germany proved far more successful with France than with Britain in this respect. Many French troops fought bravely, notably at the Meuse, Somme, and Aisne, and also at Lille, a key position in protecting what became the Dunkirk defensive perimeter. However, the necessary political will to fight on, while displayed by the Free French under Charles de Gaulle, was largely absent. With General Maxime Weygand, the commander in chief, critical of the political system and pressing for an armistice, and Marshal Henri Pétain, the deputy prime minister, also pessimistic about the future and opposed to fighting on, the cabinet, on June 15, agreed to find out what armistice terms the Germans would offer. This sold the pass. There would be no union with Britain, no attempt to mount continued resistance from a Breton redoubt, no guerrilla warfare, no retreat of the government to the North African colonies, from which, protected by their powerful navy, they could have continued defiance.

This collapse was of global significance. French control of Syria, Lebanon, Madagascar, French North and West Africa, and French Indochina (Vietnam, Cambodia, and Laos) created the possibility of German and Japanese penetration into the Middle East, Africa, and Southeast Asia. The Japanese aircraft that sank British warships off Malaya in December 1941 operated from bases in South Vietnam.

This collapse also made the British decision to fight on of greater significance, and also far riskier. German naval and air forces could now be moved far closer to Britain. The German hope for a negotiated settlement with Britain reflected the difficulties of invasion but also Hitler's interest in war with the Soviet Union. Despite the hopes of right-wing Germans who were interested in geopolitics, notably Karl Haushofer and Foreign Secretary Joachim von Ribbentrop, redressing the 1919 Versailles peace settlement was at best a tactic for Hitler, as was cooperation with Russia in 1939–41. The ideological thrust of his policy required war with the Soviet Union and would be served by a peace in which Britain retained her empire in return for accepting German dominance of the Continent. There was interest in Britain in a compromise peace, but it was pushed aside by Churchill. In part, the weakness of the Far Left was an element. Left-wing trade unionists looked to the example of Stalin, who was then allied to Hitler, but Communism was relatively weak in Britain, while both the Conservatives and Labour were characterized by a robust patriotism.

DUNKIRK: CONTEXTS, REALITY, AND IMAGES

Having broken through to reach the English Channel on May 21, 1940, and thus cut off the forces to the north of their advance, the Germans nevertheless were deprived of much of their surrounded prey by the successful evacuation of 338,226 troops, mostly British, from the Dunkirk beaches (May 27–June 4). Over another two hundred thousand British troops were saved by evacuation from other French, mostly Channel, ports. A firm defense, by both British and French units in outlying positions, such as Calais and Lille, combined with the misconceived German policy of relying on aerial attack on the troops on the beaches to allow the British to retreat from Dunkirk. The Germans also wanted to rest their tanks before turning south to conquer France. Much of the German tank force consisted of Czech equipment, captured in 1938–39, and its maintenance posed major logistical problems.

The appearance and success of the film *Dunkirk* (2017) added to the list of war films that are both impressive and harrowing,[8] but, like many war films, it has not done much to explain the significance of the episode. Indeed, precisely because of the overwhelming focus in the film on the beach at Dunkirk and on the immediate military conflict, there is a failure to consider the wider military context, let alone the political one. This is an aspect of a more widespread neglect of strategy.

The ability to evacuate so much of the British army from Dunkirk was important. It created an impression of heroic resilience, but it also ensured that there were not, as there might otherwise have been, a large number of prisoners to provide, as it were, German hostages. There was the important effect on domestic morale, notably the realization that everyone, even those who messed about in boats and could help save soldiers from Dunkirk, could do something useful. The voices urging Britain to seek terms with Germany would have been a lot louder if Britain had lost its army. Moreover, German confidence would have been higher, and this might have encouraged the

Germans to stage an invasion of southern England had there been no negotiations.

Evacuations are one of the most difficult military activities. They are a form of combined operations, always in itself problematic, but one in which the other side has set the agenda and it is necessary to evade this. They are also strategic: you withdraw in order to fight again. This is a key element in military history on land and at sea, one that at sea is best handled by powers with a strong amphibious capability. The ability to withdraw after failures on land, for example from Gallipoli in 1915–16, was important. It became even more difficult to do so in the Second World War due to hostile air power, and this was a major factor at Dunkirk and at Crete in 1941. Nevertheless, in each case, large numbers were withdrawn. Conversely, a failure to evacuate could be a serious disaster, as with Singapore and the Philippines in 1942, for the British and Americans respectively, and, for the Germans and Italians, Tunisia in 1943. Each reflected the local superiority of opposing sea and, in particular, air power. As a result, large numbers of men were lost, which affected the issue of mass.

Mass had a value of its own, and in 1940 this was true at sea, on land, and in the air. The mass of troops available, thanks to Dunkirk and other evacuations, was, despite defeat in France, important in helping to protect Britain from invasion. So was the size of the British navy that survived having taken part in the evacuation. Only six out of forty-one destroyers were sunk, and the navy took much less damage in evacuating Dunkirk than the Germans had done invading Norway that April: ten German destroyers had been destroyed at Narvik, the heavy cruiser *Blücher* in Oslo Fjord, and so on. This was highly important to the situation as far as the invasion of Britain was concerned, and it offset some of the advantage Germany gained in winning the support of Italy and taking France from the British side. Moreover, land operations affected the naval balance. In 1940, as the Germans advanced, 170,000 tonnes of French warships in construction, including the cruiser *Joffre* and the battleship *Clemenceau*, were sabotaged to prevent them from falling into German hands.

The 2017 film, which was shot on the beach used in 1940, captures the difficulty of the task and the fortitude involved. Withdrawal is particularly difficult for troops who do not know what is going to happen but can clearly hear the menacing sound of approaching foes. That was certainly the case with the Dunkirk perimeter, which was under serious attack and bombardment.

THE FALL OF FRANCE

The Germans rapidly regrouped after breaking through to the English Channel, before pressing south into France. After strong initial French resistance on the Somme and Aisne Rivers, areas where there had been much fighting in the First World War, German superiority in generalship and equipment, especially in the use of tanks, prevailed. There was to be no repetition of the blocking of the German advance in 1914, an advance that had lacked the benefit of mechanization and where the French use of rail to redeploy troops from their right flank could not be challenged from the air. In 1940, the faster-moving German advance meant that such a redeployment was not possible.

Instead, rapidly advancing into central and southern France, seizing cities as far south as Bordeaux, the Germans were able to force France to accept an armistice that was far harsher than the terms imposed on it in 1871 or envisaged in 1914. Part of France was occupied, while a government cooperative with Germany was established in Vichy in order to rule the remainder. In a deliberate echo of the terms imposed on Germany in 1919, Vichy France was only permitted a small and weak military, and, crucially, was not allowed strength in tanks or aircraft. In part, 1940 was an end of the First World War, a fulfillment of its eventual geopolitical and military potential that left everyone faced with a new and completely unexpected strategic situation. How they reacted to it determined the character of the new war that followed, and who was to win.

The effectiveness of the German blitzkrieg attacking methods in 1939–41 was exaggerated by contemporary, and later, commentators, both German and other, under the spell cast by the sheer shock and drama of the German offensives.[9] As far as outcomes were concerned, and notably on the Western Front in 1940, the situation certainly contrasted greatly with the First World War. As a result, commentators then, and subsequently, have overrated the impact in 1939–41 of military ideas and methods that, in practice, represented more of an improvisation than the fruition of a coherent doctrine, or, at most, an evolution rather than a revolution. Rather than focusing on blitzkrieg, particularly on the use of tanks and ground attack aircraft, the Germans benefited in their early campaigns from the army's doctrine, training, and leadership, and, notably, from the stress on flexibility, personal initiative, and action. Germany's opponents could not match these elements, either individually or in combination. It was the combined characteristic of German strengths that gave them particular advantages, which had also been the case for the British in 1918.

However, in 1940, aside from issues of preparedness, the margin between success and failure was closer than was generally appreciated, while the potential of weaponry and logistics based on the internal combustion engine, the tank, and the lorry (truck) was less dramatic than talk of blitzkrieg might suggest. Artillery, for example, remained a key factor, as was to be seen on all military fronts. It was the major killer among weapons systems. German success against Poland, Norway, the Netherlands, Belgium, France, Yugoslavia, and Greece in 1939–41 also owed much to poor strategic decisions by Germany's opponents, notably in terms of defensive planning and the allocation of reserves, particularly as a consequence of having to defend an overlong perimeter. Moreover, German generalship and organization displayed serious shortcomings in 1940. Indeed, there was a parallel between French and German military conservatism. More seriously for Germany, in invading the Soviet Union, from June 22, 1941, German strategy and fighting methods proved deeply flawed.

These were not the only issues. There were related doctrinal problems. German doctrine was based on the notion of a rapidly obtained and decisive land battle. This goal was realizable if the opposing power was readily accessible, focused its strength on the army, lacked adequate space in which to retreat or maneuver, and accepted the same doctrinal suppositions. These factors, however, were absent in the case of Britain, the Soviet Union, and the United States; and German war making was the story of failure to suppress the will of others: the inability to make opposing states accept German assumptions. In the case of Germany, will could not be a substitute for the ability to set sensible goals.[10]

WAR IN THE WIDER MEDITERRANEAN

Meanwhile the war had spread in a new direction, as Italy, under its Fascist dictator, Benito Mussolini, came in on the German side on June 10, 1940. However, the Italian attack on France in June was thwarted by a firm resistance resting on good prewar defensive positions in the Alps.

The umbrella nature of the war was indicated by the number of struggles it included. This number included the Italian attack on Greece on October 28, 1940. This attack was mounted at Mussolini's insistence, despite the Italian forces used being outnumbered and also lacking supplies, as the General

Staff had been warned. There was a lack of good ports in Albania through which the Italian navy could land supplies and a shortage of trucks to move sufficient supplies from the ports. Within two weeks, the advance was stopped by a lack of supplies. The Greeks counterattacked. The Italians had nine divisions, the Greeks thirteen plus additional forces, while the individual Greek divisions had more soldiers than the Italian ones. Finally, when the Greek government realized that it did not have to fear Bulgarian or Turkish intervention, it concentrated the entire army against the Italians. The terrain added further difficulties. Albania and Northern Greece have mountain chains running north to south, and the front ran west to east, perpendicularly cut by mountains. Due to its lack of numbers, the Italian army concentrated its forces in the valleys to stop Greek attacks along the roads, only for the Greeks to attack along the ridgelines and overwhelm any Italian troops that might be there.

By December, the Italian army had been driven from Greece and a third of Albania. In bitter cold, the Italians lacked food, artillery, and organization. In late January 1941, the situation stabilized, although an Italian counteroffensive in early March failed. The Italians were not able to prevail until, attacking on April 15, they took advantage of the German invasion of Greece earlier that month. Italian total casualties were 155,172, the majority wounded or ill.

Furthermore, in December 1940, the Italian forces that had invaded Egypt from Libya were driven back by the British, a term that should be taken to include Dominion and Empire forces, particularly, in this case, Australians. The British went on to conquer eastern Libya and, in early 1941, to reconquer British Somaliland and overrun Eritrea and Italian Somaliland, finishing the conquest of Italian East Africa in northern Ethiopia that November, after overcoming formidable logistical difficulties as well as those posed by the environment and the shortage of good roads.[11] As a reminder of the significance of linkage between different fronts, the skills developed there proved of value for the British when later operating in Burma.[12]

More generally, the Italian military lacked good equipment, in part due to the limitations of its industrial base.[13] There was also an absence of realistic political direction by Mussolini, a shortage of able commanders, and serious problems with morale.

Hitler responded to Italian defeats by sending help to the Italians in Libya, which led to the British being driven back and, on April 6, 1941, attacking Greece and, on the same day, Yugoslavia, which had defied German wishes.

Virtually surrounded by its opponents, the strung-out Yugoslav defense proved vulnerable, and the country fell rapidly, as Poland had done. The Germans also benefited from both the international and the domestic political situation. Bulgarian, Hungarian, and Italian forces joined in the invasion, each receiving part of Yugoslavia as their reward. Within Serb-dominated Yugoslavia, there was considerable division, and many Croats were unwilling to fight against the invaders.

The British sent an expeditionary force to help the Greeks, but, with inadequate air support, it was pushed back with fifteen thousand casualties. The tempo of the German advance, especially its rapid use of airborne troops and armor, brought a decisive advantage, as did the effective use of ground-support aircraft. This enabled the Germans to overcome successive defensive lines in Greece.

At the same time, due to poor weather and roads, among other factors, German aircraft and armor had only a limited impact. In practice, the weakness of the Greek army, notably in command, equipment, and logistics; the lack of coordinated Anglo-Greek command; and the readiness of the hesitant commanders of the British forces to withdraw in the face of fear of being outflanked combined to lead to failure.[14]

The campaign culminated with the capture of the Greek island of Crete by German parachute and air-transported troops. This was a risky attack, launched on May 20, 1941, as such forces were unable to bring heavy arms with them, while the formidable British naval presence thwarted the planned maritime support for the invasion. German air attacks, however, inflicted serious damage on the British navy, while the German assault force, although it took heavy casualties, was able to gain the initiative from a poorly directed resistance, to seize airstrips, and to secure resupply by air. The Crete operation was a close-run thing as the parachutists were nearly beaten, but a failure of communications led the British to believe that the situation was never as close to failure for the Germans as it was. The British evacuated their forces, those remaining surrendering on June 3. Because of the very high casualties suffered by the paratroops, Hitler never engaged in a major parachute-landing operation again. The paratroops became, in effect, conventional infantry thereafter, albeit of a more elite nature than those in the regular army.[15]

The conquest of Crete took the Germans forward into the eastern Mediterranean. However, the possibility of exploiting this advance was lessened by successful British action to secure Iraq (April–May 1941), Lebanon, and Syria (June–July 1941), the first from a pro-German government and the latter two from Vichy France. Moreover, the German focus on war with the Soviet Union, which broke out on June 22, 1941, directed German priorities. The Mediterranean was no more than a sideshow for Hitler, one where he acted in order to prevent Britain from exploiting Italian weaknesses.

THE SOVIET UNION ATTACKED

Hitler jeopardized the multiple German geopolitical, strategic, operational, and tactical successes of 1939–41 by declaring war on first the Soviet Union and then the United States. However, to Hitler, these successes were of scant value unless they were means to his goal: he was convinced that a clash with Communism was inevitable and was Germany's destiny, and that the Germans were bound to win. His policies were motivated by a crude and brutal racism in which Slavs were inferior to Germans. Hitler was also convinced that defeating the Soviet Union would lead Britain to negotiate, and thus avoid the need for a hazardous German invasion of Britain. Meanwhile, ignoring British advice, Stalin refused to heed signs of imminent German attack and foolishly maintained confidence in the 1939 Nazi-Soviet Pact.

On June 22, 1941, nearly 3.6 million German and allied troops, supported by 3,350 tanks and 1,950 aircraft, were launched in a surprise attack that had been postponed from May due to unusually wet weather that made the roads impassable. The badly prepared Red Army, which had about 2.7 million troops and 10,400 tanks deployed in the western Soviet Union, suffered heavy defeats at the outset and in initial counterattacks, losing large quantities of men, tanks, and aircraft. However, lulled by overconfidence in the value of a swift offensive and completely failing to appreciate Soviet strength, both numerically and in fighting quality,[16] the Germans had not planned or prepared adequately for the conflict. Much of the German infantry was not fully combat ready, in part due to a lack of sufficient training, while the armor was short of drivers and radio operators and was outclassed by the Soviet T-34 tank. Because it was assumed that the war would be over before winter, there was a lack of the winter equipment and uniforms that were to be required.

From the outset, Soviet forces, notably in northern Ukraine, fought better than the Germans had anticipated, and the large amount of Soviet territory conquered, and the millions of troops killed or captured, were at the cost of heavier-than-expected German losses. Soviet doctrine, with its emphasis on defense and its stress on artillery, proved effective once the initial shock and surprise of the attack had been absorbed. Although there was very serious failure at the operational level, the Soviets fought hard, and the Germans were unable to sustain success and, more seriously, to achieve it in a manner that would enable them to overcome the space and resolve of the Soviet Union.[17] Instead, their victories left them exhausted.

There was a serious disjuncture in the case of Germany between, on the one hand, tactical and operational effectiveness and, on the other hand, strategic folly and economic preparedness, a disjuncture also seen in other cases during the period covered by this book, but never at this scale. The problems posed by the vastness of the territory to be conquered by the Germans were compounded by a lack of consistency in German strategy. Operation Barbarossa was launched to give effect to Hitler's murderous determination to destroy Communism and Jews, to create a greater Germany, and to put pressure on Britain, which continued to hold out. The German invasion plan represented an attempt to seize all objectives in the Soviet Union simultaneously, but this reflected a serious source of confusion that arose from the failure to settle the core target of the operation and the mistaken assumption that the Soviet Union would fall rapidly. The inconsistently conceived and executed offensive stemmed from a failure to set sensible military and political goals. Even if the Soviet Union was defeated, there was no viable peace policy on offer for its leadership or people other than total submission.

Policy was consistent: destroy the Soviet Union, annex territory, seize resources, and kill Jews. Strategy, however, shifted over the emphasis between seizing territory or defeating Soviet forces, and also over the question of which axes of advance to concentrate on. This led to a delay in the central thrust on Moscow in September, while forces were sent south to overrun Ukraine and destroy Soviet armies there: the gain of the resources of Ukraine (notably grain) and the crushing of Soviet forces there then appeared more important than a focus on Moscow. Hindered by Stalin's refusal to consider advice to withdraw, the Soviet army lost three-quarters of a million men, killed or captured in Ukraine, but victory was won at the cost of serious losses in the German armored forces.[18] Large numbers of Jewish civilians were slaughtered by the Germans, and many by their Romanian ally.

The delay in the advance on Moscow hindered the Germans when they resumed it in late 1941 in Operation Typhoon,[19] not least because the Soviets, helped by the transfer of troops from Siberia where they had faced the Japanese, proved better than the Germans at operating in the difficult winter conditions, and that winter proved very difficult. The Germans, moreover, had very poor logistical support. More seriously, it was unclear what their attack could achieve. Although the Soviet government was evacuated to Kuibyshev on the Volga, the Red Army was able to hold the assault on Moscow, their communications and command center, and to mount a counterattack launched on December 5–6, 1941. At the end of the 1941 offensive, the Germans had captured neither Leningrad nor Moscow. Moreover, the Soviet counteroffensive revealed the continued vitality of the Red Army, with its effective artillery and increasingly potent tanks.[20] This vitality encouraged resistance activity in the occupied territories. The counteroffensive was eventually held, but the Germans never again came so close to Moscow as they had done prior to its launch.

Once their advances had been held, the Germans lacked strong operational reserves to cope with counterattacks, and they found it difficult to stabilize the front in the face of these attacks. Further south, having captured the city of Rostov on the Don River on November 21, 1941, the Germans evacuated it a week later as Field Marshal Gerd von Rundstedt, the Army Group commander, feared they had become overextended. Rundstedt was sacked.

To the north, Leningrad (St. Petersburg) held off German attacks but was besieged, and its inhabitants suffered grievously as the Germans sought to starve out the city, the birthplace of Soviet Communism. About one million people died there. The German operations against Leningrad, however, used up troops to scant strategic purpose.[21]

AXIS ATTACKS HELD, 1942

In Russia, the Germans were able to recover from the Soviet counterattacks of the winter of 1941–42 and mount a major new offensive, whereas the Japanese failed to recover comparably from the first defeats they encountered. The new German attack, however, was to be disastrous. From the outset, the 1942 offensive, Operation "Blue," was jeopardized by a poorly conceived and executed plan. In this, the Germans planned the seizure of the Caucasian oil fields, notably around Baku on the Caspian Sea, in order better to prepare for the lengthy struggle that American entry into the war appeared to make inevitable: most of the world's oil supplies were under Allied control or closed to the Axis by Allied maritime strength. The Allies dominated oil production in the Western Hemisphere (United States and Venezuela) and also in the Middle East (Iran, Iraq, and Saudi Arabia), which helped to make the seizure of oil fields in Borneo and Sumatra important for Japan.

Hitler, however, underestimated Soviet strength and also failed to make sufficient logistical preparations, both consistent problems with his military leadership. Furthermore, there were serious flaws in the development of the operation, specifically in the decision to attack simultaneously toward the Volga River as well as the Caucasus. As the British and Americans showed in advancing against Germany through and beyond France in 1944, the Germans were scarcely alone in their difficulty in fixing on an axis of advance. Nevertheless, the German failure to do so on the Eastern Front was of particular seriousness due to the size of the opposing forces and the extent of the area of operations. Moreover, in 1941, the German advance had already suffered greatly from this factor. However, as with the determination to devote so many resources to destroying Leningrad, Hitler's conviction that the city of Stalingrad, on the Volga, had to be captured foolishly substituted a political goal for the necessary operational flexibility: German strategy was both misguided and poorly implemented. Despite a massive commitment of resources, the Germans were fought to a standstill at Stalingrad, which had been turned by their air and artillery attacks into an intractable urban wasteland that, in practice, offered major advantages to the Soviet defenders. The fighting there became attritional, and the German force was "fixed." This was an appropriate image of strategic failure.

Soviet losses in combat at Stalingrad were heavy, but they helped stop the Germans. Moreover, the Russians had mass, some good commanders, and effective artillery. At Stalingrad, as elsewhere, the Soviets benefited from their ability to take heavy casualties, an ability that owed something to the willingness to shoot commanders and ordinary soldiers for failure: about fifteen thousand in the battle for Stalingrad and at least two hundred thousand during the war as a whole, while in 1945, many tens of thousands of surviving prisoners freed from German captivity were shot or sent to the gulags (Soviet concentration camps).

In the Second World War, the attritional character of the conflict was particularly pronounced on the Eastern Front after the initial German successes in late 1941 and mid-1942. This was not least because that was the European land sector in which conflict lasted longest, as well as the largest in Europe, although, in the world as a whole, the Chinese-Japanese conflict lasted the longest. In Europe, the human mass and cost involved was throughout greater on the Eastern Front[22] than in the Mediterranean or Western Europe. The Germans had not planned for such an outcome, for neither their military and its doctrine nor the military-industrial complex was prepared for the lengthy conflict that resulted. Instead, the Germans sought the *Kesselschlacht* (battle of encirclement and annihilation) that they had pursued in earlier conflicts, and, as in 1914, there was no Plan B, along with a failure to give adequate weight to other possibilities.[23]

In a separate conflict, the German invasion of Egypt was blocked and subsequently defeated at El Alamein. Moreover, Operation Torch, an American-British invasion of Morocco and Algeria in November 1942, achieved rapid success in transferring Vichy-run Northwest Africa to the Allied camp and thus greatly lessened Axis dominance of the Mediterranean. In addition, by causing a disillusioned Germany to occupy Vichy-run France, it led to a breakdown of the German alliance system.[24]

THE EASTERN FRONT, 1943

Although the Americans and British dominated the struggle at sea and in the air, and made a very important contribution on land by their successes in the Mediterranean and, from 1944, in Western Europe, the Red Army absorbed the bulk of the German army: over two-thirds were always engaged on the Eastern Front after Germany attacked the Soviet Union. After Stalingrad, this front was largely a prolonged struggle of attrition, although there was usually much more obvious movement than on that front in the First World War. Formidable foes on the defensive, the Germans succeeded in stabilizing the front in early 1943 after the loss of Stalingrad. In part, this was thanks to Field Marshal Erich von Manstein's skilled employment of counterattacks,[25] but it was also due to the difficulties the Red Army encountered in sustaining the offensive, difficulties already seen in early 1942. The relationship between these factors was complex, and this enhances the difficulties in analyzing the respective weight of these factors. Thereafter, however, the Germans were outfought.

The German generals agreed with Hitler that Germany could not afford to relinquish the initiative in Russia. The Battle of Kursk was fought in July–August 1943 to win a victory, but it also represented the last chance to stabilize an economical front line. The Germans launched formidable tank assaults on the northern and southern sides of a large Soviet bulge or salient on the front line, intending not only to shorten the front line but also to strengthen their prestige and strike a major psychological blow. However, the Soviets were well prepared. They had constructed concentric lines of defenses, and these weakened and finally stopped the German assaults. The

Germans suffered especially badly at the hands of Soviet artillery, yet again demonstrating that artillery is the most underrated arm in the war; antitank guns indeed were the most underrated weapons. The availability of large Soviet armor reserves was also important to the flow of the battle. The Germans did not fight well. There were many command mistakes. For example, in accepting battle at Prokhorovka on July 12, Lieutenant General Hermann Hoth, the commander of the Fourth Panzer Army, knowingly gambled on the tactical skills and technical superiority of the outnumbered and unsupported divisions of II SS Panzer Corps because he remained committed to his view that the decisive engagement would be fought there. In the event, the Germans failed to break through.[26]

Once the German offensive had been blocked, the Soviets rapidly switched over to the attack, making far more gains than the Germans had done in the battle. The Soviets crossed the Dnieper River and drove the Germans out of eastern Ukraine. For the remainder of the war, the Germans stood on the strategic defensive on the Eastern Front. Meanwhile, the Red Army proved increasingly successful in attack, adept at developing cooperation between armor, artillery, and infantry; at making the latter two mobile; and at developing logistical support so as to maintain the impetus of attack, the last a key element.

Defeat for Germany at Kursk was followed on the Eastern Front by longer fronts defended by weaker forces, notably so when the Soviets pushed into the Balkans in 1944. German losses rose and, as a percentage of army strength, were at 15 percent in 1943, heavier than in 1941 (less than 7 percent) or 1942 (10 percent). This was largely due to the conflict on the Eastern Front.

NORTH AFRICA AND ITALY, 1943–45

Meanwhile the Germans and Italians in North Africa had been forced to surrender by American and British forces in May 1943. The Germans had initially made good use of their interior lines in Tunisia in order to fight the advancing American and British forces separately, and their attack on the Americans in the Battle of the Kasserine Pass in February 1943 had inflicted much damage on units that were not adequately prepared for high-tempo conflict. In part, this was a matter of the blooding or experience that the Germans had gained through earlier conflict, just as Japanese effectiveness in 1941–42 owed something to earlier experience in China, not least in amphibious operations. American combat effectiveness rapidly improved, however, while the Axis forces in Tunisia suffered from the impact of Allied air superiority, especially on their supply links from Italy, and once the Allies had gained the initiative, they were able to win a speedy victory. The Allied success in Tunisia hit Japanese confidence in its Axis allies hard.[27]

The Allies pressed on to invade Sicily that July and mainland Italy that September. Amphibious power and air support allowed the Allies to seize the initiative. However, while the overthrow of Mussolini by his own ministers in September 1943, in response to the Allied success, temporarily wrecked Axis cohesion, a rapid German response gave them control of central and northern Italy. This response left the Allies in a far more difficult position. The mountainous terrain and the east–west river lines made Italy excellent defensive terrain. Prefiguring the situation in Korea in 1950–53, much of the fighting proved to be conventional infantry combat, with artillery playing a major role: the terrain was not well suited to armor.

The Allied attempt to bypass German defenses with the Anzio landing in January 1944 proved very risky, as the exploitation of the landing to create and secure a strong defensive perimeter was difficult. A series of hard-fought offensives were required to surmount successive German defensive lines, and Milan, the major city in northern Italy, only fell in April 1945. The Germans not only resisted Allied advances but also suppressed resistance by Italian partisans. In turn, the latter also fought the puppet, pro-German republic of Salò to which Mussolini had been reduced. Thus, the war in Italy was both a civil war and a struggle between regular forces.

Although the latter did not fulfill Allied hopes until the very close, the German units sent to Italy were not available to fight the Soviets, nor to resist the Allies in France. Moreover, the Italy campaign was not a strategic irrelevance as far as the goal of the defeat of the Germans in France was concerned. Allied amphibious operations in the Mediterranean in 1943 provided valuable experience in planning and execution, notably in air support, airborne attacks, and the use of landing craft. The landings of 1943, especially that at Salerno, also provided warnings about the difficulty of invading France, not least in terms of the German response. The interdependence of land and air warfare was shown by Hitler's concern to retain control of as much of Italy as he could in order to keep Allied bombers as far from German targets as possible.

Chapter 6

NORMANDY LANDINGS, 1944

On June 6, 1944, in Operation Overlord, Anglo-American forces landed in Normandy. J. F. C. Fuller, the leading British military thinker of the period, was to claim, in the *Sunday Pictorial* on October 1, 1944, that

> had our sea power remained what it had been, solely a weapon to command the sea, the garrison Germany established in France almost certainly would have proved sufficient. It was a change in the conception of naval power which sealed the fate of that great fortress. Hitherto in all overseas invasions the invading forces had been fitted to ships. Now ships were fitted to the invading forces. . . . How to land the invading forces in battle order . . . this difficulty has been overcome by building various types of special landing boats and prefabricated landing stages.

To Fuller, these boats and landing stages matched the tank in putting the defense at a discount. He argued that Operation Overlord marked a major advance in amphibious operations, not only because of its unprecedented scale, but also because Allied capability transformed the nature of the task in taking the war to the Germans in France. There was now no need to capture a port in order to land, reinforce, and support the invasion force. The unsuccessful Dieppe operation, an attack across the English Channel on August 19, 1942, on the French port of Dieppe, had shown that attacking a port destroyed it, which indicated that such a goal was inappropriate; but in 1944, the Germans mistakenly still anticipated that the Allies would initially focus on seizing ports.

The invasion of Normandy benefited from the experience gained by the British and Americans in North African and Italian landings in 1942–43, although the scale of the operation and the severity of the resistance, both anticipated and actual, were each more acute in Normandy. This resistance ensures that, although the overlooked significance of Soviet offensives in Eastern Europe in 1944 requires due attention, nevertheless, it is still necessary to underline the importance of Overlord.

Overlord was a triumph for combined operations, but also a product of the success of the Allied military over the previous two years. In part, this success was a matter of victory in conflict. The British, Canadian, and American navies had won the Battle of the Atlantic, without which it would not have been viable to sustain the major preparations required in Britain prior to the launch of any invasion. In order to confront the German forces in

France, it would be necessary to land and support far more troops than had been the case with Operation Torch in North Africa in November 1942, although at a much closer distance to base, which greatly affected the shipping possibilities. The ability to arm and support these numbers was an aspect of the Allied success in mobilizing the productive resources of much of the world's economy, but especially that of the United States. The Allied ability to mount amphibious operations, and in both theaters at the same time, rested ultimately on American shipbuilding capacity, and most of the forty-two million tons of shipping built by the Allies during the war was constructed by the Americans.

The United States also produced 297,000 aircraft during the war. Numbers alone, however, did not suffice. It was also necessary to take the war to the Axis and outfight them. By the summer of 1944, absolute air superiority over northern France had been obtained. The effectiveness of Allied ground-support air power there owed much to the long-term strategy of gaining air superiority over the Luftwaffe.

As important as success in conflict was the process of training and other preparations that contributed to an increase in confidence in the overall fighting quality of land forces and, crucially, to a major expansion in the effectiveness as well as size of the armies.[28] Uneasiness over this factor remained, however, and unsurprisingly so, because, as in the First World War, the use of large numbers of men with little or no combat experience posed major problems for prediction. Training is the factor most underrated in discussing Allied competence.

Prediction was at issue for both sides. Anticipating an attack, which Hitler was confident could be repelled, the Germans, nevertheless, could not prioritize it because of the serious Soviet pressure in Eastern Europe. Soviet successes forced a reallocation of German units intended for the West.

In France, although they had developed the wide-ranging Atlantic Wall system of fortifications, many of which were built of ferroconcrete, the Germans lacked adequate naval and air strength to contest an invasion. Indeed, the Germans were in a far worse state for both naval and air support than the British had been when threatened with invasion in 1940. Furthermore, much (although by no means all) of the German army in France was of indifferent quality, as well as short of transport, training, and, in many cases, equipment.

These problems made the quality of German command decisions particularly important, but these proved inadequate. For long, such failings during the war, for example during Operation Barbarossa in 1941, were generally blamed, notably by captured German generals being questioned, on Hitler's untutored and maladroit interventions. More recently, alongside this factor, there has also emerged a stress on drawbacks in German planning as a frequent aspect of more widespread deficiencies in German war making.

In the particular case of Overlord, the German failing related both to their assessment of where the attack was likely to fall and about how best to respond to it. The Germans were surprised by the Normandy landing. In part due to Allied attempts, including the apparent buildup of units in South East England, they had concentrated more of their defenses and forces in the Calais region, which offered a shorter sea crossing from Britain and a shorter route to Germany. Normandy, though, was easier to reach from the invasion ports on the southern coast of England, particularly Plymouth, Portland, and Portsmouth. Even after D-Day, Hitler remained anxious about a subsequent additional landing near Calais. As another instance of German intelligence failures, the Germans anticipated a Soviet assault in Ukraine in 1944, instead of in Belarus further north where it actually came, and to devastating effect.

The German commanders in the West were also divided about how best to respond to any landing, particularly over whether to move their ten panzer (tank) divisions in France close to the coast so that the Allies could be attacked before they could consolidate their position or whether to mass them as a strategic reserve. The eventual decision was that the panzer divisions, whose impact greatly worried Allied planners, should remain inland, but their ability to act as a strategic reserve was lessened both by the decision not to mass them and by Allied air power. This decision reflected the tensions and uncertainties of the German command structure, those around Hitler and around the army leadership at many levels as a whole.

The German response was also affected by Allied operations, which again underlined the significance of combined operations. Air power helped ensure that the Allies were able to secure the flanks of their landing by the use of parachutists and glider-borne troops. These landings were particularly important to the landing on the right flank of the Normandy operation, at Utah Beach on the eastern base of the Cotentin Peninsula, as the Germans were unable to bring up reserves to support their coastal defenses there. The disorganized nature of the American airdrop, which matched that of the Sicily operation the previous year, further handicapped the defense, as it disorientated it, not least because there were no coordinated targets to counterattack. The Americans took very few casualties on Utah, in large part because the crucial fighting had already taken place inland.

On the next beach, Omaha, the situation was less happy. The Americans were badly prepared in the face of a good defense, not least because of poor planning and confusion in the landing, including the launching of assault craft and Duplex Drive (amphibious) Sherman tanks too far offshore, as well as a refusal to employ the specialized tanks developed by the British to attack coastal defenses, for example, Crabflail tanks for use against minefields. The Americans sustained about three thousand casualties, both in landing and on the beach, from German positions on the cliffs that had not been suppressed by air attack or naval bombardment. The experience of Mediterranean and Pacific landings had not been taken on board. Air power could not deliver the promised quantities of ordnance on target on time, and ferroconcrete was highly resistant to bombardment. Eventually the Americans on Omaha were able to move inland, but, at the end of D-Day, the beachhead was shallow and the troops in the sector were fortunate that the Germans had no armor to mount a response. This lack of support owed much to a failure in German command that reflected rigidities, in part stemming from Hitler's interventions.

The Canadian and British forces that landed on Gold, Juno, and Sword Beaches further east (the Canadians on Juno) faced active opposition and equipment issues but benefited from careful planning and preparation; from the seizure of crucial covering positions by airborne troops, who landed within their planned drop zones; from the effective use of specialized tanks; and from German hesitation about how best to respond, although there was particularly hard fighting on Gold, where D-Day objectives were not attained.[29] The Twenty-First Panzer Division, the sole German armored division in the area, did not counterattack until the early afternoon. German tanks approached the Channel between Juno and Sword Beaches but were blocked. At the cost of 2,500 troops killed that day across the entire invasion zone, the Allies were back in France: 132,000 troops had been landed, while the airborne force was 23,000 strong.

The over eleven thousand sorties flown by Allied air forces that day had a major impact: the Luftwaffe was kept away, while air support, though not always able to suppress defensive fire, made a valuable contribution. Had invasion been attempted in 1943, it would have been a more serious problem in France than it was to be in 1944 as, although the Germans had not proceeded so far with their defensive preparations as they were to have done by D-Day, the Allies did not yet have sufficient air dominance to seek to isolate the area of operations. The naval armada, largely British, both provided heavy supporting fire—heavier fire than from air attack—and also prevented disruption by German warships.

This brief summary of what occurred also helps indicate what was distinctive about Overlord. In Operation Dragoon, the large-scale Allied landing in Provence in the south of France on August 15, for example, the weakness of the defending force ensured that there was no major battle comparable to that at Normandy: resistance both on the beaches and inland, where an Anglo-American parachute force landed, was light, and casualties were few. An assault on a fortified coastline on the scale of Overlord was unique.

Had the projected invasion of Japan gone ahead as planned, however, the Allies would have confronted an even more formidable challenge. Indeed, General Douglas MacArthur, the American commander in the Philippines, told a British visitor, Major General William Penney, in April 1945 that his troops had not yet met the Japanese army properly, and that when they did they were going to take heavy casualties.[30] As a consequence, General George Marshall, the American chief of staff, considered using atom bombs in tactical support of a landing on Kyushu: this island was seen as the site for the first landings in Japan, and it was there that the Japanese had concentrated most of their forces. Such an invasion appeared absolutely crucial to the defeat of Japan.

Due to the importance of the Eastern Front, that was not the case with Germany and the Normandy landings, but if the Western Allies were to play a major role in the defeat of Germany on land, they had to invade France. However valuable, operations in Italy could not engage the major German forces in Western France, and once the Germans had responded speedily and successfully in 1943 to the fall of Mussolini, the possibility of an effective rapid Allied exploitation of successes in Italy was limited.

BATTLE FOR NORMANDY, 1944

If Overlord was unique in scale, it also indicated the unpredictable nature of force requirements. There had been interwar interest in enhancing amphibious capability, but it had been a low priority. For both the British and the Americans, it was highly unlikely at that stage that there would be a future need to invade a hostile French coastline. Were Germany to attack in the West again, the more likely scenario was, as in the First World War, of France resisting and receiving assistance from Britain, and maybe the Americans, through the Channel and Atlantic ports.

Instead, France had fallen. The unexpected nature of the challenge facing the Allies in 1944 was a problem, as, very obviously, it had been earlier for the Germans when they had planned an invasion of Britain in 1940, and, as the latter showed, improvisation was not an option. It could not be a substitute for the necessary capability and preparations. In contrast, the Allies benefited in 1944 from a purposed process of planning that applied resources to tasks clearly defined in the light of experience. This achievement, however, sounds easier than was the case, not least because each invasion posed unique issues and problems. Furthermore, by 1944, the combined experience of such invasions, which included American amphibious operations in the Pacific, ensured that very different lessons could be drawn, for example concerning the desirability of surrendering surprise by mounting a lengthy prior bombardment, which was, in particular, to be an issue in discussions over how best to prepare for the landing on Omaha Beach. The targets in Pacific landings were small compared to those in Italy and Normandy in 1943–44, and there was no strong prospect of resupply for the Japanese defenders.

Even with the success of Overlord, it proved difficult for the Allies to break out of Normandy, and they both faced a hard battle and fell behind the anticipated phase lines for their advance. Allied casualty rates were far higher than in the initial landings. Despite air attacks, especially on bridges, the Germans were able to reinforce their units in Normandy, although the delays forced on them both ensured that the Allies gained time to deepen their beachheads and obliged the Germans to respond in an ad hoc fashion to Allied advances, using their tanks as a defense force rather than driving in the beachheads. In the Battle of Normandy, the Germans learned how to adapt in the face of concentrated firepower and air attack and adapted well to defending the *bocage*, whereas the Allies, notably the British and the Canadians, found it difficult to break through and restore maneuver. The American capacity to innovate tactics stood them in good stead in defeating the Germans.[31]

SOVIET OFFENSIVES, 1943–45

Alongside improvements in organization and equipment,[32] the Soviet learning curve in implementation was apparent in 1943 as they developed the theories of "Deep Operations" that had been advanced in the 1930s, neglected in 1941, but now implemented and refined in the cauldron of war.

Rather than seek encirclements, as the Germans had done in 1941–42, the Soviets deployed their forces along broad fronts, launching a number of frontal assaults designed to smash opposing forces and maintain continued pressure.[33] This was similar to the Allied offensive on the Western Front in 1918.

The Soviets denied the Germans the ability to recover from attacks, lessened their ability to move units to badly threatened positions, and searched out the weakest points in their positions. As in 1918, at the tactical level, this lessened the value of German defensive "hedgehogs." While they had an operational importance on narrow-front campaigns, narrowing the advance and challenging its flanks and rear, these "hedgehogs" were less significant in resisting broad-front attacks, particularly when they could not rely on air support or armored counteroffensives. The loss of air support also ensured that it would not be possible to reinforce encircled positions by air.[34]

The degree of success increasingly enjoyed by Soviet offensives instilled uncertainty in their opponents. This helped to ensure that the defensive effort required by the Germans on the Eastern Front meant that the mobile reserve necessary to oppose successfully a second front in France was being destroyed.

Although not always successful,[35] the Red Army indeed achieved what has been seen as its own blitzkrieg. This was especially so in the breakthrough attacks in June–September 1944 (Operation Bagration), which overran Belarus and took the Soviets close to Warsaw. In the process, the Red army destroyed much of the German Army Group Center and caused over half a million casualties.

The Germans were badly outgeneraled and totally outfought. In less than two and a half years of fighting, the Red Army drove the Germans from the Volga to the Elbe, a distance greater than that achieved by any European force for over a century, and one that showed that a war of fronts did not preclude one of a frequent movement of those fronts. This was not simply an advance on one axis, but one from the Black Sea to the Baltic across much of Eastern Europe, and an advance that destroyed much of the German army. The achievement was greater than that of the German advance east in 1941–42, not least because the opponent was unable to recover and instead was totally defeated.

Germany's allies were also defeated and knocked out of the war. The Soviet advance into the Balkans led in 1944 to the overthrow of pro-German governments in Romania, Bulgaria, and Hungary, and to the German evacuation of Greece, Albania, and Yugoslavia. Thus, the campaign of that year was important to the fate of a number of states. It does not receive matching attention. Moreover, under pressure, Finland responded to the shift of fortune by abandoning Germany in 1944. The Finns subsequently joined the Soviets in attacking German forces based in Arctic Norway. Once they had changed sides, the Romanians also provided considerable numbers of troops to fight the Germans.

Soviet operational methods toward the end of the war stressed firepower but also employed mobile tank warfare: attrition and maneuver were combined in a coordinated sequence of attacks in which heavy losses were accepted. Once broken through, mobility and the sustained pace of the offensive allowed the Soviets to prevent their opponents from falling back in order, while strong German defensive "hedgehogs" were enveloped and then bypassed.

MILITARY STYLES AND STRENGTHS

The difficulty of making general statements about military style, and notably about national characteristics, is underlined by the different conclusions of detailed studies. For example, American fighting quality in the winter of 1944–45 against the Germans has been underlined in a study of the Vosges campaign but questioned for the Huertgen Forest operation. Command skills in the latter have been rendered suspect. In part, such differences can reflect scholarly emphasis. However, there is also the frequently underrated issue of variations between units, as well as the extent to which particular command decisions could accentuate the nature of such differences.

The relatively small size of the American army ensured a lack of reserve divisions, and the resulting duration of combat without a break for individual units in 1944–45 created serious difficulties as well, again, as variations between units. At the same time, the Americans did not suffer the heavy losses the Germans were hit by, losses that affected their fighting quality and lessened the earlier capability gap in Germany's advantage. Allied strength, including in air power, meant that the Germans, forced onto the defensive, were no longer able to demonstrate their earlier superiority in maneuver warfare. Pushed into attritional warfare, the Germans were unable to match Allied tactical and operational skills.

The war repeatedly demonstrated the value of doctrine and, very differently, of training. As far as the former was concerned, Major General Eric

Dorman-Smith, deputy chief of staff for the British Eighth Army in North Africa in 1942, and a critical commentator, then and subsequently, saw doctrine as a crucial factor in conflict there in 1941:

> In the Middle East Command, during the autumn of 1941, there arose the tactical heresy which propounded that armour alone counted in the Desert battle, therefore the British . . . should discover and destroy the enemy's equivalent armour, after which decision the unarmoured infantry divisions would enter the arena to clear up what remained and hold the ground gained.

Dorman-Smith contrasted this situation with Rommel's Afrika Korps and its tactical preference for a "mixed formation of all arms" and attributed British deficiencies to the sway of generals with a cavalry background: "the romantic cavalry mystique of horsed warfare" led to "basic tactical fallacies . . . the dichotomy between the unarmoured infantry divisions and the relatively 'un-infanterised' armoured divisions."[36] Dorman-Smith correctly picked out the impact of earlier cavalry practices in British armored warfare. However, just as cavalry had been hit by infantry firepower, so tanks were stopped by antitank guns.

In practice, armored divisions that were balanced between the arms were more effective, rather as the Napoleonic division and corps had been. The British eventually adapted their doctrine and closed this capability gap, dismissing some commanders in the process, although the initial doctrine for infantry-armor operations imposed by General, later Field Marshal, Bernard Montgomery, Commander of the Eighth Army in 1942–43 and of the Allied Ground Forces (Normandy) in 1944, was flawed and required change after the serious problems encountered in Normandy in 1944. There armor too often advanced without adequate support. This was despite commanders urging their officers to wait for support, which was a sensible response to the German skill in defensive warfare, especially the careful siting of guns to destroy advancing tanks. In July 1944, Lieutenant General Sir Richard O'Connor, the commander of the Eighth Corps in Normandy, instructed the commander of a British armored division to "go cautiously with your armour, making sure that any areas from which you could be shot up by Panthers [tanks] and 88s [antitank guns] are engaged. Remember what you are doing is not a rush to Paris—it is the capture of a wood by combined armour and infantry."[37]

The learning curves successfully followed by Allied forces[38] helped not only to close the capability gaps with their Axis opponents but also to provide gaps in favor of the Allies. This element tends to be ignored because of the widespread presentation of the war in terms of superior German and Japanese fighting quality that was only overborne by greater Allied resources. The latter interpretation faces many problems, including the failure to make any sense of the ultimately flawed Italian contribution to the Axis. Aside from the failure to address variations within armies, there is a more general lack of appreciation of changes in overall effectiveness, a situation also seen with the assessment of the First World War. In the case of Japan, American, Australian, and British-Indian fighting effectiveness on land all greatly increased between early 1942 and 1944. So also with the Allies fighting Germany.

Training was very important, and success in it had tactical and thus operational consequences. Training helped condition men to machines (and to the machine, at once complex and simple, that is the army); to enable troops to assimilate new tactical thinking and to convey an instructive response; to provide experience of the unit in, and with, which troops would fight; and to provide a psychological form of empowerment, providing an understanding of what was to happen as troops became "combat wise." Night training and the use of live firing in training were both significant. It was necessary to overcome the civilizing effects of peacetime and to prepare troops for killing. Bayonet drill was a classic instance, even though bayonets were rarely used for that end other than by the Japanese. German riflemen in action usually had their weapons slung across their backs, and the Soviets, British, and Americans used light automatic weapons effectively rather than bayonets.[39]

Training was far more complex than in the late nineteenth century. In large part, this was because the nature, range, and challenge of combined-arms operations were more difficult, on a battlefield that included not only indirect fire but also tanks and aircraft. The nature of formations, and the responsiveness of troops to officers and noncommissioned officers, also changed as close-order formations, whether lines, squares, or columns, were replaced in the "empty battlefield" by more dispersed formations. As a result, officers could not readily give orders, and individual soldiers as well as noncommissioned officers now had to make their own choices. That troops were more educated, better read, and less familiar than in the past with the rural experiences of coping with weather, understanding terrain, and seeing death in the case of animals was also significant.

RESOURCE TARGETING

The importance of resources helped provide direction to the land war. Thus, planning for the German offensive in 1942, Hitler included an advance on the Soviet oilfields at Baku, although it was not clear how this oil would be transported. This advance ensured that there were fewer tanks available for operations near Stalingrad and also increased the vulnerability of the German offensive to flank attack. In the event, the Germans did not reach Baku. They conquered territory in the northern Caucasus, but to no strategic effect.

Attacking industrial resources, by land and air, was also important to Allied strategy. In his general situation memorandum of January 21, 1945, Montgomery, now commander of the Twenty-First Army Group, wrote of the leading German industrial region: "The main objective of the Allies on the western front is the Ruhr: if we can cut it off from the rest of Germany the enemy capacity to continue the struggle must gradually peter out."[40]

THE CLOSE OF THE WAR, 1944–45

The German army, like that of other states, was expanded very rapidly, and this caused problems for its training. From 1.1 million strong at the start of 1939, it reached 5.76 million in June 1940, an expansion that worried German commanders. Combat effectiveness, however, was helped both by the training that took place during the "Phony War" of inactivity between the conquest of Poland and the attack on Scandinavia in the spring of 1940, and by the limited number of casualties, which meant that the experienced manpower was not chewed up, as had happened in 1914. Between the start of September 1939 and the end of August 1940, the German army lost seventy-six thousand dead and very few prisoners, low figures compared to what had been expected as a result of the experience of combat in 1918. In contrast, French combat effectiveness did not improve during the "Phony War."

As far as Germany was concerned, there were improvements, tactically and operationally, on the part of the British, Soviets, and Americans, such that it proved repeatedly possible to defeat German forces in 1944 and to inflict heavy casualties upon them. The German position in Europe was reasonably strong in the spring of 1944 as, despite the Anglo-American invasion of Italy in 1943, the Germans were still largely fighting a one-front war, that with the Soviet Union. Despite the decline in the strike power of the German navy and air force, the army was still effective, and there was no serious threat from the hostile population of occupied areas. However, Allied effectiveness had greatly improved. Success in part reflected preparation, as with the Anglo-American invasion of Normandy which benefited greatly from extensive preliminaries, notably in developing amphibious capability and in intelligence gathering.

Despite the July 20, 1944, bomb plot, an effort by some senior officers to kill Hitler and overthrow his regime, the war did not end that year as was overoptimistically hoped by some Allied commentators. A lack of command coordination hit the Allies, as did supply problems. Moreover, the German defense hardened as the campaign of maneuver in the West was forced to a close in late 1944. The German army did not collapse. Its units, both large and small, retained cohesion.[41] Although they knew they had lost, the German commanders fought on, at great cost, because they wished to avoid a shameful defeat and because many were committed Nazis. Following a pattern clearly shown from Operation Barbarossa on, senior officers tended increasingly to disregard military reality when they took decisions. So, even more so, did Hitler, who responded to the Bomb Plot by taking more control and determining to take the offensive. This was very apparent with the Ardennes offensive in late 1944, the Battle of the Bulge launched on December 16, which was followed, on January 1, 1945, by Operation Nordwind, an offensive in Alsace. Confused German command structures did not help. Allied combat quality and responsiveness, such as the superb American defense of the town of Bastogne in the Bulge campaign,[42] were both underrated. Nevertheless, German propaganda still managed to suggest to the people that the fate of the war was still undecided.

Despite flaws, the Allied achievement in 1944 was formidable, not least in comparison with the extent of Allied advances in 1918, although, in 1918, the Allies had the disadvantage that Germany was essentially fighting a one-front war and that the Germans took the initiative for part of the year. In 1944, the German army lost 1.8 million troops, a third of its strength. This hit experience and training, notably affecting the quality of officers and men. The Wehrmacht found itself on the defensive, trapped in an attritional war it could not win, and attempts to regain mobility, notably by means of the Battle of the Bulge in December, failed. This attempt to break through to Antwerp and inflict defeat on the Western Allies was designed to strategic effect, notably to persuade Britain and the United States to abandon the war so that Germany could focus on the Soviet Union. In practice, this was a total misreading of the political situation. In addition, in the face of Allied military power and resilience, there was not room for the maneuver warfare the Germans had earlier used so well.[43]

Alongside, for the Allies (and the Axis), the significance of resources and the role of improvements in fighting technique, it is also important to note other factors, including the extent to which the quality of officers improved under the serious pressures of their tasks, while there were also improvements in the steps taken to monitor and maintain troop morale.[44] The fighting remained costly and brutal until the close. In April 1945, nearly as many American soldiers were killed in action in Europe as had been killed in June 1944.[45] The Germans and Japanese continued to fight hard until the end, which helps explain the decision to continue bombing them so much.

WEAPONRY

The roles of cultural and doctrinal differences were seen in weapons procurement, although other factors were also involved, including the nature of links between the military and industry. Unlike the Germans, the Americans and Soviets concentrated on weapons that made best use of their capacity because they were simple to build, operate, and repair, for example, the American M-1 Garand infantry rifle and Sherman M-4 tank and the Soviet 120 mm Type 38 mortar. In contrast, German tanks were complex pieces of equipment and often broke down, compromising their operational value. For example, the unreliability and high maintenance requirements of the Tiger tank weakened it. The Americans emphasized tanks that were fast and maneuverable, rather than heavily armored, and produced the Sherman, which exemplified these characteristics, in large quantities. The Americans also benefited in late 1944 from the introduction of high-velocity armor-piercing shells for their tank armament.

Tanks were not alone. Motorizing antitank weaponry was important. The resulting self-propelled tank destroyers had a major impact: effective German versions were matched by American tank destroyers armed with 76 mm and 90 mm guns.

More generally, the absence of adequate mechanization, at nearly all levels, reduced the effectiveness and range of German advances; although, even had there been more vehicles, there were the issues both of their maintenance and, more seriously, the availability of petrol (gas).

A very different example of German overprovision from that of tanks was provided by uniforms. The uniform of German soldiers looked good but required far more wool than its British counterpart. The Germans also lacked the winter clothes that the Soviet troops had. This hit them especially hard in the very hard winter of 1941–42.

Returning to weaponry, the Allies had important advantages in artillery and in motorized infantry. Artillery was more effective than in the earlier world war because of better shells and fuses, for example proximity fuses, which were used by the Allies in land warfare from the Battle of the Bulge. Benefiting from impressive guns, such as the American 105 mm howitzer, Allied artillery was more intensive and overwhelming in firepower, although the British lacked an adequate modern heavy artillery. The Soviets had particularly plentiful artillery and, in 1945, used short and savage artillery bombardments to prepare the way for tank assaults. The British, Americans, and Soviets were very keen on using big artillery bombardments to accompany their offensives. The Germans, who employed artillery when they could, had no real answer. In the Pacific, the Japanese relied on the terrain, frequently digging in underground. In contrast, Allied firepower there was largely provided by warships and air attacks, although the plunging fire of mortars was important to conflict on the islands.

Artillery fire, especially that of the Americans, benefited from improved aiming and range, which reflected not only better guns, but also radio communication with observers and meteorological and survey information. The Americans, with their high-frequency radio, were especially adept at this combination. The use of self-propelled and mechanized guns increased the mobility of artillery. Artillery dominance remained a decisive factor into the closing campaigns of the war.[46] It tends to be underrated in film portrayals of the war in favor of tanks.

The Germans were not without good weapons, although their value depended on fighting conditions. For example, on the Eastern Front, the impact of the effective German long-range antitank guns was lessened by the close distances of actual engagements. However, in the MG-42, introduced in 1942, the Germans had a flexible, easy-to-use machine gun. This gave considerable strength to their defensive positions and made it important to suppress their fire before they were stormed.

Whereas the Americans, who first used the Bazooka antitank rocket in 1942, failed to upgrade it as tanks got heavier, the Germans developed the design into the more powerful Panzerschreck rocket grenade. They also developed the handheld Panzerfaust rocket launcher. The British lacked a satisfactory antitank weapon. The ranges at which rifles were used were often no more than four hundred yards, and often much less. This led to the development of the assault rifle, firing a round of intermediate power with a range of about four hundred yards.

MOVEMENT

American weapons production was closely linked to the objective of movement. Building on their prewar peacetime society as well as on military developments, the British had made impressive advances with mechanization, while American forces were motorized to an extent greater than those of any other state, and this was not only a question of the armor. German success in 1940 led American tank commanders to foster a doctrine in which their armor alone brought success. However, American force structure and training was organized by Lieutenant General Lesley McNair, the head of Army Ground Forces from 1942 to 1944, to emphasize combined-arms attacks. McNair was not in favor of heavier tanks with bigger guns. Instead, he favored antitank guns and tank destroyers. He also created airborne units and light divisions.[47]

American infantry and artillery were fully motorized, which helped maintain the pace and cohesion of the advance. The Germans, Japanese, and Soviets, and even the British, could not match this integration, although that did not prevent major Japanese advances in China in 1944–45. Panzergrenadiers were only a minority of the German infantry. Most of the German infantry were slow-moving infantry, dependent on horse-drawn transport. In contrast, the Soviets were able to make much of their infantry and artillery mobile, in part thanks to the American provision of trucks.

American mobility was intended to allow for "triangular" tactics and operations, in which the opposing force was frontally engaged by one unit while another turned its flank, and a third, in reserve, was poised to intervene where most helpful. British observers were impressed by the value of motorized infantry and, in late 1944, some individual commanders, such as O'Connor, sought to find ways to follow suit.[48] In its planning in 1940–42, the Vichy army had responded to German victory in 1940 by envisaging a more motorized force so that the infantry and artillery could move at the same speed as the armor.[49]

American force structure and tactics were a direct product of the economy's ability to produce weaponry and vehicles in large numbers and were closely related to American logistical capacity. The force structure and logistics also helped to ensure the strength of the economy, as the relatively small number of combat divisions, eighty-nine, made it easier to meet demands for skilled labor. President Franklin Delano Roosevelt's call, in his radio broadcast on December 29, 1940, for America to be "the great arsenal of democracy" was fully met.

Given the size of the United States, it was necessary for the economy there to be effective at transportation and logistics. This experience helped the Americans greatly in the war. The flexibility of both economy and society had direct consequences in terms of American production and fighting quality.[50] Institutional and cultural factors were very significant, notably the widespread existence of management abilities stemming from the needs of the economy, as well as a high degree of appointment and promotion on merit, albeit not as far as African Americans were concerned. In addition, there were widely disseminated social characteristics that had military value, including a can-do spirit, an acceptance of change, a willingness to respond to the opportunities provided by new equipment, a relative ease with mobility, and a self-reliance that stemmed from an undeferential society.

At both tactical and operational levels, mobility and firepower were seen by the Americans as multipliers that compensated for relatively few troops. These facets had resource and logistical implications, not least in the need for oil (gas), ammunition, and shipping. Thus, the *relatively* small size of the American combat arm increased its mobility, although there was need, on the part of Americans, for a substantial backup and for a higher level of resources than enjoyed by other armies.

That account of American fighting style, however, does not allow for the variety of methods employed by the Americans in response to many military environments. For example, it was not only against the Japanese that the Americans employed close-in infantry techniques. At the same time, these techniques became more significant in the Pacific in 1944–45 as the Japanese on the islands increasingly focused on resting on the defensive in well-fortified positions rather than attacking landing forces. From 1944, the Americans employed "corkscrew and blowtorch" tactics, involving satchel charges and flamethrowers, in order to kill Japanese in situ or force them into the open to be killed by overwhelming fire.[51] At the same time, the expansion of the range of weaponry and capabilities included, very differently, decrypting encoded radio messages.

RESOURCES

Allied resource superiority and economic sophistication[52] affected the conduct of the war at the strategic, operational, and tactical levels. For example, as the Americans advanced across France in 1944, they generally did not storm villages and towns where they encountered resistance. Instead, they stopped, brought in aerial, armor, and artillery support, and heavily bombarded the site before moving in, with limited loss of American life, although this did not lessen the contribution made by their effective infantry.

To some British commentators, the Americans were overly keen on waiting to bring up artillery, a course that could lead the Germans to disengage successfully and retreat. However, American artillery moved forward close to the line of advance, while the British had learned by hard experience at German hands in North Africa in 1941–42 the wisdom of methodical preparation and superior firepower when closing with the Germans. Montgomery used artillery and air support to preface his attacks in 1944–45. His employment of the former reflected First World War doctrine and practice as well as the defensive strength of the Germans.[53] At the same time, Montgomery adapted to new ideas from subordinate officers and created doctrine accordingly, notably with combined-arms doctrine.[54]

Resource superiority made it easier for the Americans to support combined-arms operations, although it was also necessary to have the relevant doctrine and training. In part, this entailed knowing how best to respond to the combined-arms tactics of opponents. The Germans proved unable to do so. In particular, their moving armor was vulnerable to Allied close-air support, which helped to close the capability gap from which the Germans had initially benefited. This was an instance of the manner in which resource factors were very important in providing the basis for successful combined-arms operations, although, again, they could not, in themselves, provide the necessary doctrine. Doctrine had to adapt to weaponry, but it also involved other factors.

CONCLUSIONS

The role of subsequent assessment of the war remains significant to the perception of land warfare because, for all leading powers bar China, which was to wage a large-scale civil war in 1946–49, it was the last existential conflict they waged. At the level of the personal experience of individual soldiers, the memory, or rather memories, have been kept alive in part by publications[55] but, more commonly, by extensive treatment in the media. Unfortunately, this process can not only be misleading for the war itself, but it can also lead to a neglect or underplaying of the significance of what happened. There are also the persistent issues arising from different national and other treatments of the same episodes or developments.[56]

As a result of the interest in mechanized warfare shown by societies for whom such mechanization was, with the motor car, part of the experience and facts of life, the impression of combat changed. Images created at the time also proved highly seductive. These images were of movement *and* force, and the war was very much seen in these terms, and thus as different from the First World War. With the tank, firepower became an aspect of mobility, and the combination dominated the image of fighting and, more particularly, of success. Plucky infantry could be shown as defeating armor, as in the American film *The Battle of the Bulge* (1965). However, the general theme, not least, later, in television documentaries on the History Channel, was that of armor advances.

This theme led to an underplaying of the role of artillery, which in both world wars was the principal killer of combatants, although not generally a significant killer of civilians. The role of artillery was classically underplayed in accounts of battles, but it proved of importance not only in suppressing defenses as used by the British against the Germans and Italians at El Alamein in North Africa in 1942, but also in thwarting counterattacks. This role was one of the principal aspects of the continuity between prewar circumstances and the world wars, as well as between the two of them, of which it is all too easy to lose sight. A sense of continuity can be seen in an extract from the draft report of 30 Corps, part of the British Eighth Army. Dated November 21, 1942, this report was drawn up after its victory in Egypt at El Alamein, the key battle in the North African theater in the war:

> The operations proved the general soundness of our principles of training for war, some of which had been neglected during previous fighting in the desert. In all forms of warfare, new methods should never disregard basic principles. The operations involved a reversion, with the difference due to the developments in weapons, to the static warfare of the war of 1914–18. This reversion should not be regarded as an isolated exception unlikely to recur. . . . Our organisations and weapons must remain suitable both for mobile and periodical static operations.[57]

Moreover, the use of armor could in part be countered by the development of antitank defenses, notably in the form of antitank guns and minefields. The quality and quantity of each increased greatly during the war. Artillery, however, was employed to suppress both.

Although the Second World War was a unit, there were major changes in land operations during it, as there had been during the previous world war and as were also to be seen in other conflicts, for example the American Civil War and the Iran-Iraq War. In the world wars, these changes reflected the inability of Germany and Japan to translate their initial victories into lasting political or military success. In each case, this failure helped to give an attritional character to the war, both at the strategic level and in the nature of the fighting. Even then, differences in war aims, operational culture, force structure, and resource availability combined to ensure great diversity in conflict.

The American development of the atomic bomb, a formidably expensive task that required much scientific, technological, industrial, and organizational capability, reflected the extent to which the war saw the mobilization of societies across the full range of their capabilities.

Targeting civilians, however, was taken to far more brutal levels by the harsh occupation policies of Germany and Japan, policies that reflected a racism and racist sense of mission that were central to their attitudes and policies. The Holocaust was a totally one-sided German war on the Jews that led to the slaughter of over six million of them. They were not alone. There was also much slaughter of non-Jews, notably of Russians. Overall deaths during the war were twenty-two to twenty-five million military and thirty-eight to fifty-five million civilians.

Aside from these instances of policy, the very scale of the Second World War and the nature of operations, including air attack and submarine blockades, put unprecedented pressure on societies, although most military manpower remained in the armies. The role of states increased at the same time that they faced major challenges in directing economies and in maintaining social cohesion and morale. This was not least in the face of unprecedented bombing, in particular on Germany and Japan. As a separate issue, strategic choices posed many difficult issues, notably of prioritization. These issues were voiced publicly in some states, but in Germany, the Soviet Union, and Japan, there was no allowable criticism of government policy.

Chapter Seven

The Cold War, 1945–71

Due to policies and events, the frictions of war and its destructiveness, the Second World War transformed the world. It saw the United States and the Soviet Union become more powerful, while the European imperial powers were greatly weakened, even though Britain was, and saw itself as, one of the victors. As a result of their new weakness, the European powers both wished to retain colonies and were less able to do so than prior to the war. The shift in strength in 1940–45 was a key background to the Cold War, which was increasingly the rivalry between American-led democratic capitalism and Soviet-led Communism, as opposed to the pre-1941 situation when Britain and France had been the leading opponents of Soviet-led Communism. The United States and the Soviet Union competed to try to control, or at least influence, the former European empires.[1]

This rivalry dominates attention in the period 1946–89. It spanned the world and extended from the 1950s to include the space race. The numerous conflicts and confrontations of the period, most prominently the Vietnam War and the nuclear arms race, but also conflicts in the Middle East, sub-Saharan Africa, Central America, and South Asia, tend to be considered in terms of the Cold War. While valuable, not least in explaining foreign intervention and the provision of arms supplies, each of which was frequently crucial, this interpretation can fail to allow for the distinctive and different nature of these struggles. In particular, decolonization, the cause of many of the conflicts in the period, had contrasting origins, causes, courses, and consequences to the Cold War, and it is important not to run them together.

The Cold War can in practice be dated to the Bolshevik Revolution in Russia in 1917, a revolution that led to the Russian Civil War in which fourteen foreign powers intervened. This was the "hot" stage of the Cold War, and, in part, from 1921 there was the long after-echo in terms of what is generally called the Cold War. Thus, the situation after 1945 was a revival of the earlier Cold War after the brief interval of German-imposed Soviet-Western cooperation in 1941–45, albeit a revival in which the United States took the leading role in opposing the Communist powers, a group that was absolutely and relatively stronger than prior to the Second World War. This strength was particularly apparent after the Communists won the Chinese Civil War in 1949.

NUCLEAR CONFRONTATION

The United States enjoyed a monopoly of nuclear power from 1945 until 1949 but only used this monopoly in order to force Japan to surrender in 1945, a successful employment of new technology. The possibilities that nuclear weapons might be employed in order to stop Communist victory in the Chinese Civil War (1946–49), or to prevent the takeover of Eastern Europe by the Soviet Union and its local Communist allies (1945–48), were not pursued. Nevertheless, America's nuclear strength provided an opportunity for post-1945 American demobilization and for a degree of American confidence about the world system.

This confidence was rudely shattered in 1949 when it became clear that the Soviet Union had been able to develop a nuclear device. This achievement reflected not only a major effort, in part based on the slave labor of political prisoners, but also extensive spying on the Western powers.

The highly disconcerting Soviet success encouraged the Americans to press on with their development of a thermonuclear device, a hydrogen or H bomb, which was much more lethal than the A bomb. However, in a race in the early 1950s, the Soviets followed suit and did the same, and even more speedily than with the A bomb. Other powers, beginning with Britain and followed by China and France, developed nuclear and even thermonuclear capability, including the relevant delivery systems. Nevertheless, the key powers were always the United States and the Soviet Union. This situation became a crucial context for land warfare between the major powers.

Initially, the form of delivery that was intended was as bombs dropped by aircraft, but from the late 1950s, this was supplemented by missiles, either ground launched or fired from submarines. These missiles, which moved far faster than aircraft, were much harder to track or intercept. The two powers built up a formidable array of missiles in the 1960s and, as everything was nuclearized, an entire world of preparation and theory followed suit, one in which land warfare played a scant role. Planners considered targeting that would have killed hundreds of millions, and civilians became used to drills for preparations that would in fact have saved them neither from the blast nor from the subsequent radiation. Children, including myself, were taught to take shelter under their desks at school.

At the same time, as a crucial instance of what was to be called deterrence, the nuclear arsenals may well have prevented a full-scale war, a high-specification war, due to the very obvious destruction it would have caused. Arguably, the increase in their destructive power made the use of nuclear and thermonuclear weaponry of limited value other than as a deterrent threat of "mutually assured destruction." Indeed, in 1955, President Dwight Eisenhower of the United States, a former general, warned his Soviet counterpart of the risk that human life in the Northern Hemisphere might come to an end in the event of such a war. Eisenhower, president from 1953 to 1961, abandoned the idea of the "rollback" of Soviet power in Eastern Europe precisely because he feared nuclear devastation. As a result, NATO did not intervene on behalf of the Hungarian rising against Soviet control in 1956, a rising that was crushed.

Although those who argued that nuclear warfare meant an "end of war" forgot the capability to "scale back" to conventional weapons and continue war, in practice deterrence lessened the prospect not only of a nuclear war but also of a large-scale ground war. Instead, the great powers fought indirect wars, notably in Korea and Vietnam, without committing the full range of their forces or pressing home the attack. Eisenhower did, however, threaten the use of nuclear weapons in order to bring the Korean War (1950–53) to an end. Moreover, their use appeared imminent during the Cuban Missile Crisis of 1962, when the United States and the Soviet Union came very close to war over the deployment of Soviet missiles on nearby Cuba, a war that would have included an American invasion of Cuba and a Soviet move into Western Europe.

The United States and the Soviet Union were the major sources of weaponry, doctrine, and training in this period. This provision could prove influential with their allies, for example, Israel for the United States after 1967 (prior to that, France was the source) and Egypt and Syria for the Soviet

Union. However, Syrian failure at the hands of Israel in 1973 provides a good instance of the major differences in the effectiveness with which Cold War weapons systems were used, in this case tanks. Moreover, as the Soviet Union found with both China and Egypt, the provision of arms did not prevent abandonment of a Soviet alliance by former allies.

In turn, China sought to offer a different, less technological approach to war, one focused on people's war and the linked mobilization of revolutionary enthusiasm. This approach was influential in the decolonization struggles of the 1940s to 1970s, especially in sub-Saharan Africa in the 1970s, and was to become the doctrine of radical regimes, as in Libya. The influence of different doctrines was important in the structuring of armed forces and in strategic planning.

There was no paradigm state of conflict or of capability in this period. At the same time, it is the task of the historian to do more than simply note the variety and offer a potted narrative on that basis. Instead, there is a requirement to try to shape the past and make it understandable, even if this coherence might have been elusive at the time, and this elusiveness might require more attention today when looking at the past, present, and future. Several points emerge. Most significantly, it is important to consider, as a major part of events and developments, the conflicts that could have occurred and, as a linked point, were being planned for. Indeed, doctrine, procurement, training, and preparation, whether strategic, operational, or tactical, focused on such conflicts. In some cases, the course of actual warfare was not too different from the relevant procurement, training, and preparation, but there was one central difference. Unlike in the 1910s and 1930s, the biggest war that was anticipated did not occur. This was a full-scale conflict between the Communist bloc and the West.

The impact of the possibility of such a war, however, should not mean that discussion automatically and exclusively switches to an account of the potential conflict between Warsaw Pact and NATO forces in the North European Plain, and the preparation and planning for it, highly important as these certainly were. Instead, it is also necessary to note the other full-scale wars linked, at least to a degree, to this confrontation, or separate from it, that did not happen but that were considered. These included a full-scale war between China and the United States, a prospect that greatly concerned Chinese policy makers in the 1950s. Both sides assessed how best to respond to amphibious attack, in the case of the United States, a Chinese invasion of Taiwan.

In the 1960s, however, Chinese policy switched as antagonism developed with the Soviet Union. The ground forces on both sides of their frontier increased greatly from 1964, and fighting broke out in 1969. However, although the accounts from both sides are contradictory, the fighting was small scale and contained. Nevertheless, animosity remained strong, as, in a very different context, it indeed remains. The nature of Chinese plans in the crisis of the late 1960s is unclear. The Soviet emphasis in the event of escalation was on an attack on the Chinese nuclear training facilities in Xinjiang. However, there would also have been a significant land warfare component. The Soviet Far East was highly vulnerable to a Chinese land attack, but if the Chinese had mass, the Soviets had the possibility of using maneuver, as in the Manchurian crisis of 1945, to gain and use the initiative. Aligned with the United States from the early 1970s, China continued close to conflict with the Soviet Union, which offered the United States a key strategic advantage. A border agreement was not signed until 2003, an additional agreement following in 2008.

There were other scenarios that were considered as part of the Cold War, notably conflict between Japan and the Soviet Union. Japan prepared to resist a Soviet invasion of the northernmost island, Hokkaido. Separately, there were other possibilities for conflict between major powers, for example, large-scale conflict between China and India as opposed to the limited war that broke out in 1962. All of the possibilities for conflict between major powers entailed planning and preparations. Both were significant, as far more than resources were involved in success.

The context for planning and preparations was set by a changing present, changing in particular in terms of technology and geopolitics, but also with reference to the experience of conflict. Thus, in the late 1940s, the experience of note was the Second World War, although what that might mean was far from clear as it looked in different directions: from large-scale land operations to the dropping of nuclear bombs. In part as a result of different legacies, but also linked to contrasting geopolitical possibilities and threats, there was a dichotomy in the late 1940s. The Soviet Union had no nuclear capability but a large army, and its preparations remained focused on the latter. This was especially so as Soviet goals, in the event of war, centered on the invasion of Western Europe, which was vulnerable to land attack. On the other hand, the United States concentrated on air power and actively demobilized its wartime land forces.

Chapter 7
CHINESE CIVIL WAR, 1946–49

In East Asia, the Second World War had rapidly led to decolonization struggles, notably in Vietnam (against the French) and the Dutch East Indies (Indonesia), as well as to the Chinese Civil War (1946–49). This, still the largest conflict in terms of combatants and area fought over since the Second World War, led to a total victory for the Communists. The war received insufficient attention from analysts, in part because it did not appear to be between cutting-edge forces. Subsequently, in a pattern that drew on earlier, often unreasonable disparagement of Guomindang forces,[2] the war was explained and understood, not so much as a military struggle, but as one in which the very different political ideologies on offer meant that the Communists were bound to prevail over the corrupt and unpopular Nationalists. Such an account was very much that offered by the Communist Party, and this underlines the role of politics in the presentation of lesson learning about war. This account was also that provided by Dean Acheson, the American secretary of state, who argued that the Communist victory was due to powerful indigenous forces while the Nationalists were flawed by corruption and beyond American help, and for that reason the United States needed to show strategic restraint and pursue containment.[3]

This account, however, was less than a full one of a conflict that was not only important in its own right but also involved a large amount of fighting that could not be explained as part of a quasi-automatic process. The Communists benefited from their development of an effective operational method in which large numbers were used to help win campaigns that involved both maneuver and attacks on opposing positions.[4] Although the Chinese were to emphasize the significance of the military ideas of Mao Zedong and to present them as distinctive, in practice Soviet operational methods in 1944–45, notably as successfully used in Manchuria in 1945, proved important to the Communist offensives in China in 1947–49, albeit without the degree of mechanization shown by the Soviet forces.

American views of the fighting in the Chinese Civil War were somewhat distant. The conflict was very much treated as subordinate in some military hierarchy to the fighting in the recent world war and therefore as having relatively little of significance to offer the United States.

KOREAN WAR, 1950–53

Attitudes changed considerably on June 25, 1950, when Communist North Korea invaded South Korea. The Communist dictator of North Korea, Kim Il Sung, believed that the war would end rapidly, thanks to a rising in the South he foolishly expected. Indeed, there had been a Communist-led partisan rising in 1948.[5] Operating in force, the North Koreans drove the South Koreans down into a perimeter in the south of the peninsula around the town of Pusan. The Americans, however, intervened, which the North Koreans had not expected. Aside from moving troops to protect Pusan, the Americans were successful that year in regaining the initiative by means of a large-scale amphibious landing at Inchon behind North Korean lines. Nevertheless, subsequently, large-scale Chinese intervention, from October 1950, designed to prevent America from dominating a united Korea, rapidly turned the scale and pushed the Americans, the South Koreans, and their United Nations allies down the peninsula.

In this conflict, the American army had to learn on the job. It was in a poor state at the beginning of the war, in part because it was really only preparing for a Third World War. Command and combat skills, however, improved in 1951.[6]

Once the front had been stabilized in 1951, the conflict became more positional. Chinese human-wave frontal attacks fell victim with heavy casualties to American firepower, and in late May, the Chinese abandoned their large-scale offensives.[7] Thereafter, the war became more static and attritional. The advantages given to the defense by Korea's mountainous terrain were accentuated by the politics of the conflict, as the United States did not wish to move to the total war that might cause the outbreak of the Third World War. Operational intensity and casualties both fell, and lengthy negotiations became more important, with offensives tied to their course.

As trench replaced maneuver warfare, the role of artillery became more important. Moreover, as the defenses on both sides became stronger, the tendency for a more fixed front line was accentuated. There were elements of the First World War, not least because of the combination of manpower and firepower and the limited mobility associated with positional fighting. In August–October 1951, United Nations (UN) forces captured a series of mountainous positions in assaults that recalled the methods of Western Front trench conflict. Casualty rates became too high to justify the continuation of the advance, and the front line thereafter changed little. In the summer of

1953, the Chinese mounted a series of attacks in order to win advantage in the closing stages of the war. They made territorial gains, but only at the cost of very heavy casualties.

The war demonstrated to the United States both the need for an effective standing (permanent) army and the extent to which it could not necessarily deliver a verdict. Instead, the American threat to use atomic bombs played a role in bringing the conflict to a close in 1953. An armistice left two rival states: North and South Korea. The highly destructive war led to the death of 2.5 million civilians and 1.2 million soldiers, including thirty-four thousand Americans.

AFTERMATH OF THE KOREAN WAR

In combination with the Soviet development of nuclear weaponry, this situation, and the lessons drawn from it, encouraged the United States to press ahead with its increasing reliance on air power and nuclear arms. This process had been enhanced by the American commitment of land forces to Europe as a result of membership, from 1949, in NATO, a membership that took forward the implications of postwar American occupation zones in Germany and Austria. The Korean War, following on from the Czech coup in 1948, in which the Communists seized power in Czechoslovakia after armed trade union militias and police took over Prague while the army was confined to barracks, had led to more urgency about how best to defend Western Europe from Soviet attack.[8] However strong the American commitment, it was regarded as highly unlikely that NATO forces would be able to defeat an invasion of Western Europe by the Soviet army. As a result, the strategy became that of a nuclear response, with the American army there to demonstrate resolve and to force this response. This is a pattern seen today with the American commitment to South Korea in the face of a far larger, but not very well armed, North Korean army that is likely to launch human-wave attacks.

Under President Eisenhower (1953–61), the emphasis was on the army as a force for civil defense at home and as a NATO commitment, and the marines were seen as the overseas expeditionary force. The major American military commitment to Europe was linked to the development of a nuclear capability by armies, notably in missiles. In part, this development reflected an attempt to demonstrate relevance, notably in the face of the focus of expenditure on the air force. The army was cut from 38 percent of total American military expenditure in 1953 to 22 percent by 1959, with the biggest fall occurring in 1955. The latter percentage included nuclear weapon systems for the army, which further cut down the money available for nonnuclear items. Tactical nuclear missiles became a key tool in the Cold War, being deployed for example from the late 1960s by the Americans in South Korea against the threat of attack by the North. Army manpower was cut, and the role of army leadership in strategic policy making was reduced.[9]

In the case of the United States, moreover, there was a lack of interest in the lessons offered by contemporary wars of decolonization. They appeared to have little to teach the United States, which had ended its colonial presence in the Philippines in 1946, was moving Alaska and Hawaii toward statehood, and did not face an independence struggle in Puerto Rico or its other colonies. Indeed, the Americans treated colonialism and imperialism as European, old fashioned, redundant, distant from American values, and different from a world of free-market capitalist, independent democracies that they were seeking to create and lead. As a consequence, the Americans did not devote sufficient attention to the wars of decolonization in the period, nor to those between non-Western powers. This failure to learn lessons doctrinally was to hit them hard in the Vietnam War.

INDOCHINA

That terminology, the Vietnam War, was a reflection of this very problem of inattention because the Vietnam War in which the Americans played a leading role from the mid-1960s to the early 1970s was in fact but one in a sequence that ended only at the close of the 1970s, or, if more obscure hostilities in Cambodia and Vietnam are included, at the close of the 1990s. To America's Communist opponents, the sequence was clear, but not so to the Americans. Most significantly, in the first war, the French were involved in a bitter and, ultimately, unsuccessful effort to retain colonial control of Vietnam, Cambodia, and Laos, a struggle that focused on Vietnam. This was one in which the Americans came to provide much financial support to France, but to which, in 1954, they refused to commit troops. Had they done so, the United States would have had earlier experience of the issues involved in such conflict. Such experience would have stood them in good stead subsequently, doctrinally, in terms of command experience, and with reference to organizational priorities, training, and procurement.

The commitment of American troops in 1954 would also have led to a different narrative of military history, and thus, possibly, to a different analysis. On a related point, had France been the leading Western, or even just West European, military power in this period, that might also have led to another analysis.

As with the Korean War, a key element was geopolitical, or, rather, geopolitical as set by a recent sequence of wars. The defeat of Japan in 1945 and of Nationalist China in 1949 were crucial, as they meant that, in both Korea and Indochina, the anti-Western forces had the benefit of neighboring support, unlike the Communist insurgency against British rule in Malaya in the 1950s. Chinese assistance during 1950 helped to ensure that the Communist and nationalist Viet Minh pushed the French back with heavy casualties from their border posts in the Le Hong Phong II offensive in northern Tonkin in late 1950. The struggle was linked to the Korean War, where the French played a role in the UN contribution, notably in supporting American and South Korean forces in capturing Heartbreak Ridge in late 1951. Indeed, Chinese support for the Viet Minh was a way to put pressure on the UN force and vice versa. The Americans, who had begun to supply assistance to the French in Vietnam in May 1950, pressed France not to make peace with the Viet Minh. This was an aspect of the new American strategy of containment, one readily seen in the deployment of forces in Western Europe but made more serious for the Americans by Communist success in China.

At the tactical level, the French benefited from defensive firepower, notably in defending the open areas of the Red River delta in 1951–52. In the Battle of the Day River in May–June 1951, Viet Minh conventional attacks in large numbers proved vulnerable to French firepower, and the Viet Minh retreated with far heavier casualties. The standard narrative emphasizes the folly of the French forward airborne deployment to an exposed forward position in Dien Bien Phu in late 1953 and the fall of this position in May 1954 to adroit Viet Minh attacks, helped by innovative tactics and superior engineering skills. This struggle, which is still difficult to assess due to the role of propaganda, became the center of attention even though it was peripheral in terms of location and manpower.[10] French will was broken by this defeat, and, although the French were still in control of all the cities, they abandoned the struggle in 1954 and accepted a provisional partition of the country between the new independent states of North and South Vietnam. Cambodia and Laos also became independent.

The standard account of this Vietnam war focused on French weaknesses, notably the lack of recent experience in sustained, large-scale counterinsurgency operations; operational deficiencies, particularly in maneuver; and poor command choices. These factors were all pertinent, but so was the success of their opponents. The Viet Minh's dynamic synergy of guerrilla and conventional warfare, a warfare that reflected their organizational and doctrinal flexibility, and their successful logistics were also highly significant. So also was a political resolve that was greater than that of France and that was not matched by French success in efforts to create a political system in Vietnam to support their efforts. An aspect of this resolve was an ability to take heavy casualties and maintain tactical, operational, and strategic energy.

INSURGENCY WARFARE

This outcome, however, did not mean that the French were predestined to lose. Indeed, in terms of territorial control, they had certainly not done so by the beginning of 1954. As so often with historical interpretation, there is a tendency to make victory appear clear cut and the defeat of the other side inevitable, and from those to fashion a teleology. That process ignores the narrow margin of much success, the complexities involved, and the difficulty in determining key factors in causation.

Far from there being any inevitability of success for insurgents, or, indeed, for left-wing insurgents, there were many failures in this period, notably with large-scale Communist insurgency movements in Greece, Malaya, and the Philippines. Specific political and military factors within individual states were important, as were those in a wider geopolitical context. The latter included the key element of supplies. Limiting the flow of munitions to insurgents proved important in all the examples just given, as well as in those of anti-Communist insurgents in Eastern Europe in the late 1940s and 1950s, Tibet in the 1950s, and Cuba in the 1960s. This flow was also highly significant psychologically and politically to insurgencies in overcoming a sense of isolation and inconsequence.

With the Soviet Union in the late 1940s and early 1950s, the emphasis had been on conventional confrontation with the West, and there was a belief that full-scale war might break out soon. As a consequence, Soviet support for decolonization struggles was of relatively little consequence; they appeared a "long-war" alternative and not one that captured the experience or doctrine of the Soviet army. The situation changed as a result of the Communist victory in China, as Mao Zedong backed such struggles, and notably so after the failure of full-scale operations to bring victory in Korea. In the short term, this support for decolonialization struggles was very important in Southeast Asia, but it subsequently also became so in sub-Saharan Africa.

In contrast, attempts to foster insurgency in Latin America had scant success between those in Cuba in the late 1950s and in Nicaragua in 1979. Thus, in Venezuela, the army and American-trained rangers helped defeat Cuban-backed rebels in the 1960s, and they were also defeated in Bolivia.

Right-wing insurrections, in the shape of military coups, could be more successful, as in Brazil in 1964. However, in Venezuela in 1959–61, conservatives supported by the dictator of the Dominican Republic, Rafael Trujillo, failed to overthrow the Social Democratic government, which was supported by the United States.[11]

There was a significant change in Soviet policy after the death of Stalin in 1953 and as a result of subsequent negotiations with the United States about nuclear limitations and the rocket race. These developments suggested that full-scale war was not imminent, an assumption encouraged by President Eisenhower's pragmatic opposition to supporting the risky idea of the "rollback" of Soviet power and by his refusal to act in support of the Hungarian rising against Soviet control in 1956.[12] The option for such action was essentially closed by the strength of the Soviet military.

Soviet interest in the Middle East and Africa increased from the late 1950s, and this interest helped make the decolonization struggles of that period more clearly part of the Cold War. This interest also made it harder for the counterinsurgency side to win, however that was defined, because support for the insurgents could be maintained by outside powers that could not be attacked. The Soviets also became more committed to states in these regions, notably Egypt and Syria, and armed and developed their militaries. So also with Soviet commitment to India, whereas the United States and China backed Pakistan.

After Vietnam, France failed totally in defeating insurgency in Algeria despite a major commitment of resources and withdrew in 1962. This failure again received insufficient attention elsewhere, notably in the United States. In part, this was because of the assumption that colonial rule was redundant, but there were also pejorative views of French power, views that owed much to French defeat by Germany in 1940 and in Vietnam in 1954.

The British compared themselves favorably to the French. However, there were parallels in British conduct. Although the emphasis for both was on managed decolonization or orderly transfers of power, the reality was often a mixture of harsh resistance to change and the rushed abandonment of power.

For every instance of violence avoided by the British and French, there were examples of conflict chosen, even positively embraced. These choices were made in the light of lessons drawn from other places and other empires. Prosaic terminology, notably that of law and order, was intended to depoliticize anticolonial rebellion and make the resultant repression, often with large-scale incarceration, appear limited and excusable.[13] In Portuguese Africa, a far more persistent effort was made to retain imperial control.

A broader comparative account might raise a few questions. The largest slaughter of civilians in the 1950s occurred in China and was scarcely due to imperialism. This was seen by the Communist regime as warfare against reactionary elements. Moreover, areas that became independent of imperial rule frequently saw higher, far higher, levels of violence than during the struggle for independence. This was the case for example, each very differently, with India, Congo/Zaire, and Nigeria. In the last, the Biafra War of 1967–70, in which nearly a million people were killed, drew on earlier rivalries, as well as the impact of postimperial developments. Long-lasting divisions can also be seen in other cases, such as Sudan, Cyprus, Algeria, Indochina, Ethiopia, and, later, Sri Lanka. There were also separatist struggles in states that had not been colonies, for example Iran.

Decolonization itself was mutually dependent, in the sense of being intrinsically linked to a wider global process and not nationally distinctive. Moreover, the end of empire triggered wider and deeper changes to the postwar international system than arose from solely the Cold War or more familiar interstate rivalries.

VIETNAM WAR

As nuclear confrontation escalated, limited war in Vietnam in the 1960s and early 1970s proved far less successful for an American-led coalition than the Korean War had been for a very different American-led coalition. The analysis of the war continues to be highly controversial and interacts with the debates since about how best to conduct military operations. In particular, the inherent viability of guerrilla warfare and, conversely, of counterinsurgency strategies both became an issue. The Vietnam War also led to much discussion of the merits and limitations of air power, notably bombing. Although it could bring significant tactical and operational advantages, the Americans failed to use bombing to bring victory or, indeed, to direct the responses of the North Vietnamese, except for an investment in antiaircraft capability.

The American image of land warfare during the Cold War as a whole is dominated by the Vietnam War, and for a number of reasons. This was a lengthy conflict, one in which the United States, the world's leading military power, was a major participant and the one in which it was involved most intensively. The war, the sole major televised ground conflict during the Cold War, was extensively reported from on the ground, with print journalism supported by impressive photography, and was followed with great attention around the world. As the war was also a failure for the United States, it was both analyzed there and attracted great attention elsewhere, being indeed seen as an augury of a new age of land warfare, that of revolutionary warfare, and more particularly as a victory for Maoist ideas of revolutionary violence and strategy.

Moreover, American failure appeared to demonstrate that air power had not redefined warfare and predetermined wars to the extent that its protagonists argued, nor that nuclear capability had closed down the significance of warfare, whether conventional or not. All of these points had, and still have, considerable value, but none justifies the extent to which the Vietnam War, this Vietnam war, dominates discussion, and notably so at the popular level.[14]

The American-supported government in South Vietnam faced a Communist rebellion by the Viet Cong, which led to more overt American intervention. In turn, in a process that had begun before American intervention, forces from North Vietnam moved south to help the Viet Cong. By 1963, there were sixteen thousand American military advisers, but the South Vietnamese army was not in command of the situation. In part, this was because it was having to respond to its opponents and had a large area to defend, but there was also a command culture focused on caution and firepower that could not grasp the dynamic of events. Being on the defensive meant that its opponents were able to dictate the pace of campaigning.

By 1965, in the face of the North Vietnamese and Viet Cong moving, as they thought, into the last phase of Mao Zedong's theory of revolutionary war and accordingly deploying large forces, the South Vietnamese army was on the verge of collapse. This situation led to a major increase in American commitment in order to preserve the credibility of American power and to force war on the Communists in an area where the Americans could intervene. Thus, to President Lyndon B. Johnson, the war was a necessary demonstration of resolve, a strategic goal that rather swallowed the specific problems of winning success in South Vietnam.

The Americans faced tactical and operational difficulties in operating in South Vietnam but overcame them. Initially, the Americans focused on defending coastal areas that were strongholds of South Vietnamese power and essential for American deployment, but gradually, having built up an impressive logistical infrastructure, they moved into the interior. The Americans were able to advance into parts of South Vietnam that had been outside the control of Saigon and to inflict serious blows on the Viet Cong in the Mekong Delta. In addition, direct mass Viet Cong attacks on American positions were generally repulsed with heavy casualties, for example at the siege of Plei Me in the Central Highlands in 1965.

The Americans sought to advance throughout South Vietnam, establishing "firebases" from which large-scale search-and-destroy operations could be mounted to defeat the large units being deployed by their opponents, to inflict casualties on them, and to erode their strength. The helicopter played a major role in this extension of activity, especially with the use of the new First Cavalry Division (Airmobile). Land warfare was becoming far more mobile than it had been as a result of the internal combustion engine. In addition, the environment, notably the forest cover and the lack of good roads, was generally not appropriate for armor. The use of the helicopter represented a successful operational and tactical engagement with the situation. It was so, however, only because the North Vietnamese did not have human-portable surface-to-air missiles until late in the war. Had they done so earlier, the usage of helicopters would have been extremely difficult, which would have forced the Americans to change their tactics to more conventional methods of advance, supply, and retreat.

In the event, against the background of the very different experience of the Korean War, the American army had gradually learned the necessary tactical skills to campaign in South Vietnam, albeit, in turn, squandering this lesson by the practice of rotating units out of the combat zone. However, the strategy underpinning American land warfare was problematic, as, in parallel, was the very different strategy involved in American air warfare against North Vietnam. American activity on the ground was somewhat apt to conceal the extent to which the initiative was, in practice, shared with the Viet Cong and North Vietnamese. Moreover, although heavy casualties were inflicted, in what could be presented as attritional warfare linked to American "scientific" operational research and the related "kill statistics," opposing numbers rose, as North Vietnam responded to the American buildup by sending troops south down the Ho Chi Minh Trail, thus avoiding the strong

American presence in the Demilitarized Zone between North and South Vietnam.

There was also the problem of forcing conflict on opponents, a problem underlined by the politically imposed necessity of using air attack, but not ground forces, in attacking the opponents' base area of North Vietnam. Within South Vietnam itself, there was no concentration of opposing power that could be rapidly fixed and readily destroyed as, in very different circumstances, the Israelis were to do against Egypt, Jordan, and Syria in 1967 and the Indians and Pakistanis were to seek to do in successive conflicts.

Denying American success was presented by the North Vietnamese as a way to bring victory, on the grounds that American willpower to sustain the struggle was less than that of their opponents. However, that did not suffice for the North Vietnamese and, more particularly, ensured that they found it difficult to shape the conflict, a position accentuated by American claims that the war was going well. This situation helped to ensure the launch of a major offensive by the North Vietnamese in 1968, one designed to show to the American public that their army was failing, and also to demonstrate to the South Vietnamese that this army could not protect them.

There were obvious fundamental contrasts between the Tet Offensive and that of the Israelis in 1967, not least in terrain and outcome, but there was a similarity in that the ability to take the offensive disorientated opponents and provided a political message accordingly. The Israelis were not up against a superpower with superior technology or united command. Given the constraints within which they had to operate, the North Vietnamese and Viet Cong did well, helped, as with the Israelis, by strong morale.

The attacks mounted under cover of the Lunar New Year celebrations of Tet were launched in the mistaken belief that they would engender a popular uprising. In turn, overoptimistic American assumptions about enemy casualties in the border battles of late 1967 were matched by an inability to believe that a full-scale attack on the cities would be mounted. About eighty-five thousand Viet Cong and North Vietnamese troops attacked from January 30, 1968, being eventually defeated with heavy losses over the following month. There was a recurrence of the failure of attacks on French positions in 1951. Nevertheless, North Vietnamese military and political strategies did not depend on continual success.

Having defeated these attacks, American effectiveness in counterinsurgency increased from 1968, but, in part for tactical and operational reasons,[15] it still proved difficult to "fix" opponents and to force them to fight on

American terms. Nevertheless, in 1969, the Americans inflicted serious blows on the Viet Cong, who had lost many of their more experienced troops in the Tet Offensive. The Viet Cong achieved little in 1969, and their attacks suffered heavy losses.

Yet, although the Americans were able to repulse attacks, their counterinsurgency strategy was hit by the unpopularity of the South Vietnamese government, by Viet Cong opposition and intimidation, and by increasingly vocal domestic American criticism of what appeared to be an increasingly intractable conflict. The last encouraged the Americans to shift more of the burden back to the South Vietnamese army. This army had some good commanders and units but was not up to American expectations. Thus, prefiguring the situation in Afghanistan after the Soviet withdrawal in 1989, although the Viet Cong and North Vietnamese did not win in the field in 1968–72, they benefited greatly from shifts in the military and political contexts. At the strategic level, these shifts included growing pressure on American interests elsewhere, and notably so as a result of Soviet support for Arab rearmament and intransigence after the Six-Day War of 1967. The Soviet deployment of more warships in the Mediterranean increased the pressure.[16]

The issues facing the United States in South Vietnam were matched by the experience of their allies, albeit with the complication of the impact of particular approaches and combat styles. Analysis of the Australian pacification activity in Phuoc Tuy Province, as of the Americans in Binh Dinh Province, questions the thesis that the policy had succeeded and was therefore wrecked by the eventual pullout. At the same time, it is clear that the Viet Cong, which had been able to compete openly with the government in 1966, was, by the close of 1972, forced to operate clandestinely. Yet there has also been a focus on the "inherent weaknesses in the South Vietnamese state," which in part was a matter of webs of patronage and corruption, but that, more generally, was a consequence of "the immaturity of the South Vietnamese state." This situation greatly affected military preparedness and morale.[17] Training was also poor, and the army depended on the Americans for firepower and logistics.

The balance of failure in Vietnam, that of failure by both sides, continued, and was demonstrated by North Vietnam in 1972 in one of the major offensives of the period, one that stands comparison, as a military and political move, with the Egyptian and Syrian assault on Israel in 1973. The casualties inflicted on the Viet Cong in and after the Tet Offensive, as well as the inability of American air attacks to destroy North Vietnam's war-supporting capability and logistical system, had ensured a greater reliance on North Vietnamese forces, rather than on the Viet Cong, while also creating the possibility for the use of conventional forces in a standard Soviet-style operation. In March 1972, the North Vietnamese launched the Nguyen Hue campaign (or Easter Offensive) across the Demilitarized Zone between North and South Vietnam. The surprise nature of the attack, and the strong forces deployed, brought initial success. Quang Tri, a provincial capital, was captured and another, An Loc, besieged. President Nixon briefly considered using nuclear weapons.

A standard view, notably in the United States, emphasizes the role in the eventual North Vietnamese failure of the American Linebacker I air campaign, which hit the supply system, and thus the support, of the invasion force, particularly with fuel. This account underplays the role of South Vietnamese defenders, who held off the invasion, and the problems the North Vietnamese confronted in mastering high-tempo maneuverist warfare. Both were also to be issues for Egypt and Syria when attacking Israel in 1973, and for Iraq when attacking Iran in 1980. The Soviet Union could provide impressive weaponry, particularly tanks, but it proved far more difficult to transfer the doctrine and techniques of effective operational warfare, and notably so if faced by a determined opposition. As more generally in military history, capabilities, whether in attack or defense, were focused, accentuated, minimized, or offset by the characteristics of the opponent.

In particular, in Vietnam in 1972, there was a failure to make the best use of tanks, which reflected both an operational inability to use them in a maneuverist capacity in order to gain mobility and achieve particular objectives, and a tactical failure to get and utilize infantry-armor coordination. Instead, as with the Iraqis in 1980, the tanks were used by the North Vietnamese as an assault force on South Vietnamese positions, indeed essentially as mobile artillery. This had the effect of squandering the initiative in operational terms while providing targets for American air attack.[18] On the eve of the American withdrawal in 1973, neither side had won the war on the ground, a repetition of the situation for the French in 1954, which was not a comparison the Americans would have welcomed. However, the Americans, like the French in 1954, were under serious fiscal pressure and were suffering from rising domestic problems.

NON-WESTERN CONFLICTS

The period witnessed a series of conflicts between non-Western powers. These included wars between India and Pakistan in 1947–48, 1965, and 1971, and between Israel and at least some of its Arab neighbors in 1948–49, 1956, and 1967. There were also attempts to maintain state control over autonomous or would-be autonomous regions. Thus, Iran suppressed Kurdish rebellions in 1946 and 1979, while in Iraq, Kurds were attacked in 1959.

Some conflicts had the potential to be of particular significance. Fought in the Himalayas, in terrain unsuitable for tanks, the war between China and India in 1962 was short and limited, but it could easily have been far greater in scale. The Chinese heavily outnumbered the Indians and benefited, as a result of road building, from superior logistics, at least in the zone of conflict. The struggle arose from a long-standing dispute over the mountainous frontier, which dated back to colonial days and was exacerbated by a regional struggle for predominance. The Indians began the war, on October 10, with an unsuccessful attempt to seize the Thag La Ridge, and the Chinese then responded with an offensive launched on October 20, defeating and driving back the Indians. An Indian counteroffensive on November 14 was defeated and, on the next day, the Chinese outmaneuvered the Indian defensive positions near Se La, inflicting heavy casualties. Having revealed that the Indians would be unable to defend the frontier province of Assam, the Chinese declared a unilateral cease-fire on November 21 and withdrew their troops. Theirs was a limited operation in which prospects for exploitation were gravely restricted by environmental and logistical factors. In total, the Indians had lost 6,100 men, dead, wounded, or prisoners. This war was analyzed subsequently, notably in 2017, as conflict between the two powers again appeared a prospect.

The results of the successive India-Pakistan wars indicated the value of the far larger Indian military, but other factors also played a role in Indian success, underlining the point that far more than resources cause success in war. In 1965, for example, the Indians chose to advance not in Kashmir, as the Pakistanis had anticipated, but instead in the Punjab, using tanks to drive on Lahore and Sialkot. The Pakistanis had been encouraged by India's defeat by China in 1962, but the Indians, with their Soviet T-55 tanks, fought better than had been anticipated. Indeed, victory over Pakistan led to a recovery of Indian confidence after defeat by China. In 1965, unlike in 1947–48, there was large-scale conventional conflict between Pakistan and India, including the use of large quantities of tanks and artillery. The Pakistani army proved more successful in mounting coups than in fighting India.[19]

In contrast, Latin American states did not go to war with each other; indeed they have not done so on any scale since the Paraguay-Bolivia Gran Chaco War of 1932–35. In part, this absence of conflict was a product of an American hegemony that continued despite Cuba going Communist. Moreover, the lack of ideological division as a reason for any conflict between the states was important, for example in avoiding war between Argentina, Brazil, and Chile. Their militaries devoted much of their effort to controlling their own states, each, moreover, mounting successful coups.

Non-Western conflicts in part involved the use of the legacy of the Second World War, notably in terms of experience and weaponry. Thus, Indian and Pakistani commanders had come out of the British imperial military system, as did those of African states that gained independence without conflict, for example Uganda. The military of Papua New Guinea, independent from 1975, developed out of the Australian army's Papua New Guinea units. That transition worked for a while, but the military, from 1984, found itself increasingly playing a role in internal security. That role contributed to a difficulty in being a capable and stable force.[20]

In the initial wars of the late 1940s, the emphasis in non-Western conflicts was more clearly on infantry. However, independence, resource accumulation, and military aid from leading powers as they sought allies rapidly brought a greater degree of mechanization and particularly the development of tank forces. Israel was to use the mobility of its army, and the tank-killing skill of its own tank forces, with great success when defeating Egypt in 1956. It was helped, however, by the wider context, not least in having no other Arab states to fight in 1956, unlike in its wars of 1948–49, 1967, and 1973.

WAR IN YEMEN

South Vietnam was not the sole defeat for counterinsurgency forces in a conflict made even more difficult by international intervention. Indeed, in an instructive episode that showed much about military capability in the second half of the twentieth century, and which also demonstrated many of the characteristics of conflict between non-Western powers, President Nasser of Egypt, a veteran who had served against Israel in 1948 and whose power derived from the overthrow of the monarchy in a coup in 1952, sent troops to Yemen. This was in an attempt to support the new revolutionary regime established in September 1962 by a military coup against the conservative rule of Imam Muhammed al-Badr, and, more generally, as part of Nassar's radical pan-Arabism. The Royalist opposition to the new regime was backed by neighboring Saudi Arabia, which provided money, weapons, and bases, while Jordan, another conservative Arab monarchy, sent military advisers. The Egyptians had anticipated a commitment of only three months but found themselves in an intractable situation that offered a parallel to other counterinsurgency operations of the period.

Aside from the inherent difficulty of the task, which owed much to the bellicose and fissiparous character of Yemeni society and to the harsh nature of the arid terrain, the Egyptian army was not prepared for operations in Yemen. It lacked adequate planning for operations there, was critically short of information about both Yemeni political alignments and the terrain, was short of adequate communications equipment, and was not prepared, by training, doctrine, or experience, for a counterinsurgency conflict. Instead, Egyptian military experience was in conventional operations against Israel, most recently in 1956, and then only briefly. Alongside obvious contrasts, there were also instructive parallels with the later Soviet and American commitments in Afghanistan.

The attention devoted to Yemen, a war generally ignored in such global histories as these, here serves as a corrective to the tendency to put the Six-Day War first in the discussion of the 1960s in the Middle East, and thus underlines the problems inherent in any process of assessing relative significance. The standard approach often in practice rests on facile assessments of relative significance.

In the initial operations in October and November 1962, the Egyptians found their attempts to control the entire country thwarted by opposition that made more effective use of the terrain in Yemen, not least by ambushing road-bound Egyptian columns: the mobility that mechanized vehicles brought was often inflexible and brought vulnerability. This mobility therefore had both tactical and operational consequences.

The Egyptians responded at the close of November by focusing on a defensive triangle of key cities where they intended to build up the Republican army, but this army failed to realize their hopes, performing worse than the South Vietnamese military and only becoming an important element from 1966. Royalist successes instead led the Egyptians to build up their forces and return to the offensive in February 1963, regaining, in Operation Ramadan, control over most major towns and much territory. To secure these gains from Royalist counterattacks, the number of Egyptian troops rose from fifteen thousand in the winter of 1962–63 to thirty-six thousand.

In many respects, there were instructive parallels with the Vietnam War, as well as precursors to later conflict in Yemen, notably in the 2010s. The Royalists had bases in neighboring Saudi Arabia (the equivalent of North Vietnam) and supplies from there, and they made good use of the terrain, not least in mounting ambushes. The Egyptians, in contrast, like the Americans in the Vietnam War, had control of the air, which they used for bombing, ground attack, and air mobility, the last, for example, seen with the seizure of the town of Sadah after paratroopers had established a runway on which troops could be landed.

The Egyptian ability to take the initiative, however, was not matched by success in achieving results. As with so many counterinsurgency struggles, territory, unless occupied, could not be retained, but the occupation of territory itself did not produce benefits and it also meant a major commitment of manpower. Furthermore, the difficulty of achieving results, combined with the absence of an exit strategy, hit the morale of the Egyptian forces, although there was no coup in Egypt, unlike in 1952. To the soldiers, Yemen appeared a hostile environment, both physically and culturally, and, as with the Americans in the Vietnam War, difficulties in identifying the enemy contributed to this sense of alienation. Discipline was weakened, corruption developed in the officer corps, and military and domestic support for the war fell. The inflexibility of the Egyptian military—an inflexibility, tactical, operational, and strategic, also seen against the Israelis in 1967—made it difficult to adapt doctrine and tactics to engage the guerrillas. Nevertheless, there were some improvements in tactics, not least with the use of helicopter-borne aerial resupply.

In 1964, the Egyptian forces in Yemen were increased to fifty thousand men, but they still faced problems in using the roads; and indeed, early in the year, the capital of Sana was besieged by the Royalists. The Egyptian attempt that summer to kill the imam led to the capture, successively, of two of his headquarters, but he was able to escape into Saudi Arabia and the campaign did not lead to the end of the war. Once the Egyptians withdrew from the areas they had captured in the northwest, they were reoccupied by the Royalists. In 1965, despite deploying seventy thousand troops, the Egyptians again faced problems in responding to ambushes that cut supply routes and left their positions isolated and vulnerable. Much of the east was overrun by the

Royalists, and Egyptian frustration led to plans for an attack on Royalist bases in Saudi Arabia, which had already been repeatedly bombed.

At the same time, and the parallel with the Vietnam War is instructive, the Egyptians tried to negotiate. In August 1965, Nasser and King Faisal of Saudi Arabia signed the Jeddah Agreement, in which they undertook to stop helping their protégés, and as a result, by the summer of 1966, there were only twenty thousand Egyptian troops in Yemen. However, the hopeful signs of the previous autumn were wrecked by the failure of peace talks between the Republicans and the Royalists, as well as by Nasser's interest in using Yemen as a base for seizing control of the strategic port of Aden after the British, in response to an anticolonial insurgency there, withdrew from their colony in neighboring South Yemen. This interest reflected a revival of the expansionist interests seen under Mehmet Ali in the early nineteenth century. As a result, the Egyptians reoccupied parts of Yemen they had abandoned, although it was the increasingly effective Yemeni Republican troops that played the major role in operations against the Royalists in 1966–67.

Israel's total and humiliating victory over the Egyptian forces in Sinai in June 1967 in the Six-Day War led to pressure for an evacuation of Yemen so that Egyptian forces could be concentrated in preparation for a future conflict with Israel, and indeed this was to occur. The fig leaf of an agreement with Saudi Arabia (which, despite its promises, continued to supply the Royalists) allowed them to do so, mostly in October, although not finally until December 1967. Once the Egyptians had left, the Republicans, ironically, proved more resilient than had been anticipated, successfully defending Sana against siege in the winter of 1967–68. Saudi support for peace finally led to the end of the war and the formation of a coalition government for Yemen in 1970. Thus, the latter stages of the war were very different from the situation in South Vietnam and, indeed, in Afghanistan in 1989–92. At the same time, in Yemen, as in South Vietnam and Afghanistan, it was the international context that was highly significant, not least the question of prioritization, for Egypt, the United States, and the Soviet Union, respectively.

In contrast to Egypt's lengthy commitment to Yemen, Syria's unsuccessful invasion of Jordan in 1970, in support of a rebellion by Palestinian guerrilla forces, was a struggle between conventional forces. The Jordanians fought well and benefited from effective air support against Syrian ground forces, which in turn lacked air assistance. The Jordanians, who enjoyed important American diplomatic support, succeeded in expelling the Palestinian guerrillas. Syria, in contrast, was aligned with the Soviet Union.[21]

Chapter 7

ARAB-ISRAELI WARS

A series of wars between Israel and its Arab neighbors (1948–49, 1956, 1967, 1973, and 1982) arose because the Arabs proved unwilling to accept the culmination of the Zionist movement in the form of an independent Israel. Rejecting the UN partition resolution of November 29, 1947, they sought to drive the Jews from Palestine as the increasingly ineffective colonial power, Britain, withdrew. Fighting broke out throughout Palestine in December 1947 and became full scale when the British mandate ended on May 14, 1948.

From 1948 to 1949, Israel was able to establish its independence in the face of poorly coordinated and badly prepared moves by the regular forces of Egypt, Iraq, Jordan, and Syria, along with the irregular forces of the Palestinians and the Arab Liberation Army. The Arabs benefited from more weaponry and firepower, as well as from taking the initiative, but the Israelis had more troops by the last stage of the war, and also the determination born of a conviction that their opponents intended genocide; they certainly, at least, planned what was later to be termed ethnic cleansing. More mundanely, the Israelis, as in their wars in 1967 and 1973, had interior lines of communication, while the supply of Czech small arms and, to a lesser extent, aircraft was crucial to their ability to do well.

It is, however, important to note that the Israelis were less successful in their fighting with Iraqi, Jordanian, and Syrian forces than in conflict with the Egyptians, the Palestinians, and the Arab Liberation Army. This contrast, which underlines the mistake of aggregating different circumstances into a supposed unitary "Arab" military culture that does not in practice exist, was responsible for the postwar shape of Israel, notably expansion across the Negev desert to the Red Sea, which was the result of the defeat of Egyptian forces. Lacking a unified command, the rival Arab forces suffered from serious problems with logistics, but the Israelis found the Jordanian regulars formidable opponents.

The war ended with the partition of Palestine between Israel, Egypt, and Jordan. Determined to make the Palestinian home a Jewish homeland, Israel gained, as a result of relative success in the war, far more than had been envisaged in the UN partition resolution in 1947. Egypt and Jordan each also gained part of the proposed Arab state. The latter was not established. Indeed, Jordan's army, the Arab Legion, was more concerned with seizing the West Bank of the Jordan than with destroying Israel, and its forces only operated in the territories allocated to the Palestinians. Although Jordan, which annexed the west bank in 1950, was able to reconcile itself to the existence of Israel, Egypt and Syria were far less willing to do so. This refusal ensured a high level of tension, as did the presence of Palestinian refugees, most of whom had been driven from their land by Israeli action. These refugees threatened not only relations with Israel, but also the stability of neighboring states, especially Lebanon. Terrorist attacks and the robust Israeli response greatly increased tension.

In 1956, Israel attacked Egypt on October 29 in concert with Britain and France, overrunning the Sinai Peninsula, but then withdrew in the face of American and Soviet pressure. The weak resistance put up by the Egyptians reflected Israeli success in gaining the initiative, as well as the poorly trained nature of the Egyptian army and its inability to use the Soviet and other weapons it had received effectively. In particular, the Egyptians, who fought well in prepared positions, suffered from inadequate combined-arms training and from the rigid tactics of their armor, while Israeli success indicated that the reserve system, which provided the bulk of their army, worked. Peacetime training was shown to be effective.

The Israelis also benefited from having numerical superiority in Sinai, in part because Nasser, Egypt's leader, correctly anticipated an Anglo-French invasion of the Suez Canal zone to the west. When Britain and France attacked, Nasser indeed ordered his already embattled troops in Sinai to retreat. Prioritization again was a key issue. The whole of the Sinai Peninsula was conquered by the Israelis in under one hundred hours, at the cost of 172 fatalities. After the campaign, however, Israel, badly let down by the failure of Britain and France to sustain their invasion, agreed to withdraw in return for the deployment of United Nations peacekeeping troops along the frontier.

After the 1956 war, both Israel and, even more, her Arab neighbors, who were helped by greater oil revenues, increased their military expenditure. Moreover, Egypt's unification with Syria in 1958 created, in the United Arab Republic, the prospect of more united Arab action, especially in 1960. However, pan-Arabism was always weaker in practice than in rhetoric: the union was overthrown by a coup mounted by Syrian officers in 1961, which began a series of coups and countercoups that lasted until 1963, while the United Arab Command, created in 1964 by a meeting of Arab leaders in order to prepare for war with Israel, faced acute national divisions.

Nevertheless, a serious Israeli-Syrian border clash in 1964 was followed by an upsurge of Palestinian guerrilla attacks on Israel in 1965–66, with

Israeli reprisal attacks on Palestinian bases in Jordan. In November 1966, an Egyptian-Syrian defense treaty seemed to move Egypt closer to Syria's desire for war: a coup in February had led to radical Ba'athists, who dominated the army, seizing power.

Meanwhile, Israel developed a military able to underwrite a doctrine that called for a rapid advance in the event of war. Wanting any conflict to be swift, so as to avoid large casualties and the economic disruption of calling up reservists for a long period, the Israelis built up their air power and their tank force so that they could take the offensive and maintain this control of the operational dynamic.

In 1967, rising regional tension, particularly Egyptian saber rattling, led to a preemptive Israeli attack on Egypt. Nasser was encouraged in his blustering by the supply of Soviet equipment and by his desire to retain the leadership of the Arab cause: the aggressive attitude of the Syrian government toward Israel challenged his prestige. Nasser also felt under pressure from economic problems arising from his misguided attempt to force-start the economy through state planning. His expulsion of the UN peacekeeping force from the Sinai frontier, as well as the closure of the Gulf of Aqaba to Israeli shipping, provoked Israel and reflected a failure to appreciate the limitations of the Egyptian military, which in turn was overly concerned about Yemen, where several of its leading units were deployed. The Israeli attack began on June 5, 1967, with a surprise attack on the Egyptian air bases launched by aircraft coming in over the Mediterranean from the west—not the direct route of attack. The Egyptians, who had failed to take the most basic defensive precautions, lost 286 aircraft in just one morning, and in addition their runways were heavily bombed. Claims that America and Britain were responsible for the air attack were totally unfounded.

As the war spread, it led to the Israeli conquest not only of the Gaza Strip and Sinai from Egypt, but also of the West Bank section of Jordan as well as the Golan Heights from Syria. Gaining the initiative was crucial to the execution of Israeli's well-prepared plans, as were training and morale that were better than those of their disunited opponents. In Sinai, the Egyptians suffered from a failure to appreciate the caliber of the Israeli military and the nature of Israeli operations, and from an absence of adequate, effective reserves: the large number of poorly trained Egyptian reservists in the Sinai were no substitute, and, more generally, Arab armies were affected by a lack of adequately trained troops and certainly of troops trained for such conflict.

The war in Sinai was also a large-scale tank conflict. Soviet T-54 and T-55 tanks used by the Egyptians were beaten by American Patton and British Centurion tanks used by the Israelis, who showed greater operational and tactical flexibility, not least in successfully searching for vulnerable flanks and thus overcoming the strength of prepared Egyptian defensive positions. The Israelis displayed their skill at tank killing. The Egyptian command system, weakened by cronyism and complacency, proved totally inadequate to the challenge, a situation that prefigured that of Iraq in 1991: domestic political considerations, notably of military patronage, had taken precedence over battlefield effectiveness. The successful use of Patton and Centurion tanks against T-54s and T-55s contrasted with the India-Pakistan War of 1965 in which the Patton (Pakistan) was opposed to the Centurion (India). The Soviet tanks were not particularly good, and the T-54 was very poor, as it lacked gun stabilization. The American and British tanks were superior.

Having broken into the Egyptian rear, the Israelis ably exploited the situation, and they also benefited greatly from the destruction of the Egyptian air force at the outset of the war: Egyptian ground forces were badly affected by Israeli ground-support air attacks, for which operations in Yemen had given them no experience. When Field Marshal Mohamed Amer, the chief of staff, instructed the army to retreat from Sinai to the Suez Canal on June 6, the unplanned withdrawal was chaotic, the cohesion of the army collapsed, and resistance to the Israelis disintegrated. The Egyptians lost about ten thousand men dead and five thousand captured, as well as much of their equipment: about $2 billion worth was destroyed (at a time when $1 billion still meant a lot), while Israel captured 320 tanks. Many were refurbished and later served the Israelis as infantry fighting vehicles. Amer was sacked and subsequently arrested for allegedly plotting a coup. He appears to have been forced to commit suicide.

The conflict in Sinai also underlined the key role of field maintenance and repair in mobile warfare, the Israelis proving more effective than the Egyptians in every case. As always, overnight repair of equipment and its return to the battle line proved a key element in the war-making ability of a modern army. Nonbattle losses through mechanical failure are apt to be more costly than battle losses.

Given misleading assurances by Nasser, Jordan joined in on the Egyptian side on June 5, only to have its air force destroyed and the West Bank overrun. The Israelis had not anticipated a ground war with Jordan, but misguided Jordanian support for Egypt led the Israelis to attack once they were certain that the Egyptians had been defeated and that it was therefore safe to move units. Syria refused to provide assistance to Egypt, but it shelled Israeli positions, and, on June 9, the Israelis, keen to take advantage of an opportunity to occupy the Golan Heights, attacked. As Egyptian and Jordanian forces had already been wrecked, with the Jordanians accepting a ceasefire late on June 7 and Egypt early on June 9, the Israelis were able to focus on the Syrians, reflecting the importance of sequential warfare and of Israel's ability to respond rapidly to problems. Gaining the initiative, and using their aerial superiority for ground attack, the Israelis benefited from a collapse in Syrian morale. The failure of Syria's patron, the Soviet Union, to intervene was also important, not least because the Soviets had stirred up Syria against Israel and had made some preparations to intervene. At the end of the war, having lost about one thousand men, Israeli forces were fewer than 60 kilometers from Damascus and less than 110 kilometers from Cairo.

Israel remained in occupation of the regions conquered in 1967, providing it with strategic depth but ensuring that it now controlled a large and disaffected Arab population. In the long term, the presence of a substantial Arab population within Israel and, even more, in Israeli-occupied territories was to challenge the security of Israel, leading to Arab risings called the intifadas, while the consequences of the occupation helped to destabilize Israeli politics.

In addition, over six hundred thousand Arab refugees, many of whom had fled Palestine in 1948–49, were based, mostly in refugee camps, in neighboring Arab states, where they challenged the stability of Jordan and Lebanon. Furthermore, the failure of the Arab regular armies encouraged some of the Palestinians to resort to terrorism, not only in the Middle East but also further afield. Terrorist attacks on Israelis included those at the Munich Olympics in 1972 and the hijacking of aircraft to Entebbe in Uganda in 1976. Meanwhile, Egypt and Syria, totally unwilling to accept Israel's gains in 1967 and to negotiate peace, had been rearmed by the Soviet Union, which, in pursuit of Cold War objectives, did nothing to contribute to regional stability.

CONCLUSIONS

To stop this chapter in 1972 underlines the theme of variety, not least in terms of national styles and strategic cultures,[22] as well as serving the point that the conflicts of the Cold War years are too big a topic, and cover too many years, to handle in just one chapter as otherwise might seem appropriate. By the end of 1972, the intractability of warfare was particularly apparent. Neither side had won the Vietnam War, nor indeed the Cold War. The Israelis had heavily defeated their opponents in 1967, only to find them swiftly rearmed and resolute. Warfare had been most successful in aiding, sometimes achieving, decolonization and in settling conflicts within states. The future of war appeared unclear, but it had certainly not been rendered obsolete by nuclear armaments, which, in practice, had not been used since 1945, although they were extensively and expensively deployed, while extensive preparations had been made to fight using tactical nuclear weapons.[23] The geopolitical matrix of the next decade rested uncertain.

Chapter Eight

The Cold War, 1972–89

The military pace in the second half of the Cold War again was high, but it was also different. With the exception of the closing stages in the decolonization struggles in the African empires of Portugal and Spain, such wars had come to an end. Nor was there any recurrence of a clash between major powers as had occurred in the Korean War, although there was still to be a use of the rhetoric, for example by Argentineans when attacking the British-held Falkland Islands in 1982.

There was, however, an extension of conflict into parts of the world where it had hitherto been relatively limited since 1945, notably Central America and Northeast Africa, but also Afghanistan and Iran. Moreover, there was an increase in conflict between, and within, independent states.

In terms of doctrine, technology, and methods, there was change, as with the American shift in 1973 to an all-volunteer army,[1] but little innovation. Most important was the rise of terrorism and also the development, by Iran, of a new fundamentalist Islamic strategy. Land warfare was affected by the post-Vietnam repositioning of the American military and, in particular, by the army's creation of a strategic rationale, operational doctrine, and military history that were designed to enable it to fight a nonnuclear major war with greater effectiveness so that there was no need to rely on the first-use nuclear option. Greater effectiveness was linked to an abandonment of conscription and to a consequent emphasis on a smaller but more professional and mechanized army. As in other periods, the linkages between these (and other) trends were often indirect and sometimes contradictory, while there is no clear order of priorities in treating these conflicts.

SOUTHEAST ASIA

Northern Europe, the epicenter of Cold War confrontation, and the Middle East, the site of many conflicts, generally engage most attention first. However, the most instructive starting point is Southeast and East Asia, because there a conflict in which the United States was to the fore was replaced by a situation in which regional powers, notably the regional superpower, China, were the key players, while the American role was essentially offshore. That is a situation that has continued to the present.

The failure of the Nguyen Hue campaign in South Vietnam in 1972 meant that the North Vietnamese would need to follow the route of negotiation in order to move forward in the Vietnam War. This course was encouraged by the 1972 American rapprochement with China, a step of great strategic significance that, like the earlier overthrow of the left-wing nationalist government in Indonesia in 1965–66, made it less serious for the Americans to abandon South Vietnam. The Paris Peace Agreement of January 1973, during the negotiation of which in December the Americans threatened to use nuclear weapons, was followed by American withdrawal two months later.

The conflict continued, with the two Vietnams the combatants and with heavy South Vietnamese casualties. In April 1975, South Vietnam was overrun, in the Ho Chi Minh campaign, by a renewed invasion from the North. Conventional North Vietnamese divisions achieved what they had been unable to do in 1972. They made good use of tanks in 1975 and ably integrated them with infantry and artillery. Unlike the North Vietnamese, the South Vietnamese military was politicized, without equivalent gains in motivation. The South Vietnamese also faced important doctrinal and operational problems, including a failure to seize, and use, the initiative, which amounted to a widespread reluctance to take combat to their opponents. Moreover, in March 1975, the South Vietnamese followed an unwise strategy with the abandonment of the Central Highlands, where the North Vietnamese had launched their attack. Instead, the South Vietnamese focus was on defending the south near Saigon, a strategy that gave their opponents a powerful impetus and gravely weakened their own morale and cohesion.

Again, this account does not put the American failure to continue providing military support, notably air power, front and center. The contrast between 1972 and 1975 suggests that it was the key factor, but that analysis offers too limited a reading of the situation in each of those years, as one that overly puts the focus on the United States. To change just one variable does not necessarily explain success.

The withdrawal of American forces and the total fall of South Vietnam were not the limits of conflict in the region. In 1975, the Communists also overthrew their opponents in Cambodia and Laos. There was, however, a major falling out, with Vietnam, which looked to the Soviet Union, in 1978–79 conquering Cambodia, which looked to China. In response, believing that Vietnam ought to be taught a lesson and fearing a fundamental Soviet threat to Chinese security, in February–March 1979 the Chinese attacked Vietnam with five hundred thousand troops, inflicting much devastation, only to find that greater Vietnamese guerrilla warfare experience, combined, on the part of the Chinese, with poor logistics, inadequate equipment, and failures in command and control, led them to withdraw, and without forcing the Vietnamese forces to leave Cambodia. Although larger in scale and longer than its attack on India in 1962, this was also a more limited war than the Chinese intervention in Korea in 1950–53, notably because it was not fighting a major power. It proved far easier for China to restrict its commitment in Vietnam than in the case of the United States in Vietnam or the Soviet Union in Afghanistan.

Low-level conflict continued in Cambodia, with China backing rebels after its protégé, the Pol Pot government, was overthrown by a Vietnamese invasion in 1978–79. Moreover, border conflict continued between China and Vietnam until 1991, with much of it on a large scale and very costly in lives.[2]

Nevertheless, there was no major conflict in East or Southeast Asia after the 1970s. Partly as a result, the capacity of the region to lead to conflict was underplayed until the situation dramatically changed in the mid-2010s. Indeed, the focus on the Islamic world in the meanwhile was a product not only of the inherent importance of warfare there, but also of a relative significance arising from a lack of conflict in East and Southeast Asia, an area of far greater and rapidly growing economic weight. China's economic rise in the 1970s–2000s was very much achieved through integration with the American-dominated global system and without conflict. The situation did not alter until the 2010s, when tensions rapidly escalated.

Another approach would be to ask how best to define a major war. The Vietnamese invasion of Cambodia in 1978–79 involved 150,000 troops and followed conflict between Cambodia and Vietnam in 1975–78. This 1978–79 invasion was initially resisted by conventional means, leading to the loss of about half of the Cambodian army, until recourse was had to guerrilla operations from bases in Thailand. Subsequently, the Vietnamese retained a large force in Cambodia, indeed 180,000 of their 1.26-million-man army in 1984, a year in which major efforts were launched against the guerrillas. In 1989, the Vietnamese withdrew their forces, a change that was linked to a cut in the Vietnamese army by about half. About fifteen thousand Vietnamese troops had been killed during the occupation. Peace came in 1999 when the Khmer Rouge, the key resistance element, no longer enjoying Chinese support, was completely dissolved. A conflict on this scale would have been regarded as major elsewhere in the world.

THE ISLAMIC WORLD

In the Islamic world, there were very different issues at stake, although there were the same dynamics arising from the complex interactions between local power struggles and Cold War rivalries. Communism was a far weaker ideology in the Islamic world, and sectarian ethnic and religious tensions were far more significant. To outsiders, the defining element at the start of the period appeared to be that of the Arab-Israeli struggle, an assessment accentuated by the Yom Kippur War of 1973. However, this focus underrated the significance of rivalries within the Islamic world, rivalries already militarily apparent in the 1960s, most notably in the Yemen conflict in 1962–70. So also with Syrian intervention in Lebanon from 1976. Ideological factors interacted with great and regional power rivalries. Thus, in the Dhofar region of Oman in 1963–76, Britain, Iran, and Pakistan supported the sultan against rebels backed by Communist powers, notably neighboring South Yemen.[3]

Alongside the range of factors that encouraged conflict and intervention, there were similarities at the tactical and operational levels. Thus, despite the emphasis on mobility, fortifications were used to prevent advances by opponents. Sometimes this was successful, as with the Hornbeam Line in Oman, a series of fortified outposts designed to hinder rebel movements, and at other times much less so, as with the Yom Kippur War.

YOM KIPPUR WAR, 1973

The Yom Kippur War (the Ramadan War for the Arabs) was a land attack in which antiaircraft missiles were designed to neuter Israeli air power. The surprise attacks launched by Egypt and Syria on October 6, 1973, broke through Israeli positions, notably the weakly defended Israeli Bar Lev Line on the east bank of the Suez Canal, which was imaginatively assaulted by the Soviet-trained Egyptians who used technological ingenuity in order to wreck the defenses.

Established in the western fringes of the Sinai Peninsula, the Egyptians then repelled a series of Israeli counterattacks. They inflicted serious damage on Israeli armor, which suffered from a doctrine that, based on the experience of 1967, exaggerated the effectiveness of tank attack and failed to provide adequate combined-arms capability, especially sufficient artillery support and mobile infantry. Israeli attitudes reflected wishful thinking. The Israelis were happy to believe that they could focus on tank warfare and therefore lessen the risk of suffering infantry casualties. As the Israelis had deployed French antitank missiles in the 1960s, they were aware of their capability, but they did not build on this experience.

In 1973, Egyptian infantry units equipped with Soviet Sagger antitank guided missiles proved deadly and destroyed over eight hundred Israeli tanks and other combat vehicles. The point about combined-arms capability has already been made in this book when discussing the Second World War. It needs to be understood in terms of the contrary attraction of the distinctive feature of firepower mobility offered by tanks. That feature was to be challenged by air power, but the latter lacked the sustained presence provided by tanks.

The Israelis, in 1973, however, were able to drive the poorly performing Syrians back, advancing into Syria and repelling counterattacks.[4] In response to Syrian pressure for help, the Egyptians changed their strategy, operational method, and tactics and moved their armored reserve forward, attacking on October 14. This was a mistake, as the Israelis were strong in defense, not least once the Egyptians advanced beyond the antiaircraft cover offered by the Soviet SAM-ZSU air defense system. In an attack that highlighted the deficiencies of their tactics, the Egyptians lost heavily in what is known as the "Chinese Farm" battle. The Israelis also used concentrations of artillery fire to overcome the Sagger units. Gaining and using the initiative, the Israelis further took the advantage by outmaneuvering their opponents, crossing the Suez Canal, overrunning the Egyptian missile defense units, and imposing a result on their opponents.[5]

Although the 1973 war proved far less one sided in its course than that of 1967, it still indicated significant differences in fighting quality, differences that were clearly to the advantage of Israel. Moreover, these differences suggested again that the quantity of resources was less important than their quality and use. This was an interpretation that greatly interested American observers, as the Israeli military, with its American tanks, was treated as a representative of the Americans against the Egyptians and Syrians, both of whom used Soviet tanks, doctrine, and training. A similar pattern of learning was employed as far as the air conflict was concerned.

SUB-SAHARAN AFRICA

The collapse of the Portuguese Empire following the April 1974 revolution in Portugal indicated the complexity of assessing reasons for success. While insurgents became more effective on the ground in Africa, events in Portugal were crucial. The Portuguese rapidly withdrew from the colonies.

In southern Africa, anti-Western decolonization struggles continued after the end of the Portuguese Empire. In order to maintain control by its minority-white settler population, Southern Rhodesia (now Zimbabwe) had unilaterally declared independence from Britain in 1965. Initial African guerrilla opposition, which began in 1966, suffered from the extent to which the Zambezi valley offered a difficult approach route to Southern Rhodesia in terms of both support for the guerrillas and terrain. From late 1972, however, it proved possible to operate against Southern Rhodesia through Mozambique as Portuguese control there was slackening. As in insurgencies more generally, the nature of nearby bases was a very significant issue. Full-scale guerrilla warfare was waged from then until 1979.

As in other decolonization struggles, the African opponents of the government were largely divided on tribal lines, and this was also linked to contrasts in foreign bases and support, as well as in military strategy. The Ndebele-based ZAPU (Zimbabwe African People's Union) sought to apply Maoist concepts of guerrilla operations, while the Shona-based ZANU-PF (Zimbabwe African National Union–Patriotic Front) under Robert Mugabe preferred more conventional operations. Rivalry between them was linked to that between the Soviet Union and China. The Southern Rhodesian military proved better at attacking infiltrating guerrillas than its government was successful in winning "hearts and minds," while the burden of the war was accentuated when South African military support was withdrawn in 1975. Increasingly isolated, not least because, under Jimmy Carter, president from 1977 to 1981, the American government was opposed to white-minority-rule states, the Southern Rhodesian government conceded majority (African) rule.

Southern Rhodesia briefly returned to British control before, in 1980, becoming an independent state as Zimbabwe. Robert Mugabe, the Chinese-backed head of ZANU-PF, unleashed a bloody reign of terror on the Ndebele in 1982 using Korean-trained troops.

In South African ruled South West Africa (now Namibia), SWAPO (the South West Africa People's Organization) had begun guerrilla attacks in 1966. SWAPO received Soviet assistance. The Communist powers believed that the overthrow of Western colonies and pro-Western states would weaken the capitalist economies by depriving them of raw materials and markets and would also challenge their geopolitical position and strategic advantages. In the event, with the exception of Zimbabwe under Mugabe, the successor governments found it economically necessary to trade with the West and actively sought Western investment.

Opposition to minority white rule had become more vigorous in South Africa, with the Soweto rising of 1976 spreading to major cities. On June 16, in Soweto, a township in Johannesburg, between ten and twenty thousand black students rallied to protest against being obliged to receive education in Afrikaans, the language of apartheid. The government responded with a mixture of firmness and concessions. The former involved murderous policing, the recruitment of local auxiliaries, intelligence, subversion, and military strikes against foreign guerrilla bases. The heavily armed police used armored vehicles and helicopters in Soweto. Many of the marchers were shot dead.

As with the British in India, however, political factors, not military failures, led to a major shift in control in South Africa. The minority white government eventually chose to pursue a policy of peaceful change, in part because the end of the Cold War had robbed the government of the international ideological justification (the key in its relationship with conservatives in the United States) underpinning its racist policies. As part of an agreement to limit the conflict in Angola, South Africa withdrew from South West Africa in 1990. In South Africa, the first majority-franchise election followed in 1994 and led to the African National Congress peacefully gaining power under Nelson Mandela. As with Indonesia and most states that experienced decolonization, the boundaries of the colonial state were maintained, and there was no return to precolonial political units.

NEW DOCTRINE

As always with military history, there was no one cause for developments, or indeed their course, or the consequences of them. Nevertheless, just as German military doctrine and strategy were affected by victory in Poland in 1939, so Israeli successes encouraged already-existing American and NATO interest in a more flexible practice of land warfare. A critical approach would emphasize a wish on the part of the Americans to move away from the experience of the Vietnam War and, instead, toward the more familiar opposition to the Soviets in Northern Europe, with a concomitant stress on conventional warfare defined in terms of symmetrical conflict focused on tanks. This was seen as likely to involve fewer casualties and to require less manpower than an infantry war, and this outcome was important given the ending of conscription. That approach can then be taken forward to claim that, as a result, the Americans proved far less prepared for the "wars among the people" that became more significant in the 1990s and far more of a problem for them in the 2000s.

This narrative, and the linked analysis, is not without value and will be considered where appropriate. However, with particular reference to the years 1973 to 1989, from the end of American participation in the Vietnam War to the fall of the Berlin Wall, it would have been feckless for the American army to focus on warfare such as that in Vietnam or the conflicts in sub-Saharan Africa that occurred in the period. Instead, the strength of Soviet conventional forces in Eastern Europe posed a continuing threat and, indeed, had been a backdrop element during the Vietnam War. There was the possibility, both in 1967 and in 1973, that the Arab-Israeli conflicts in the Middle East would lead, with a deliberate or accidental escalation, to full-scale rival superpower interventions. There was also concern about the Soviet Union possibly exploiting the Portuguese revolution of 1974, a course, however, made more difficult by the lack of any land link for intervention. In 1983, there were to be strong fears that the Soviets were planning to launch an attack in Western Europe.

This element of great-power rivalry was sharpened politically and militarily by the failure of hopes based on the détente seen in the mid-1970s and, instead, by the strengthening of Cold War tensions. These became more potent from the Soviet invasion of Afghanistan in December 1979 and focused greatly on the deployment of tactical and intermediate-range nuclear missiles in Europe. For the American army to have failed to focus on this challenge would have been to invite the charge of redundancy in the face of military and political developments and to have entrusted NATO defenses to nuclear missiles, and that at a time in which Soviet missile strength was markedly increasing.

The Americans advanced the doctrine of Active Defense in 1976 and then, from 1981, that of AirLand Battle. These concepts, through which careers were helped and weapons planned for, sold, and relied on, led to a stress on the integration of firepower with mobility. This was a marked development of the process termed ROAD (Reorganization of the Army Division) seen in 1959–63, not least because of the emphasis on the coordination of air and land fighting. To give teeth to the process, there was a modernization of conventional weaponry. Moreover, the doctrinal innovation focused on the consideration of how best to direct and win the operational level of war, that between tactics and strategy.

In this, the Americans were not only advancing concepts that made sense of their own commitment to a maneuverist approach, as opposed to fixed defenses for Western Europe, but also seeking to match, counter, and overcome the Soviet development of operational art. This development took forward ideas that had been untried in conflict in the 1930s but used in 1944–45 in order to sustain a successful offensive and to overcome the problems posed by the defenders by forcing continual disorientation on them. The Soviet focus was on moving forward second- and third-echelon forces in order to replace those in the initial attack and thus sustain the offensive. Under Marshal Nikolai Ogarkov, the perceptive chief of the General Staff from 1977 to 1984, the Soviets developed earlier concepts of "Deep Battle," which had been made more possible by the spread of mechanization in their army and by the growth of airborne forces.[6] He sought a more compact, technologically advanced military, rather than one focused on the techniques of mass conflict.

In turn, American AirLand doctrine and strategy proposed the engagement and destruction of the second- and third-echelon Warsaw Pact forces at the same time that the main ground battle was taking place along the front line. Stopping the movement forward of Soviet reserves was seen as crucial. AirLand became the battle plan in 1984.[7]

What this would have led to is unclear, not least due to multiple military and political factors on both sides, including the operation under pressure of both alliance systems, as well as tensions within military and political systems. These tensions, for example, led to the ousting of Ogarkov in 1984.

Uncertainty ensured that planning had to address multiple options, which included the extent to which both sides were deploying coalition forces that were composed of units of varying quality. Moreover, each had to deploy along long fronts.

At the same time, the very absence of any conventional conflict between Western and non-Western forces in this period, and, indeed, not until the American-led coalition in 1991 destroyed the Iraqi army with its Soviet arms and doctrine, means that the possibility of such a war tends to be downplayed in the military history of the period. Instead, the emphasis is on conflicts that were short and/or relatively small scale, notably the Anglo-Argentine Falklands War of 1982, Israeli operations in Lebanon, and the Soviet intervention (long, but small scale) in Afghanistan. Each was more generally instructive about the capability of weapons systems under the strain of conflict. However, it was not easy to read from them to more general questions of what would have happened had a major war broken out in Europe, although efforts were made to do so, notably with reference to Israeli operations.

It would have been very difficult to prevent such a conflict from becoming nuclear, not least as Soviet forces would almost certainly have used nuclear weaponry from the outset, while the United States, Britain, and France would probably have done so had the defense been put under great pressure. It was assumed that the Soviet Union would advance in part through neutral Austria.

This situation arises again today when considering the Russian threat to NATO. Moreover, the idea of fighting a limited nuclear war had scant purchase in reality. There were no agreed conventions on what such a limited war meant, and it would have been difficult to maintain such limits under the pressures of conflict, including the fear of imminent changes in the war making of other powers. Given this scenario, it is unclear that the planning of either side for large-scale ground conflict was realistic. In addition, there were factors of speed. Although it was widely assumed that any Soviet advance would be rapid, it would not be as speedy as a nuclear exchange and was therefore unlikely to preempt the latter.[8]

Allowing for these points, it is worth returning to the question of likely effectiveness, not least because there is a widespread assumption that Soviet operational art would have proved highly successful. There is a parallel with assumptions about German blitzkrieg methods in the absence of greater opposing resources. The evidence cited with reference to Soviet operational art relates to 1944–45, when, however, both Germany and Japan were also facing other opponents, were under very heavy pressure from them, and had only limited air power. The later applicability of this success is unclear. It is difficult, for the Cold War, to disentangle the advantages stemming from Soviet resources, notably tank numbers, and those arising from Soviet doctrine. It is also unclear how far there was a ready ability to implement the doctrine.

In addition, there were issues arising from the interoperability of Warsaw Pact forces, with the Soviets being justifiably doubtful about their allies, including the Poles and the Hungarians. Only the East Germans were regarded as reliable. So also for the Germans and their allies in the Second World War. There were also questions about the effectiveness of nonelite Soviet divisions. Although it can be mistaken to read from one conflict to another, such questions were encouraged by the deficiencies seen with the Soviet army in Afghanistan in 1979–89. Moreover, the Russian army proved somewhat unimpressive in Chechnya in the 1990s.

Soviet planning could be bold but also formulaic, inflexible, and mechanistic. Plan Granite, which they helped produce for the Egyptians, included, in its last phase, the reconquest of the whole of the Sinai from Israel. In the event, in 1973, the Egyptians settled for far more limited goals. Though mishandled, this might well have been a sensible decision. In 1987–88, more impressively, but against weaker opposition, Soviet planners and weaponry, alongside Cuban troops, helped lead to the checking, in the large-scale Battle of Cuito Cuanavale, of the South Africans intervening on behalf of their UNITA protégés in the Angolan Civil War.[9]

THE AFGHAN WAR

Soviet intervention in Afghanistan in 1979 was an attempt to end instability in what was seen as a client state on the Soviet border. There may well have been aspirations to derive further benefits from control of a country that also bordered Iran and Pakistan, the former of which was unstable, and that took Soviet power closer to the Persian Gulf and the Indian Ocean, but they were less significant and to the fore than the concern to achieve a favorable stability in Afghanistan and to thwart Chinese and American influence.

Given the proximity of the Soviet Union, its resource strength, and its aerial dominance, the failure of the Soviet forces to overcome guerrilla resistance is instructive. It is more so because this failure indicates the strength of the "alternative" narrative in post-1945 military history, which stretches from wars of decolonization, via the Vietnam War and the Soviets in Afghanistan, to more recent issues with Western interventionism. Soviet failure in Afghanistan also became very important to a fundamentalist Muslim narrative about military history, one in which leading powers should be, could be, and would be defeated by the "righteous." This was not a new idea, but it derived much greater strength from the Soviet failure and was to be deployed by al-Qaeda to rationalize its moves.

The Afghan war also served as an instance of the ability of outside intervention to handicap major powers, in this case of the supply of arms by the United States and others to oppose the Soviet Union. Lastly, the war, as so often, offered a very different lesson of sorts, that of the difficulties of defining as well as fixing success, but, linked to that, of the possibility of fighting a limited conflict such that a crisis could be contained. This was a lesson for interventionists in the early twenty-first century that many were unwilling to accept, in large part because they wanted closure in terms of the bringing of peace and order. Thus, aside from warning about the risks of interventionism, the Afghan War offered a lesson about the precariousness of results and, more broadly, of the shared nature of any military situation, one that threw the focus onto political understanding and skill.

Initially, the Soviets appeared highly successful in Afghanistan, indeed operating, as they had done in Hungary in 1956 and Czechoslovakia in 1968, in order speedily to impose a political solution by force, a solution that entailed the support for a faction in the Communist rivalry. The use of airborne troops served, as in Czechoslovakia, to help seize the cities rapidly and to overcome the risk of opposition to movements on land.

However, in the far-larger Afghanistan, the political, social, military, and international contexts were very different, and the Soviet intervention simply accentuated and redirected the opposition and rebellions that had followed the installation of a Soviet-backed regime in April 1978. Those rebellions, which included a serious rising in the city of Herat in May 1979, reflected opposition to attempts to change society, notably with equality for women and land reform, as well as to the power and patronage changes of the new regime. In practice, although traumatic within Afghanistan, this violence was not of wider significance. Instead, it was the Soviet inability to accept instability there, and the resulting determination to intervene, that, in the event, caused far more sustained violence, a pattern also to be seen with interventionism in the early twenty-first century.

As with the misplaced Western conviction in the 2000s about the appeal of liberal democracy, the Soviets had a misguided set of values and teleology that they sought to impose on Afghan society. This set focused on a conviction of the superiority and inevitability of progressive ideas, notably atheism. As a result, the Soviets failed to understand their opponents and their viability and had scant prospect of moving from military moves to political outcomes that had traction in Afghan society. Linked to the lack of any real "hearts and minds" approach were significant limitations in Soviet military practice.

In large part, these arose from an absence of effective counterinsurgency doctrine, strategy, tactics, training, and experience. The operations in the late 1940s and early 1950s against nationalists, especially in Ukraine and the Baltic republics, had been largely carried out by security police units at the expense of vulnerable opponents, exhausted after the Second World War, and were seen as police actions and had not entered the army's narrative and experience. Nor had opposition in Hungary in 1956 been sufficiently sustained or in Czechoslovakia in 1968 been sufficiently violent to alter this pattern. The Soviet army was designed for conventional conflict with NATO in Europe, and essentially for highly mobile operations on the North European Plain, and its commanders and officers were trained accordingly.

In contrast, in Afghanistan the Soviets faced harsh terrain, major logistical problems in supply and distribution, disease, and intractable opponents. Prefiguring the Americans in Iraq in 2003, the Soviets also deployed too few forces, in part for understandable logistical reasons. A force of 120,000 troops for a country much bigger than South Vietnam (although without facing the comparable danger of an invasion from a neighboring power— North Vietnam) was too few for the consecutive operations that Soviet war fighting envisaged. Moreover, the use of reserve troops from Muslim Soviet Central Asia in practice led to animosity with the majority Pashtun population. The pro-Soviet Afghan army, although poorly equipped, contributed to mass and security, but not always to operational effectiveness.

There were also the issues posed by the inability to force large-scale battle on the guerrillas, who generally proved able to avoid Soviet advances while, in turn, continuing to threaten Soviet supply routes. In 1980–82, the Soviets failed by pursuing a conventional attack strategy against guerrilla warfare. In 1983, they switched to an antisocietal strategy, but this also failed. Driving the population off land that could not be controlled simply entrenched hostility, while Soviet sweeps and other operations were followed by a return to base that brought no permanent benefit. The situation also deteriorated for the Soviets when the guerrillas were equipped with ground-to-air missiles by the United States and Britain, as these greatly affected helicopter and air support.

However, although they controlled most of the countryside, the guerrillas were not able to take and hold major cities, nor to block the main road from the Soviet Union to Kabul. Ultimately, it was the decision of the Soviet Union under the new leader from 1985, Mikhail Gorbachev, that led to the ending of a commitment that it could not win but was able to maintain. The withdrawal, agreed in 1988 and completed in 1989, did not lead to the automatic fall of the client government. Instead it held on, as South Vietnam had done in 1973. The Soviets continued to provide aid, which might have been the more sensible strategy from the outset.[10]

So also, more generally, for other interventionist powers. Looked at differently, that was indeed the usual pattern, in that both the Soviet Union and the United States, as well as other powers such as France and Britain, usually took part in conflicts without taking their involvement to the point of full-scale commitment or, indeed, hostilities. This was the involvement of special advisers, training missions, the provision of weaponry, the secret dispatch of special forces, and the persuasion of allies to take a role. Indeed, much of the military history of the 1970s and 1980s can be understood in these terms. The same was true for other periods, but it was more generally true for the years covered in this chapter. This was due both to the determination to avoid any escalation to a Third World War and to American caution after the Vietnam War, particularly so in contrast with earlier interventionism.

The Soviet Union and its allies took a far more proactive stance, notably in Northeast Africa and Angola. In each case, the Soviets operated by combining their advisers and weaponry with Cuban ground troops. Victory for Ethiopia over Somalia in the former, and for the Communist-backed MPLA over the Western-supported UNITA in Angola, indicated that this was a winning formula.

Indeed, the impression in the late 1970s was of the Cold War very much going the Soviet direction. This was encouraged by the fall of the minority-white regime in Zimbabwe and by growing pressure on the minority-white regime of South Africa and on its colony of South West Africa. In each case, land warfare involved guerrilla attacks on the part of the insurgents and air-backed counterinsurgency attacks by their opponents. Neither side was able to deliver victory in the sense of stopping the other. However, the control of towns and air bases was important and left opposition in the bush as a dangerous irritant of political consequence rather than a strategic threat of immediate military significance. This was the case, for example, with the Pol Pot remnants in Cambodia in the 1980s, remnants supported by China as a way to put pressure on Soviet-aligned Vietnam.

THE NATURE OF CONFLICT

The seizure and control of ground positions could not be done by aircraft, however significant they might be for the fighting. Instead, it was necessary to win on the ground. This involved contrasting skills, and combinations with air power, as was shown in Uganda in 1979 and in Chad in 1983 and 1987. Environmental factors were crucial to this diversity. In Uganda, as a result of forest terrain, the Tanzanian invasion was largely road bound. Infantry and armored personnel carriers played key roles, with light antitank weapons affecting operations along the roads. Infantry support was therefore significant, and, correspondingly, the rate of the Tanzanian advance was about ten miles a day. The key goal was the seizure of the capital, Kampala, as doing so destroyed the prestige of Idi Amin, the megalomaniac military dictator of Uganda. Compared to that, operations in the rest of the country were of limited significance. Thus, the strategy dictated operational requirements.

In Chad, in contrast, the open, rapid landscape ensured that air power could play a greater role, in both surveillance and attack, while on land mobility was greater than in Tanzania. Neighboring Libya intervened both in order to pursue a territorial claim to a northern strip of the country and so as to support protégés trying to conquer the entire country. The Libyans employed Soviet equipment (including tanks), doctrine, and training but suffered from the greater mobility of their opponents, who used light vehicles, mortars, antitank rockets, and a raider's desire for mobility. In an echo of the employment of trucks by Ibn Saud's forces in Arabia in the 1920s and 1930s, this was known as the "Toyota War."

After Greek Cypriots keen on union with Greece had staged a bloody coup, Turkey, a regional power, successfully invaded Cyprus in 1974, partitioning the island between the Greek and Turkish Cypriots and creating a situation that has lasted until today. The Turks benefited greatly from superior air power; from eventual numerical superiority, notably in armor; and from the Greek failure to focus on attacking the invaders. Instead, the Greeks turned on Turkish Cypriot communities and their irregulars across the island.

In 1976, Syria successfully sent troops into Lebanon in response to an appeal from the president for support of the Maronite-dominated Lebanese Front against the Druze-PLO (Palestinian Liberation Organization) alliance: full-scale civil war had broken out there the previous year. The Syrians then turned against the Maronites (Christians) and occupied much of the country. In Syria itself, the army suppressed a fundamentalist Islamic uprising.[11]

IRAN-IRAQ WAR

After the fall of the shah in the Islamic Revolution in Iran in 1978–79, Iraq attacked Iran in 1980 because Saddam Hussein, the dictator of Iraq, sought to gain a favorable settlement of long-standing border disputes and to wield the regional hegemony previously enjoyed by the shah. This attack launched a struggle that lasted until 1988. This struggle was by far the longest conventional war of the period, and one that involved more combatants and casualties than other conflicts of the time, although precise figures are contested.

The Iraqis planned to use the same methods as those employed by Israel against Egypt in the Six-Day War in 1967: a surprise air attack to destroy the opponent's air force, followed by a tank offensive. However well conceived the operational plan, the Iraqis proved incapable of executing it. The surprise Iraqi attack on ten Iranian air bases on September 22, 1980, failed because of a lack of adequate expertise, training, and targeting equipment. The effective Iranian air defense was also a factor, while, as a consequence of the Israeli attack on Egypt in 1967, many of the Iranian aircraft were held in hardened shelters. On land, both sides were only capable of fighting one battle before having to stop, refit, and plan the next advance.

More seriously, Iraqi war aims were misconceived. There was no rebellion by the Arab-majority population of southwest Iran as Saddam had anticipated. In addition, there was no Iraqi plan B. Nor was there any clear exit strategy, in part because the nature of Iranian politics had been misread, for, far from collapsing, the Iranian forces fought back, helped by an upsurge in patriotism.

The Iraqis had an impressive Soviet-armed military but did not know how to use it well or, in particular, how to produce decisive tactical, operational, and strategic results. This was seen both in the air and on the ground. In particular, the Iraqis lacked the mobility and tactical flexibility shown by the Israelis in ground combat in 1967 and 1973. Instead, their advance was slower, and their tanks were frequently employed as artillery, downplaying their capacity for maneuver warfare. Iraqi forces also lacked adequate logistics and sufficiently flexible command systems. As a result, they were unable to maintain the initial disorientating advantages brought about by a surprise attack and to force their dynamic of warfare onto their opponents. The Iraqi offensive slowed further and, to take the city of Khorramshahr in fighting from October 24 to November 10, 1980, the Iraqis had to resort to hand-to-hand combat.

Tactical flaws and operational limitations were combined with a misconceived strategic assessment of Iranian determination and capability, such that what successes were achieved could not deliver results. As a consequence of the latter (a factor also seen with the Germans on the Western Front in the First World War) rather than of the particular deficiencies of Iraqi fighting, the land warfare proved indecisive, and neither air power nor armor produced a breakthrough. Looked at differently, the lack of a breakthrough itself delivered a decisive result. Moreover, the conflict on land was the most significant. At sea, both sides used missiles and attacked commercial shipping and oil platforms. This was important as economic warfare, and in the search for international support, but was subsidiary to the bitter conflict on land.

The conflict was closely linked to the politics of the period, both regional and great power. The Iranians outnumbered the Iraqis, but international isolation made it difficult to keep their equipment, notably aircraft, maintained, which was/is always a major problem with foreign sources of supply. The Iraqis benefited from assistance from most other Arab states, as well as from powers fearful of Iran and its espousal of Islamic fundamentalism, including the United States and the Soviet Union. This help was variously financial, especially from Kuwait and Saudi Arabia, and the sale of weapons, notably by France, Italy, the Soviet Union, and China, the last of which sold the Type 69 tank, which was also sold to Iran.

Iraqi expansionism and Iran's Islamic Revolution did not cause the wider tensions that had been feared. Instead, Europe, rather than the Islamic world, came to the forefront in Cold War rivalry in the early 1980s, in part because the opportunistic and unsuccessful Iraqi attack produced a conflict that lasted after the Iraqi forces were driven out of Iran in 1982. The decision was taken by the Iranians to invade Iraq in an attempt to overthrow Saddam Hussein. This commitment ensured that Iran appeared a far less serious threat to America's allies in the Gulf, particularly Saudi Arabia. The Iranians benefited from the use of missiles against Iraqi tanks, with helicopters firing missiles. From 1984, both sides fired missiles targeting opposing capitals. These missiles were not strategic in range or type, but were in purpose. Iraqi attacks led much of the population of Tehran to flee the city in 1988. Chemical weapons were also employed.

During the war, the West provided indirect support to Iraq, not least by sending warships to protect tanker traffic in the Gulf from Iranian attack. This deployment led to small-scale and limited clashes between American and Iranian forces, clashes in which the latter were defeated. However, in contrast to the situation from 1990, Southwest Asia in the 1980s required only a relatively modest outlay of American resources, which ensured that attention could be devoted elsewhere, notably to maintaining capability in Western Europe. The Iranians finally accepted international pressure for peace in 1988 because they could not sustain the costs of the offensive.

As with Communist China and the Korean War (1950–53), war with Iraq helped further to radicalize the Islamic Revolution in Iran by enabling the radicals, notably the Revolutionary Guard, to gain the upper hand. Moreover, the financial strains of the conflict led Saddam Hussein to seek a quick profit by invading vulnerable and oil-rich Kuwait in 1990, only to find that this led to war with an American-led international coalition. Thus, the Iran-Iraq War led directly into post–Cold War geopolitics and conflict.[12] By the end of the Iran-Iraq War, the Iraqis had lost maybe 105,000 dead and the Iranians maybe 262,000.

CENTRAL AMERICA

The dialogue of decisiveness and indecisiveness was also seen, albeit on a very different scale, in Latin America where, in the 1980s, Nicaragua and El Salvador survived sustained attempts to overcome their governments, attempts that reflected the combination of long-standing local political rivalries with Cold War intervention. Air power played a role, but the key operations were those on the ground. In each case, the conflicts reflected the classic weaknesses of guerrilla operations, notably the difficulty of moving from rural power and harassing attacks to dominance of the countryside and control of the towns. Ambushes and assassinations were repeated tactical moves. Guerrilla assaults on police stations and convoys were frequent events. The weaponry included submachine guns and mortars. Creating a sense of uncertainty proved easier than using it to any effect.

In Nicaragua, the rebels of the Cuban-backed FSLN (Sandinista National Liberation Front) who overthrew the dictatorial Somoza regime found initially, as in the areas of Pancasán in 1967 and Monimbó in 1978, that establishing control in a particular area led to a concentrated target for the firepower of their opponents. The disaster of 1967, when a rural guerrilla *foco* (focus) was crushed, led to the abandonment of guerrilla activities until 1974 and to a division over strategy, notably between concentrating on rural or urban insurrections and between delaying in order to build up strength or acting at once. The best strategy won out, and the regime was overthrown in 1979. However, the United States then supported the contras (formed in 1981) in order to overthrow the Sandinista government. The Sandinistas responded by greatly increasing the size of the army (up from twenty-four to eighty thousand) and militia, introducing conscription, and using American counterinsurgency manuals and practices to take the war to the contras. The latter had failed by 1988, and the civil war ended in 1989, being followed by democratic elections in 1990.[13]

CONTROLLING COUNTRIES

Any history of land warfare in this period needs to include the frequent use of military force in attempts to confront, resist, and overcome local opposition. This use was a reflection of the limited traction or availability of democratic and peaceful means to contest or change power in many societies. This was particularly the case in Africa[14] and Latin America, but not only there. Indeed, across much of the world, force was used frequently. In Europe, there were coups or attempted coups in Portugal (1974), Spain (1981), and Italy, the first successful, the others not. In Turkey, there were coups in 1960, 1971, and 1980, and unsuccessful ones in 1962 and 1963. These coups can be classified as land warfare and as part of a continuum of force that included forceful policing.

The integration of land warfare and civil conflict as analytical concepts is insecure and open to conceptual and methodological debate. However, it is especially important for these years due to the lack of large-scale Cold War conflicts. Training and arms supplies were elements, as with the effort devoted by the United States to build up Latin American armies. Following the wide-ranging 1951 Mutual Security Act, the United States signed bilateral agreements with twelve Latin American states, the latter agreeing to focus their production of strategic materials on the United States, and not to trade with hostile states, in return for American military assistance. Similarly, help was provided elsewhere. In 1950–67, the United States provided $36.7 billion in arms and services to other powers.

The pursuit of the Cold War interacted, as in Central America, with local conflicts. Force was a key element in the pursuit and defense of local interests, employment, and status. It also played a major role in rivalries between and within communities, families, and generations. To help mold the situation, governments turned to particular groups or sides, and the articulation of the resulting tensions ensured that it was not easy to isolate or limit particular quarrels. Instead, action was taken at one level in order to influence power and struggles at another. Weapons and other forms of support were moved to allies. For example, in Mindanao in the southern Philippines, a persistent problem with a Communist insurrection led the security forces to arm private forces, such as the Kuratong Balleng gang, and they, in turn, pursued local interests, including crime and politics.

In Myanmar, in conflicts that were not closely linked with the Cold War, the military regime waged war with ethnic minorities, notably the Shan. The strategy pursued was that of the "Four Cuts." This involved brutally separating rebels from civilian support by denying them food, money, intelligence, and recruits.

This was not a struggle that received much public attention, unlike the outbreak in 1987 of what became the First Intifada, a Palestinian revolt against Israeli occupation. Armed resistance, demonstrations, and civil disobedience overlapped in Palestine. Militarily, this was as unsuccessful as Palestinian terrorism, but it was helped by its duration to become a political issue.

THE END OF THE COLD WAR

The lack of large-scale conflict was notable at the close of the Cold War when major changes occurred without significant conflict. In Eastern Europe, Communist regimes were overthrown in 1989 without resistance, other than in Romania. Subsequently, the Communist Soviet Union was transformed into a series of non-Communist, independent states, many anti-Russian, also with only limited warfare. The most significant was in the Caucasus where two of the newly independent states fought a war mentioned in the next chapter.

In contrast, in China, where, unlike in the Soviet bloc, there were successful economic policies, there was no overthrow of the system, and demonstrations were forcibly crushed in 1989, notably, but not only, in Beijing. With the help of the People's Liberation Army (PLA), a Communist monopoly of power was maintained and enforced. This monopoly contrasted with the changes in long-established one-party or quasi one-party states in the period 1980–2010, with the end of National Party hegemony in South Africa, that of the Liberal Democrats in Japan, the Christian Democrats in Italy, the Congress Party in India, and the Labour Party in Israel. The circumstances were different in each case, but the contrast with China underlined the significance there not only of the use of military force in 1989, but also of the maintenance of a strong supporting network of policing and surveillance. It is particularly the case with internal conflict that land warfare must be considered in its context.

Chapter Nine

After the Cold War, 1990–Today

Once seen as a brief postscript, the period from the Cold War to today is already the second longest (after chapter 3) of those covered in this book. It has also become more complex, with changing circumstances, or at least different elements, to the fore in attention. It is easy, as suggested in chapter 1, to provide a chronology that offers three distinct periods. The first, from 1990 to 2003, is one of American success and of growing confidence, notably in the United States, in military means as a result of technological and organizational advances. The second, from 2003 to 2011, focuses on the difficulties the United States faced in stabilizing Iraq and Afghanistan and the consequent need for a rethinking of doctrine and practice.

The third, that from 2012, returns attention to the ability of the major powers to deliver results on the ground, as was done, very differently, in campaigning in Crimea, Ukraine, Syria, and Iraq, but all as part of a geostrategic picture increasingly dominated by the growing military power and assertiveness of China and the possibility of conflict in East Asia, and on multiple fronts there. Where land warfare might play a role in the latter is unclear. In the event of a sea/air missile conflict between China and, on the other hand, Japan and its ally, the United States, the answer is little if nothing. In contrast, a Chinese invasion of Taiwan or attack on Vietnam would include such a component. So, even more, would a North Korean invasion of vulnerable South Korea. Chinese assertiveness is more significant because it is combined at the strategic level with that of Russia. This was seen in joint pressure on the United States not to intervene in Syria in 2012–13.

The suggestion above of a sequence of phases should be challenged with the argument that all these stages were present throughout the period after the Cold War (and indeed during it), even if attention to them varied. Indeed, as so often with analyses, opposing tendencies to those already cited could be seen. The 1990s, for example, was the decade of American failure in Somalia in 1993. The 2000s witnessed the Russians defeat Georgia (the Caucasus republic) in 2008. Recent years have included the use of force not only in the instances mentioned but also, very differently, in other states, notably South Sudan and the Central African Republic, in neither of which was there the flow of campaigning seen in Crimea. To add, for example, Libya would be to show that campaigning covered a range of circumstances and outcomes. So also with the overlap into the world of force in politics, both in the seizure of power and in resistance to it.

At the same time, however misleading, there was discussion of the above sequence. Moreover, this sequence was grounded in the experience of the United States, the leading military power. If only for that reason, it is the most significant even if its effectiveness in power projection in part depends on understanding the different narratives of particular countries.

The Soviet system collapsed in 1989–91, not because of defeat in war, but due to economic failure on a grand scale, to failure to manage the wish for change, and to internal discontent, first in Eastern Europe and then in the Soviet Union. The reform policies of the young new Soviet leader, Mikhail Gorbachev, policies that were designed to strengthen the Communist bloc, inadvertently resulted in the fall of Communist regimes in Eastern Europe in 1989 and in the collapse of the Soviet Union in 1991. The regimes in Eastern Europe were left without the strength and support they needed in order to resist popular pressure for change. Demonstrations were followed by the opening of the Berlin Wall in 1989, and the tottering of the unpopular East German regime communicated itself to the rest of Eastern Europe. In 1989, only in Romania was a significant effort made by the governing system to resist the process, and this effort was defeated, albeit at the cost of about one thousand casualties.

On August 9, 1991, an attempt to reverse the process was made in Russia when power was briefly seized by senior generals, the KGB, and hard-line Communists. Tanks were deployed in Moscow. As with the successful Chinese use of the army to suppress prodemocracy demonstrations in Beijing and elsewhere in 1989, this was one of the most significant moments in "land warfare" over the last three decades, but one not generally seen in those terms. In the event, mounted in a very different context from the use of force in China in 1989, the coup failed. Very few came forward in support. Tens of thousands of demonstrators manned improvised antitank barricades, the dynamic of the coup failed, three young men died under a tank on August 21, the troops were withdrawn, and the coup collapsed. The end of Communist control followed rapidly. As with the failure of the Spanish military coup in 1981 and that in Turkey in 2016, opposition had not been adequately assessed, while, again as in those two cases, the military very much lacked unity behind the coup, as well as the willingness to fight for it.

In contrast, because in China the Communist government clearly retained control in 1989 and thereafter, and because China was then in effect allied to the United States, this ensured that, alongside American strength and Soviet disintegration, the 1990s were dominated by American power and talk of military transformation. American expeditionary warfare and military pressure in the period, notably in Kuwait (against Iraq), Somalia, and the former Yugoslavia, tends to be the focus of attention. Talk of a new American-dominated world order was encouraged after Soviet client states were defeated or intimidated: Iraq in 1991 and 2003, Serbia in 1995 and 1999, and, in a different context, Libya in 2011. American power appeared even more potent with the spread of American economic and financial models, particularly those linked to free-market liberalism, especially the liberalization of financial markets and the privatization of state-owned assets.

However, in practice, there was conflict around much of the world in the 1990s, much of it rather "low tech" in terms of the weaponry used. Insurrectionary conflict in a number of countries overlapped with both civil wars and a politics of force. The common currency was the use of violence to secure political outcomes. "Failed states," such as Afghanistan, Sierra Leone, Liberia, Yugoslavia, Congo, and, to a lesser extent, Ethiopia and Sudan, provided the clearest examples, in that levels of continuous violence were high. Indeed, alongside its use in order to impose control, civil warfare became a clear definition of failure, not least because of a concern that it would spread. Ethnic tension and wider geopolitical rivalries also played key roles in the bitter civil wars in Central Africa, notably in Congo and Rwanda. The Rwandan genocide of 1994, a mass slaughter of Tutsi by militias of the majority Hutu population, led to maybe one million dead, but the bloodiest war of the period was that in Congo. The regime of President Mobutu Sese Seko, president from seizing power in a coup in 1965, was overthrown in 1997, but the Rwandan invasion in 1996 that helped accomplish this led to the intervention of other powers as well as accelerating the dissolution of Congo into areas of regional control, some of which were particularly unsettled, as also was the case in Afghanistan, a situation that has lasted to the present.

In the 2000s, the "War on Terror," and the linked American-led interventions in Afghanistan and Iraq, dominated attention and led to much discussion about military capability as assessed by the effectiveness seen with these interventions. The contrast between output and outcome was particularly apparent in the failure of the invasion of Iraq, and notably the handling of the country after the invasion, to lead to a settled, pro-Western order. Instead, there was a large-scale and multifaceted insurrection that was only suppressed with great difficulty.

However, again, this focus did not capture the range of conflict, notably in sub-Saharan Africa but also, for example, in South Asia. There, the long-standing war in Sri Lanka, which had started in 1983, came to a resolution, with the separatist Tamil Tigers (Liberation Tigers of Tamil Eelam) crushed in 2009 by the army, which reflected the Sinhalese majority of the population. This war, which involved terrorism, guerrilla operations, the deliberate killing of civilians by both sides, and the key role of the regional power, India, eventually against the Tamil Tigers, was far more typical of the warfare of the period than the rapidity in 2003 of the American overthrow of the Iraqi army. Indeed, not only in Sri Lanka, but across much of the world, the significance of ethnicity and religion, as causes and indicators of division and conflict, helped explain the high frequency of attacks on civilians. These attacks were far more insistent and devastating than would have been necessary simply to accompany the extortion, seizures, and looting that were crucial to the supply methods of the armed groups. The applicability in this context of ideas and laws of human rights, and the enforcement of those laws by third parties such as the UN, generally failed to take sufficient note of the essential character of the warfare.

When these two types of conflict—high-specification conventional warfare, as practiced by the United States and its allies, notably Britain and Israel, and warfare among the people—came into opposition, as in Afghanistan and Iraq, the more sophisticated military power found that its understanding of capability and the use of force did not produce the anticipated results. Partly as a result, there was discussion about the continued viability of established military platforms and methods, although this discussion also reflected earlier advocacy for a paradigm switch in combat methods, which was termed, in the United States, first a Revolution in Military Affairs and, subsequently, a Transformation. This discussion became central to debates about procurement, doctrine, military structures, and strategy, debates held publicly in some states, particularly, but not only, in the United States and Britain, but also significant in states where there was no open public debate, for example, China.

THE GULF WAR, 1990–91

Discussion of the diversity of conflict today is a long way from the standard starting point for the warfare of the period, the Gulf War of 1990–91. A small, weak, and neighboring target, oil-rich Kuwait, rapidly fell to a surprise Iraqi invasion in August 1990. In very public diplomacy, Iraq's refusal to meet a UN deadline for withdrawal led, in early 1991, first to a successful American-led air offensive and then to a ground campaign. In this, the focus was on an attack by armor divisions. There had been predictions that Iraqi entrenchments would be difficult to capture and that the Iraqis would force attritional warfare on the coalition, causing heavy casualties. These fears were a throwback to the world wars, especially the First World War, and drew on an overestimation of Iraqi capability based on the idea that its army was battle hardened after its long war with Iran. There was also an overestimate of the capability of Iraqi equipment.

The fears proved quite unfounded as the American-dominated coalition forces were greatly superior, with their superiority compounded by mistaken Iraqi moves. The Iraqis had dug themselves in, believing that this would protect them from air and tank attack, but they failed to appreciate the capabilities of both precision munitions and up-to-date tank gun technologies that ensured a high first-shot kill capability even when only part of the turret was visible. The Iraqis fought as if fighting Iran in the recent war, which was a mistake, as the terrain and opponent were both different.

While the Iraqis were attacked on the coast on the direct route to Kuwait City, their right (on the coalition forces' left) was outmaneuvered by a rapid American advance to the west, which put tremendous pressure on the Iraqis, as the outflanking American forces turned to attack them and destroyed much of the Iraqi army. Forcing elements to retreat exposed them to armor and air attack. This was an aspect of cooperation between means of attack in order to force opponents into a condition of vulnerability. In this context, remaining static led to destruction, but so did mobility. In one hundred hours of nonstop combat, the Iraqis lost over fifty thousand dead as well as eighty-one thousand prisoners and nearly four thousand tanks. The coalition forces benefited not only from superior technology but also from their ability to maintain a high-tempo offensive in executing a well-conceived plan that combined air and land strength. Both could deliver precision attacks. Allied, particularly American, fighting quality, unit cohesion, leadership, and planning, and Iraqi deficiencies in each, all played a major role in ensuring victory. The coalition army also held together well.

Kuwait regained independence, while, in northern Iraq, the Kurds, under Western protection, gained de facto independence, only to divide into civil war. However, a Shi'a insurrection in Basra was brutally suppressed by Saddam Hussein's Republican Guards in 1991.

"WARS AMONG THE PEOPLE" IN THE 1990s

Success against Iraq in 1991 encouraged optimism in the United States about the effectiveness of AirLand Battle. The reality over the following decade was to be one of more difficult outcomes to often intractable situations. Indeed, that was also a result of the 1990–91 Gulf War, as Saddam Hussein both remained in power and continued to be defiant, which proved to be the background to the 2003 Gulf War.

The standard focus is that on the United States, which posed, for itself and others, the strategic problems, issues, and choices bound up in the high-spectrum capabilities of the modern arms race. An American intervention in Somalia in 1992 ended in failure in 1994, while the facing down of the Serbs in Bosnia (1995) and Kosovo (1999) was arguably ultimately more due to Serbian isolation, and to overwhelming American superiority in the air, than to any Serb weakness in the face of likely American/NATO ground attack. Moreover, insofar as land warfare was a key element in Serb failure, it was the operations by the Croats and the Bosnian Muslims in 1995. These large-scale operations were achieved with American support, including pressure on the Croats and Bosnian Muslims to cooperate, rather than by what would have been the more problematic use of American ground forces.

The narrative of the years from 1992 to 2000, however, could have been written without focusing on the Americans. The problems facing conventional ground forces had in fact been demonstrated by the Russians in the Caucasus. Islamic independence movements there were able to rely on considerable popular support built on a long tradition of ethnic and religious strife, as well as on the mountainous terrain. The Russians responded by invading the rebellious region of Chechnya in December 1994. The capital, Grozny, was in Chechnya's lowlands and thereby vulnerable. It was captured by the Russians in January 1995 after a lengthy siege in which they employed devastating firepower, especially artillery. Russian brutality, however, encouraged resistance in Chechnya, which also benefited from the difficult terrain. In 1996, the Russians withdrew under a peace agreement.

The 1994–96 campaigns revealed the deficiencies of the badly led, badly equipped, badly trained, undermotivated, and understrength Russian forces, deficiencies that helped account for Russian caution over Yugoslavia, which was essentially left to the United States. As in Afghanistan in the 1980s, not least among these deficiencies was the lack of appropriate training and doctrine for counterinsurgency warfare, for which it is difficult to prepare conscripts, although it is also necessary to emphasize large Chechen numbers and the extent to which the Chechens were both well armed and determined. Many had also been trained through conscription in the Soviet army. The Russian preference for firepower reflected the dominance, in their doctrine and practice, of preparations for war with conventionally armed and trained Western forces. Mentioning these factors, however, and others can be added, does not make it clear how best to evaluate their respective significance, a recurrent problem in military history but also in planning.

In response to the bombing in 1999 of apartment blocks in Moscow and other cities that was blamed on Chechens, the renewed Russian attack on Chechnya in 1999–2000 led to the fall of Grozny in January 2000 and gave Vladimir Putin a welcome boost in popularity. However, the attack indicated similar military deficiencies. As with other forces battling insurgency, the Russians suffered from the problem of inadequate intelligence, which reflected the limitations of surveillance in such contexts. In this situation, as for other powers, there was an overreliance on firepower responses, responses that were often poorly directed. Guerrilla opposition in Chechnya, including suicide bombings, continued. In turn, the Russians mounted raids on guerrilla areas and seized suspected Chechens. Opposition was firmest in the mountainous south.

However, the political and military costs of such operations were cut dramatically by increased Russian reliance on local allies, a pattern used in the nineteenth century, but one not employed during the Communist years. Having created and armed a client regime in Chechnya, the Russian government was able to reduce its own commitment. This factor was more generally true of counterinsurgency struggles, notably of the balance between political and military commitments and responses.[1]

In the Caucasus, as in Yugoslavia, the collapse of a Communist federation was also followed by conflict within and between the new states. The Russian-backed breakaway territory of Abkhazia won de facto independence from Georgia in a war in 1992–93 and has retained it ever since. In the Caucasus, Armenia and Azerbaijan fought over control of the region of Nagorno-Karabakh. This struggle, which saw large-scale "ethnic cleansing," was won in 1993 by Armenia, the more Western of the combatants. As a result, there was less anxiety in the West, but, in addition, the conflict was not fully discussed, because it was difficult of access while it was very much seen as a region within the Soviet bloc and now under Russian sway.

The situation was different in the former Yugoslavia, encouraging Western diplomatic intervention, which in turn led to military commitments. The former state split into its constituent republics, but the linked political instability was addressed (and exacerbated) by creating states that had an ethnic logic, notably Croatia and Serbia. This helped to ensure the persecution of minorities, notably Croats in Serbia, as well as related intervention on behalf of Croats and Serbs elsewhere. Such intervention proved especially destabilizing in Bosnia, the part of Yugoslavia where there was no one majority ethnic group, but instead Serb, Croat, and Bosniak (Bosnian Muslim) minorities, each of which was in a majority position in particular parts of Bosnia.

The resulting land warfare focused on the defense of communities against "ethnic cleansing" and on the pursuit of the latter by destructive means that were intended to instill terror and thus force people to flee. War involved demonstration and negotiation, a process of conflict that was intensely political, and a mixture of sudden and brief brutality, truces, and convoluted strategies of diplomacy. This conception of war was rooted in the Balkan tradition of limited operations, including raiding. In contrast, full-scale war was in the domain of an emperor or sultan, who cannot be resisted if provoked too far. Such limited warfare also reflected the politics and environments of the area as well as the forces and logistical possibilities available.

Bosnia, unfortunately, permitted the pursuit of limited warfare, not that it appeared limited to those who suffered as a consequence, because it enabled Serbia and Croatia to put pressure on each other indirectly. In addition, the degree of control that the governments of Croatia and Serbia exercised over their Bosnian protégés was limited. This was an aspect of a potent dynamic in civil and international wars that it is all too easy to overlook. Many operations were designed as much to impress or intimidate allies as to terrify opponents. The conflict in Congo from the late 1990s is a key instance, as is that in Syria in the 2010s.

The Bosnian conflict was brought to a close in late 1995 by the combination of large-scale Croat advances on land and NATO air attacks, and the impact of both on Serb resolve. There were no allies for the Serbs to turn to, unlike in 1914. This conflict was followed by a similar crisis in Kosovo where Serbian dominance over the Muslim Kosovar population was increasingly militarized and expressed in ethnic cleansing as the Serbs sought to suppress separatist demands and to destroy support for the Kosovo Liberation Army. In 1999, Western pressure led to the escalation, but then end, of the crisis, with a Serb withdrawal. There was no land invasion by NATO forces as had been called for and planned by Britain but opposed by the United States, West Germany, and France. As a result, Kosovo in 1999 is part of the might-have-beens of land warfare. The key elements appear to have been the NATO air offensive, in effect an attack to break the will to resist,[2] and the withdrawal of Russian support for Serbia. This interpretation leaves no role for land warfare. However, it has been claimed that Russian warnings to Serbia that a NATO land invasion was imminent may have played a role and that the effectiveness of the air offensive was limited.[3]

There were in practice serious doubts about the feasibility of such an invasion. These doubts are worthy of consideration as they direct attention to the issues confronted by interventionist forces elsewhere. The two key elements that emerge are not resistance by opponents but rather factors involved in deployment, notably the attitude of local powers and the strength of logistical systems. Any invasion in 1999 was dependent on the willingness of neighboring countries to provide access and bases. Seeking to win Western backing, as well as supportive of the Kosovars, who are fellow Muslims, Albania was willing to do so, but it had very poor transport infrastructure as well as mountainous terrain in the way. Greece was a better fit in both cases, but it did not wish to support the Kosovars against Serbia, a choice in which religion and geopolitics both played a role. The logistical issues faced in supporting any deployment strong enough to defeat the Serbs on the ground were formidable.

The political character of conflict was amply demonstrated again in East Timor, as the Indonesians, who had successfully invaded it in 1975 in the aftermath of the collapse of the Portuguese Empire, brutally resisted demands for independence. As such, this was another aspect of the struggle(s) to ensure and succeed the fall of the Portuguese Empire, struggles that were most sustained and large scale in Angola. In East Timor, the Indonesian reliance on force failed to assuage local separatism. It also led to international condemnation, especially after the shooting of unarmed demonstrators at a cemetery in Dili in 1991 led to hundreds of deaths and injuries and was filmed by Western journalists. In 1999, the Indonesians responded to continued separatism and to international pressure by giving East Timor the choice of independence or regional autonomy. The people overwhelmingly chose independence, despite serious pressure from militias supported by the army, a situation that represented an aspect of what would subsequently be called hybrid warfare. After the election, the coercion was stepped up, but international anger finally led the Indonesians to accept the popular verdict. This episode is not what is conventionally understood as land warfare, but it is very much so if war and politics are assessed on a continuum, which is what is necessary given the range of asymmetric warfare.[4] Moreover, the willingness of Australia to intervene on behalf of independence for East Timor, and uncertainty about what such intervention might mean, was, as with NATO in Kosovo, an important element.

At a very different scale, the Catholic terrorists of the Provisional IRA in Northern Ireland treated the Protestant community that had been there since the early seventeenth century as a colonial relic. Its terrorism was dependent on Soviet bloc arms and Irish American donations. The first ended with the Cold War and the second with 9/11.[5]

AFGHANISTAN

The withdrawal of Soviet forces in 1989 had not led to the immediate collapse of their client regime. Instead, there was considerable success in resisting the guerrillas, albeit in a very different context from that of the South Vietnamese after the American withdrawal in 1973. However, the government was affected by the strength of ethnic and, related, regional tensions, and by the lack of any means, short of conflict or the threat of conflict, to settle issues or, indeed, measure strength and debate policy. The strength of warlords was a particular problem as they focused political and ethnic tensions. There were also the problems posed by the role of foreign powers, notably Pakistan. In 1992, the client regime was overcome.

A new element was added to the resulting cauldron with the rise of the Taliban movement. This was a movement for religious orthodoxy backed by Pakistan and capable of winning support among the Pashtuns of the south. In 1996, the Taliban rapidly overran much of the country, seizing Kabul. However, in the non-Pashtun areas, especially in the north, the Taliban encountered serious resistance and were unable to suppress all opposition.

The shelter and support given by the Taliban to Osama bin Laden's al-Qaeda (the Base) terrorist movement ensured that Afghanistan came to the fore in the warfare that followed the terrorist attacks on New York and Washington on September 11, 2001. The refusal of the Taliban to hand over bin Laden and other al-Qaeda members, as demanded by the United Nations, led to an American attack.

Afghanistan coming to the fore in 2001 was ironic, as conflict there had been continual since 1978, but after the Taliban's success in 1996, it was not at a particularly high rate. The very bellicosity of Afghan society, and its experience of war and learned responses to it, helped to ensure that a new bout of outside intervention was to be of only partial effectiveness. However, that was not what appeared to be the lesson at first.

Instead, American air power attracted the most attention, not least as it appeared to demonstrate the viability of the so-called Revolution in Military Affairs, a term that was much in vogue in the United States in the late 1990s and early 2000s, as both description and prospectus. However, in 2001, the Taliban ultimately had to be overcome on the ground by rival Afghan forces, especially the United Front, the so-called Northern Alliance. Moreover, the lack of coherence of the Taliban regime and the porosity of alignments in Afghanistan were also both important. Warlords rapidly switched allegiance while Taliban defections accentuated a failure of command and control. American air power and Afghan ground attack meshed well. The willingness of President Pervez Musharraf of Pakistan to provide assistance was also significant, although Pakistan was to follow an ambivalent approach throughout the subsequent conflict.

Success in 2001 was as speedy as was to be seen with American forces in Iraq in 2003, indeed more so given the scale and terrain of Afghanistan. However, it proved difficult in both cases to move to a more stable political outcome. In Afghanistan, the recruitment of local support in order to overthrow the Taliban ensured that there was a stronger basis than in Iraq for a new order, and this new order did reasonably well for several years. Moreover, if the war had only essentially provoked a regrouping and realignment of factions, it was ever thus in Afghanistan, and not only there: war was a realignment of politics and the means to further realignment. The appearance of success in Afghanistan was such that a window of opportunity was provided for an American attack on Iraq in 2003. Obvious failure would have made this less of an option.

Looked at differently, as was frequently argued at the time, insufficient effort was made to stabilize Afghanistan in a way fitted to Afghan society and concepts of honor, and to maintain what had been achieved, due to the decision to launch the attack on Iraq and the subsequent effort to sustain it. At the same time, it is appropriate to mention the difficult choices facing the United States in identifying its main effort both in foreign policy as a whole and also specifically within Afghanistan, issues that continue to the present. The Taliban revival from 2005 to 2006 put great pressure on the Afghan government and its foreign allies, who suffered from confusion over strategy, with goals including eliminating al-Qaeda, removing the Taliban, establishing democracy, and improving the economy. More particularly, commitment to particular tribes involved taking part in the struggles between them. Although the Taliban could not win, it was able to go on fighting, which denied the coalition forces an effective initiative and left matters unsettled. Winning battles did not mean winning the war, a lesson abundantly clear from the Vietnam War.[6]

In 2009, in the face of apparent "mission failure" in Afghanistan, including the serious problems the British, who deployed insufficient forces and took on too ambitious a task, were facing in Helmand Province, the Americans arranged a major surge in their troop numbers. This produced gains, which were then put under pressure as troop numbers were cut in the mid-2010s to serve a domestic political timetable, notably that of President Barack Obama.[7] At the same time, the presence of more troops could not dictate success. Far more was involved.

In 2015, NATO ended its combat mission in Afghanistan and handed field responsibility to the 370,000-strong Afghan security forces, which took thousands of casualties as the Taliban, encouraged by Iran and possibly Russia, increased activity in 2015–16: 6,785 members of the security forces were killed and 11,777 wounded in November 2015–October 2016. In response to the deteriorating situation, the Americans, in August 2017, decided to increase troop levels, by 3,500–5,000 men, on top of the 8,400 trainers and advisers that had been left there.

Broader geopolitics remain a key element. The Pakistani army and its powerful Military Intelligence tend to back the Taliban, identifying it as the foe of an Afghan government they regard as aligned with India and the United States. The Pakistani army benefits from a war footing that also corresponds with religious partisanship. In contrast, the prime minister, Nawaz Sharif, sacked in 2017, allegedly as a result of army opposition, was close to the United States and sought to ease tensions with India. Later in 2017, the army again demonstrated its power by not backing the government in a confrontation with Islamic fundamentalists.

THE GULF WAR OF 2003

In 2003, the United States focused on Iraq—a definite and defiant target with regular armed forces—rather than on the more intangible struggle with terrorism. The attack was presented in and by the United States in terms of "drying up the swamp"—eliminating a state allegedly supporting terrorism, as well as, more specifically, destroying Iraq's supposed capability in weapons of mass destruction. In practice, Iraq had not backed al-Qaeda and did not have the reported weapons. Nevertheless, American leaders offered the terror narrative as one of American national security. The attack was also in line with an American response that can instinctively turn to force.

Predictions that the Iraqis would employ chemical weapons, that they would blow up bridges and dams to impede progress, and that it would be hard to subjugate the Iraqi cities were all rapidly disproved in 2003. These predictions rested on the assumption that the Iraqis had responded to their defeat in 1991 by deciding not to take on the United States in maneuverist warfare, in the open, where technology would give the Americans a great advantage. Instead, it was claimed, Saddam Hussein had determined to abandon the desert and focus on the cities, hoping to entangle the Americans as they had been in Mogadishu in Somalia in 1993. Both in 1991 and in 2003, Saddam Hussein counted on the Americans suffering if they could be forced to abandon the distant use of firepower for close combat, the technique the Japanese had sought in the Pacific in 1941–45. This analysis was in part to be vindicated by the problems the Americans eventually encountered in seeking to overcome the insurrection in Iraq after Saddam Hussein was dead.

However, in 2003, the coherence of the Hussein regime, its ability to intimidate the population, and the possibility of exploiting American vulnerability along their long lines of advance were undermined by the tempo of

American attacks: the tempo strategically, operationally, and tactically. The Iraqi attacks on supply lines, for example at the Euphrates bridge town of Nasiriya, attracted considerable media attention, but the forces available for such attacks were a local irritant rather than operationally significant. Despite short-term problems, which are readily understandable given the tempo of the advance, American logistics proved able to support the offensive.

The Americans gained and seized the initiative, disorientating the Iraqi military and government and hitting their capacity to respond. The 125,000 American combat troops on the ground were the key element, although Britain supplied 45,000 troops and Australia 2,000.

Much of the Iraqi Revolutionary Guard, generally feared before the war, in fact ran away in the face of American firepower. Units that redeployed or that stood and fought were pulverized, with particular effort being devoted to destroying Iraqi armor. Air attack played a key role, but there were also important capabilities in land warfare, capabilities that brought success. The Iraqi T-55 and T-72 tanks that were not destroyed by air attack could not prevail against the American M1A1 Abrams tanks. The American use of night-vision goggles enabled them to maintain the pace of the assault and thus to prevent the Iraqis from resupplying and regrouping. The Iraqis made effective use of rocket-propelled grenades, but that could not compare. Although there had been improvements in Iraqi quality, as a honed-down force was sought, their military was far weaker than in 1991. In large part, this was because the impact of American-encouraged international sanctions since then had limited the buildup of modern weaponry, in contrast to the situation prior to 1991 when the Soviet Union and France had readily provided such weaponry.

Once they had closed on Baghdad, the Americans initially launched "thunder runs," a classic instance of the use of language in order to suggest power and intimidate, and deservedly so in this case. These "runs" were armored thrusts into the city. They demonstrated that their opponents could not prevent these advances and therefore undermined their position. Maneuver warfare was thus shown to work in an urban context, again suggesting that the land was an isotropic surface, equal in all parts and thus all vulnerable to modern weaponry, which in fact was, is, and will be far from the case. Indeed, the belief that it should be is a strategic conceit based on technological triumphalism. Having captured Baghdad, American forces pressed on to overrun the rest of Iraq, without encountering the large-scale opposition that was feared, especially in Hussein's hometown of Tikrit. At a more modest scale, and against a closer target, British forces captured the city of Basra.

A prime element of debate before the campaign, which was renewed and reviewed during it when American supply lines came under serious attack, related to the number of troops required for a successful invasion. The secretary of defense, Donald Rumsfeld, and other nonmilitary commentators had been encouraged by the rapid overthrow of the Taliban regime in Afghanistan in 2001 to argue that air power and special forces were the prime requirements and that the large number of troops pressed for by the military was excessive. In the event, military pressure led to the allocation of sizeable numbers, although far fewer than in 1991. Moreover, the campaign did not see the full committal of forces originally envisaged. The Turkish refusal to allow an invasion across their frontier with Iraq ensured that troops from the American Fourth Infantry Division prepared for that invasion could not be used at the outset of the war.

Poor planning, which can be traced to a failure of American "strategic culture," proved a serious problem. In part, this was a failure of conception and in part of implementation.[8] It proved impossible to restore order and the workings of government as had been glibly anticipated. Helped by the foolish decommissioning of the Iraqi army, which threw large numbers of armed and trained men into poverty, a large-scale resistance movement gathered pace from 2003 and led to a major commitment of American forces.[9] The scale of resistance therefore helped to ensure that American military expenditure rose faster than that in other NATO powers.

In the event, Afghanistan and Iraq saw the bringing into conflict of two very different practices in military affairs. To confront their opponents successfully, the Americans needed to change their military and political approaches. In opposing guerrillas, it was militarily necessary to move from protecting troops from attack to attacking the terrorists, but the latter was both difficult and risky.[10] Apart from the hazards of offensive missions and of patrolling, target identification was a crucial aspect of effectiveness, but it was one that was far from easy, both in cities and rural environments. In Afghanistan and Iraq, armor and artillery, more particularly the first, proved of limited value, or, rather, of more limited value for the Americans than had been anticipated. They were available as key elements of force, but they could not achieve very much in terms of overcoming opponents who were very difficult to fix and who made good use of the terrain which lacked many roads. Another context for targeting by the Americans was that of attempting to recruit support by not causing many civilian casualties, an element that affected targeting. The Syrian government was not to operate with such constraints during its civil war, nor the Iraqis in recapturing Mosul from Islamic State (IS) forces in 2017.

Facing the risk of a loss of control, the Americans committed an additional twenty-five thousand troops in a "surge," which was then proclaimed a fundamental military and political success. In reality, the "surge" only brought short-term stability, although that provided the United States with the opportunity to disengage.

The mapping of insurgency and counterinsurgency struggles, and indeed terrorism and counterterrorism, was problematic, an issue that continues to this day. In this warfare, the notion of control over territory is challenged by forces that cannot be readily described in terms of conventional military units. They seek to operate from within the civilian population, and do so not only for cover and sustenance but also in order to deny their opponents any unchallenged control over populated areas. In short, they seek to disturb the territory rather than control it, and they also lack a structure that can be readily attacked. It is extremely difficult to map a situation of shared presence, one in which military or police patrols move unhindered or suffer occasional sniping and ambushes and have to consider mines, but otherwise control little beyond the ground they stand on. As another issue affecting mapping, aerial supply and attack capabilities further complicate the situation. Thus front lines dissolve. The situation was far more limited for insurrectionary groups as they did not have access to the modern facilities for mapping. Conversely, their need for maps was more limited, not least because they had more local knowledge, which brought them a huge advantage.

ELSEWHERE IN THE ISLAMIC WORLD IN THE 2010s

The problems of land warfare in civil wars were demonstrated repeatedly in what were hybrid conflicts, at once insurgencies with features of guerrilla warfare and also of more conventional conflicts with front lines. In each case, there were periods of rapid change and others of greater stasis. In Libya, the forces of Colonel Muammar Gaddafi, dictator from 1969, when he had seized power from the king in a military coup, were overthrown in 2011. He had overcome earlier coup attempts, notably in 1993 and 1996, but in 2011 the military was unable to suppress the rebels. Western air power, special forces, and weaponry played a role in support of the rebels, but compared to Afghanistan and Iraq, there was a limited Western commitment, which was an instance of lessons apparently learned.

The conflict, however, demonstrated the difficulties of moving from military activity to securing outcomes. Western intervention in 2011 was followed by chaos and division. Militias wielded great power, notably in eastern Libya. In 2017, the self-declared Libyan National Army under Khalifa Haftar, a Gaddafi-era general, won control of Benghazi, the major city in the east. He and the Government of National Accord based in Tripoli in the west are rivals. That is only an aspect of a conflict that involves powerful militias, some Islamist, as well as Islamic State. As during the Cold War, international rivalries play a role. Haftar is backed by Russia, Egypt, and the United Arab Emirates. The scale and terrain of Libya is such that, away from the coastal cities, it can only be easy to attack IS from the air. The situation in Libya is even more dangerous than before.

So also with Syria. The Assad government proved an adept political player or, rather, adept within parameters focused on violence, which made it possible for it to counter the difficulties posed by firm resistance by its opponents. The fragmentation both of Syria and of the opposition reflected not only ethnic and sectarian identities and politics but also the nature of conflict. Settlements were defended by populations most of whom proved able and willing to fight. Combined with a plentiful supply of weaponry, this made it difficult to capture settlements without the casualties that combatants generally sought to avoid.

The relationship between these conflicts and great-power tensions became intensive in the case of Syria, with American pressure for the overthrow of the Assad regime actively opposed by Russian support for it. The Americans provided funds, training, and weaponry for the Free Syrian Army, although jihadist groups, notably Islamic Front, which could draw on support from Arab powers, were more significant in the opposition. Angry that it had failed to stop the West from overthrowing the Gaddafi regime in Libya in 2011, Russia made a much greater, and more successful, effort over Syria. Iran provided key military units to help the Syrian regime, and in 2015 Russian backing became far more insistent. The Hmeimim air base near Latakia, built in 2015, became home to about thirty-five Su-24 Russian bombers and Su-25 close-support jets, while that at al-Shayrat included four Mi-24 attack helicopters and more modern Mi-28s, and an artillery brigade was located nearby. Such deployments depended on ground forces being able to control areas, which underlined the synergy of different arms and the mistake of treating air power separately.

The Syrian use of nerve gas in 2017 against Khan Sheikhour, a rebel-held position, led to a retaliatory American attack, with fifty-nine Tomahawk cruise missiles, on Syrian air power. In response, the Syrians moved their aircraft to the Latakia region, where they were under the protection, not only of troops, but also of Russia's S-400 long-range air defense system, which, in optimal circumstances, has an operational radius of 150 miles. Such a capability again indicates the problems in rigidly defining land warfare, as these missiles were also based on land and required protection there. They were a form of artillery, albeit one directed against targets in the air. Russia also increasingly deployed drones in Syria, possibly in response to the difficulties of the conflict.

Although attention focused on air power, it was the willingness of Iran to deploy thousands of troops that played a crucial role in operations, notably in the hard-fought capture of the city of Aleppo in 2016. So also with the provision of Hezbollah forces to help Assad. Iran sought to create a continuous land route of control via Iraq and Syria to the Hezbollah region in Lebanon. This was a geopolitics in which religious sectarianism was important, as Iran wanted a cohesive Shi'a bloc.

In Yemen, potent ethnic, sectarian, and regional differences, as well as large-scale intervention by several other powers, all challenged stability. The overthrow of one president, Ali Abdullah Saleh, in 2012 was followed by his return in alliance with the Houthis, a regional ethnic and religious grouping that he had previously long fought, albeit while his son had eventually developed links with them in order to undermine a powerful rival within the Yemeni military. Having driven the new president from the capital in 2015, the Houthis advanced into southern Yemen where his supporters had taken refuge, notably in the port of Aden. Neighboring Saudi Arabia intervened from 2015 as the lead power in an international alliance backed by the United States. Persistent Saudi air strikes, as well as the provision of arms and troops by the alliance, helped limit, but not reverse, Houthi success.

In turn, the Houthis were backed by Saudi Arabia's leading rival, Iran, which advanced the case of Shi'a solidarity against the Sunni Saudis. Iranian intervention played a further role in encouraging Saudi attacks on the Houthis, attacks which, in 2015, brought the new king and his second son, Mohammed bin Salman, defense minister from 2015 and crown prince from 2017, valuable prestige within Saudi Arabia, fulfilling a desire there for international assertion. Thus, the war drew on a wide range of drives, needs, opportunities, and fears, each of which made any settlement difficult. Saudi Arabia was supported by Arab states, including Egypt. As part of the equation, Iranian-backed Shi'a militants and Saudi security forces clashed in eastern Saudi Arabia.

An additional element was provided by al-Qaeda in the Arabian Peninsula (AQAP), which gained control of much of southern Yemen in 2015. It turn, it was driven out of much of the country in 2016 by five thousand troops from the United Arab Emirates supported both by thirty thousand locally held fighters, many of whom had abandoned AQAP, and by American drones.

There have been terrible civilian casualties in Yemen, notably from bombing; disease, particularly cholera; and malnutrition. The last two are products of governmental breakdown and social condition. Yemen, like Libya and Syria, exemplified the extent to which it was difficult (although not impossible) for outside powers to control developments.

In Iraq, the forces of Islamic State made rapid gains in 2014–15, capturing Mosul in June 2014.[11] The disintegration of the Iraqi army in 2014 in the face of the advance by IS forces reflected the role of political partisanship in the running of the low-caliber army. However, IS was driven back and then defeated in 2016–17 by American-supported counterattacks by the Iraqi army. These forces had to confront suicide bombers, roadside bombs, and snipers. Moreover, IS forces made good use of darkness and of tunneling in order to provide cover and to regain the initiative. In turn, the Iraqi forces first sought, as with Fallujah in 2016, to encircle IS-held towns and then to tighten the encirclement in order to cut the IS forces off from reinforcements, supplies, and escape. Then the town was attacked from a number of points. Artillery and aircraft were employed to hit targets before elite units assaulted the town and then other forces mopped up.

The fate of Mosul, which fell in 2017 after block-by-block fighting, certainly did not suggest that land warfare was redundant. Alleyways made it difficult for attackers to use artillery, armor, and air power. Iraqi troops, which made plentiful use of "Toyota tanks"—pickup trucks armed with a medium heavy piece of equipment—supported by American air power, pressed on to capture the town of Tal Afar. So also in the Qalamoun Mountains on the Lebanese-Syrian border, from where IS withdrew after being cut off by Syrian and Lebanese forces and subjected to Russian air attack. IS was also attacked by Shi'a Arab militias and their Peshmerga Kurdish counterparts. In turn, the Kurdish declaration of independence in 2017 led the Iraqi army, supported by these militias, to drive the Kurds from much territory in Iraq, including the city of Kirkuk, from which about sixty thousand civilians fled. The Turkish government also attacked the Kurds.

At a very different scale, and until 2017 attracting less international attention, the position of Muslims caused conflict in Myanmar and Thailand. In the former, the exclusion from citizenship and state care of the Rohingyas, a Muslim minority, led in 2012 to the formation of the Arakan Rohingya Salvation Army, and from 2016 it initiated attacks on border guard and police posts using machetes and handheld explosives. In response, the army began a brutal repression of the Rohingyas as a whole, most of whom had nothing to do with the terrorism. Assisted by armed Rakhines, another local ethnic group, the army murdered, mutilated, and raped people and set houses on fire, causing over half a million people to flee. This was on the pattern of previous flights in 1978 and 1991–92 in which over two hundred thousand fled. Moreover, it was on a pattern of the harsh treatment of other minorities, such as the Shan, against which there were brutal campaigns of ethnic cleansing, as in 2009.

Global and regional geopolitics were important aspects of the conflicts in the Middle East. The rivalry between the United States and Russia was a key element, notably in Syria where Russia proved more adept and determined, matching means to goals.[12] So also with the rivalry between Saudi Arabia and Iran, particularly in Syria and Yemen. Iran's quest to create an "arc of influence" or a "corridor" to the Mediterranean to extend its control, via Iraq and Syria, to southern Lebanon, where its ally Hezbollah is in power, posed a challenge to Lebanon and, differently, to Israel. In 2017, as part of these tensions, Saudi Arabia blockaded Qatar, which had strong ties to Iran and Turkey, both of which were rivals of Saudi Arabia in Syria. In 2017, Saudi Arabia had 235,000 active military personnel and Qatar only 12,000, but Saudi Arabia found it difficult to prevail.

INTERNATIONAL CONFRONTATION

International confrontation between great powers was also to the fore, with growing tension between China and Japan as a result of the Chinese show, and thus use, of force to pursue territorial claims in the East China Sea, especially from 2013. Rising Chinese military expenditure helped drive up the spending of other regional powers, particularly Japan and India, each of which has frontier disputes with China. In 2017, although a settlement was finally reached, China and India clashed over Chinese road building in a disputed area of Bhutan. Road building would enable China to deploy troops against India.

There was also serious tension between Russia and NATO, with Russian aggression and expansionism challenging its Western neighbors. There was much talk of a new Cold War. Russian's annexation of Crimea in 2014 led to a renewed emphasis on defense in Eastern Europe and Scandinavia, with pressure on NATO to focus on the issue. NATO forces were deployed in Estonia, while both Lithuania and Sweden reintroduced conscription. Sweden also moved troops to its exposed Baltic island of Gotland, ratified a memorandum of understanding with NATO in 2016, and in 2017 took part in NATO's annual Baltic training exercise. In 2017, the bellicose President Vladimir Putin, in an interview with the Russian state-run news agency Tass, warned,

> If Sweden joins NATO . . . we will consider that the infrastructure of the military bloc now approaches us from the Swedish side. We will interpret that as an additional threat and we will think about how to eliminate this threat.

There were other major regional arms races, notably between India and Pakistan.

There was a range in capabilities and weaponry between different types of power, but also a degree of overlap. For example, drones, cutting-edge technology deployed by major states, were also used by nonstate groups, including, in Syria in 2015, Hezbollah and a rival, the Nusra Front. Similarly, ballistic missiles were deployed not only by the great powers but also by North Korea.

In 2017, land warfare appeared a prospect in Korea. North Korea has the capacity for a large-scale conventional assault on the South, as well as a sustained bombardment of its capital, Seoul, by about one thousand pieces of artillery, which included long-range 170 mm guns and chemical warheads. The United States and South Korea, in turn, deployed significant forces, including a formidable missile arsenal. Lorry-based missiles provided mobile firepower to both sides. The South Korean Hyunmoo-28 missile can deliver five hundred kilograms of high explosives at a range of 310 miles, and the American MGM-140 Army Tactical Missile System, the same at a speed of Mach 3 and a range of up to 190 miles. This is an artillery that is different in type from the emplaced North Korean guns.

FORCE AND POLITICS

The role of the military in determining, or at least affecting, political outcomes remained significant in many countries. As in the 1990s, the military in many states was deployed against disorder, or what was presented as disorder. Indeed, the notion of a clear divide between war and policing is not appropriate in many. Mexico is a case in point. In 2011, as the government sought to battle the drug gangs, there were 22,852 murders, and in 2017 over 23,000. The government could not end the power of the gangs despite the deployment of the armed forces. In 2017, Mexican troops were deployed against tappers taking gas from the national pipeline network: both troops and tappers died.

Also, in 2017, after the killing of over ninety policemen in the state of Rio de Janeiro in the first seven months of the year, Brazil began deploying troops against the gangs there who focus on drug smuggling. Nine hundred fifty troops were sent to the Rocinha favela (slum) in Rio de Janeiro to stop gun violence between drug gangs that had brought orderly life to a close. In contrast, in the United States in 2012–16, there were on average nine deaths on active service for every one hundred thousand police officers. In the Philippines, the shoot-to-kill campaign against suspected drug dealers launched by President Rodrigo Duterte led to thousands of deaths. In Colombia, police killed farmers protesting against coca eradication attempts. In India, troops were deployed in 2017 after thousands of rioters in the state of Haryana overcame thousands of police and paramilitaries trying to keep order following the conviction of Gurmeet Ram Rahim Singh, a powerful guru, for rape. Such use of troops and paramilitaries is likely to become even more common in states struggling to maintain governmental control and the rule of law.

Politics was more to the fore in many states, with a more explicit political purpose in the use of the military. In 2013, the Egyptian army overthrew Mohamed Morsi, president from 2012, and then, using force, defeated the threat from the pro-Morsi Muslim Brotherhood. In Thailand, the army ousted a populist prime minister, Yingluck Shinawatra, in 2014. This was the twelfth coup since the first, that of 1932. Another coup followed in 2017.

In Venezuela, the Nicolás Maduro dictatorship used force to suppress opposition, including in 2017. This force was provided by the army, national guardsmen, police, and hired armed thugs, the *colectivos*. Clouds of tear gas and volleys of plastic bullets were fired against demonstrators in 2017. President Maduro employed bellicose language, calling on his supporters to "prepare for battle" and stating that he would arm a volunteer militia with half a million guns. In a classic instance of the process of hollowing out militaries as they focus on political control rather than fighting capability, Maduro has won over the army leadership by providing it with many opportunities to make money. The number of generals has increased from two hundred to over two thousand, and they are chosen and reshuffled to maintain loyalty. They make money from the economic control handed them by Maduro as well as from straightforward crime such as drug smuggling. Political commissars police this system, while Cuban security forces protect Maduro.

Whatever the formal structure, many military forces are in effect gangs. When gang leaders, or warlords as they are known if they are more powerful, run a state or protostate, the overlap is clear, as in Kurdistan under its autocratic president, Masoud Barzani. However, factionalism in the military to an extent that affects politics is more general across much of the world.

RUSSIA

Concern over stability can lead to the development of paramilitary forces. Thus, in 2016, President Putin, who has always relied heavily on former KGB colleagues and on its successor, the FSB, announced the creation of a National Guard, which was to have four hundred thousand plus members under a Putin client and be an alternative to the regular army of about 930,000 troops.

At the same time, Russia has sought to maintain power in the former Soviet Union by intimidating other states and, as in Georgia in 2008 and Ukraine from 2014, intervening militarily against them. The seizure from Ukraine of Crimea, by disguised Russian troops plus sympathetic locals, pushed Putin's approval rating to 86 percent, a rise of over twenty points. This can be seen as a separate process from that of maintaining strength internally, but it is not, both because Putin does not accept the dissolution of the Soviet Union and because such action helps him with his domestic image and popularity, notably with his anti-Western supporters within the KGB/FSB. The Russian understanding of warfare as hybrid, along a spectrum from irregular to regular, informational and political to military, also played a major role. It was certainly apparent in Ukraine. Hybrid warfare, a more general engagement with the possibilities of asymmetric conflict, posed a major challenge to established Western military doctrine, structures, and methods.[13]

Russia's ability in land warfare in part reflected the extent to which it was a case of operating against contiguous states. This provided opportunities for speed, surprise, and taking the initiative that contrasts with long-distance deployment. At the same time, the use of Russia's resources, notably raw materials, in particular oil, and the authoritarian nature of the state made it possible to increase expenditure on the military. In 2008–16 it rose by 30 percent in real terms as part of a drive to raise flexibility, readiness, and deployability, ensuring that its elite forces were in a good state. This was as part of a determination to mount offensive, high-tempo operations against NATO.

However, bold plans for major expansion, for example in armored fighting vehicles, were revised downward in 2016. Furthermore, major problems were posed by Russia's stagnant population and poor economy and by the obsolescence of much of Russia's military-industrial complex. These issues looked toward the future.[14]

So did the increased cult of the military under Putin and its enhanced identification with the nation. In 2017, polls indicated that about 60 percent of Russians fully trusted the army, compared to 39 percent in 2012. The unveiling in 2017 at a prominent site in Moscow of a large statue of Mikhail Kalashnikov, the inventor of the AK-47 rifle, was symptomatic.

UKRAINE

Meanwhile, the conflict in Ukraine that began in 2014 continues. By the spring of 2017, it had cost ten thousand lives and displaced over 1.7 million people. Russian-backed separatists proclaimed the Donetsk People's Republic in 2014 while Ukraine calls the conflict zone an area of antiterrorist operations. Land capability proved the most effective way to exert pressure on opponents. The deployment of Russian tanks outside Ukraine served as a way to put pressure on the latter. Moreover, within Ukraine, Russian forces defeated the Ukrainian army, such that a line of division was left. The conflict was not called a war, but it put Ukraine under a heavy burden. The firing of mortars is a way for the separatists to demonstrate their presence, but there are no current moves of any scale.[15]

CHINA

Russia (then the Soviet Union) dominated the international discussion of Communist military capability during the Cold War. China actually fought three foreign wars—in Korea (1950–53), India (1962), and Vietnam (1979) but did not then have the capability for a long-range power projection of its army. Moreover, the Chinese army appeared far stronger on mass (numbers) than weaponry. The confrontation with the Soviet Union in the 1960s–80s enhanced the Chinese concern with power in border areas, which again led to an emphasis on mass. Furthermore, the People's Liberation Army (PLA), founded in 1947, was, as the armed wing of the Communist Party, the means by which the latter kept control of the regions. This task appeared more necessary as a result of the disorder of the Cultural Revolution of the late 1960s and the challenge to party rule in 1989.

The death of Mao Zedong in 1976 permitted a change in political ideology and military doctrine, away from mass and toward a military that was explicitly modernizing to meet cutting-edge methods. As a consequence, the size of the army, by far the dominant branch of the military, was greatly reduced in the 1980s and 1990s, with the active personnel in the army falling by about a million. Nevertheless, the army remained overwhelmingly the dominant branch, with more than 1.5 million troops in the 2000s. It was upgraded with the Type 69 tank improved by adopting Western technology. This, the Type 79, entered production in 1984.

Great-power confrontation, notably with Japan and the United States,[16] led to further major changes in the 2010s. In 2015, the government announced a cut in the army of three hundred thousand troops and the replacement of the PLA's system of organization, from seven regions to five theater commands. The former had focused on regional control and military politics, while the latter were designed to emulate American practice. In 2017, there were more organizational changes. These included disbanding five of the eighteen "group armies" (army corps) and replacing divisions by smaller and more flexible brigades. Other changes have included a greater emphasis on mobility in attack, one seen with the development of aerial assault units reliant on helicopters. In 2016, the PLA took delivery of its one thousandth helicopter. Special operations forces became more significant. Cutting-edge weaponry has been bought from Russia.

As with other states, political control was a key element. The PLA is the Communist Party's armed force, not that of the state, and although the two are equivalent, this enables a system of control focused on the party. The institution in question, the Central Military Commission, has had its authority strengthened by Xi Jinping, who is general secretary of the Communist Party of China (from 2012) and chairman of the Central Military Commission (from 2012, vice chairman, 2010–12), as well as president of China (from 2013). In 2014, Xi became leader of the new Central Leading Group for Military Reform, which was designed to bypass existing systems of command and thus enable reform and improvement. The same year, at the New Gutian Conference, Xi repeated Mao Zedong's argument, made at the 1929 Gutian Conference, that the party had absolute control over the army. In 2016, Xi also became commander in chief of the new Joint Operations Command Center of the PLA. In 2015 and 2017, the Central Military Commission's power over the military was increased. This also enables Xi to enhance his ability to implement change. Xi, who greatly enhanced his power at the 2017 Party Congress, is not in practice a pursuer of "collective rule."

As yet, the consequences of these changes in terms of military capability, let alone conflict, are unclear. However, the closer identity of this government with the PLA will make it harder to back down if a confrontation, for example, with India or Japan, does not develop as anticipated.

AFRICA

As in the 1990s, Africa remained, in the 2000s and 2010s, the continent with the highest frequency of conflict and with the most deadly conflicts. It was also the continent with the highest rate of population growth. Sudan, Congo, the Central African Republic, Somalia, and Nigeria were particular areas of intense conflict. Sudan's government was threatened by a serious rebellion that broke out in 2003 by the Sudan Liberation Army, based in the Darfur region of the west of the country, which complained of the oppression of non-Arabs by the government. In response, in 2004, the government used its regular forces, including aircraft and infantry moved in trucks, to support an Arab militia, the Janjaweed, much of which rode on horses and camels, in order to slaughter the Fur, Masalit, and, in particular, Zaghawa, native tribes in Darfur. Alongside large-scale killing, especially of men and boys, even very young boys, and the systematic rape and mutilation of women, natives were driven away; their cattle, and therefore livelihood, were seized; the wells were poisoned with corpses; and dams, pumps, and buildings were destroyed. Over three hundred thousand people died as a result in violence that persisted into the 2010s, and more than two million fled, creating a very serious refugee problem. By 2009, with a UN–African Union peacekeeping mission in place, fighting had eased, but in 2011–12 it revived, with militia attacks directed anew against the Zaghawa. The rate of antisocietal attacks carried out by governmental forces rose in 2014, and in 2016 the Sudanese military allegedly launched chemical weapon attacks. China, Iran, and Russia backed the government.

The oil-rich Sudanese government employed similar violence elsewhere. In the early 2010s, in response to an armed rebellion by the SPLM-North movement in the Nuba Mountains in the Sudanese province of Southern Kordofan, the army tried to starve out the rebels and used great brutality against civilians, including large-scale killing and rape. The racial contempt of Arab Sudanese soldiers for darker Nubians is an aspect of the violence.

After South Sudan had become independent in 2011, clashes continued with Sudan, and each side accused the other in 2012 of backing rebel groups. In South Sudan, there was also ethnic conflict between the Murle, Dinka, and Nuer tribes, with many thousands killed, in large part due to competition for land and cattle and raiding for children. Full-scale civil war broke out in 2013. By 2017, reports of atrocities, such as burnings alive, had become commonplace. The UN claimed that four million of the prewar population of twelve million had fled their homes. The key violence was between Dinkas and non-Dinkas, with the government and army run by the former, while non-Dinka armed groups unsuccessfully sought to prevent ethnic cleansing. Famine and disease followed.

Ethnic rivalry played a role in internal conflict in many other African states, such as the Ivory Coast between 2002 and 2011. In Togo, where Cnassingbé Eyadéma seized power in a military coup in 1967, he or his son, Faure Gnassingbé, has been president ever since, basing their power on their minority Kabyé tribe, which has been given key posts in the expanded army. The Ewe and Mina tribes have been kept down. In Nigeria, in 2017, the government deployed the army against separatism in the region of Biafra, but its violent approach to the Igbo minority, which is based there, helped strengthen separatist tendencies. At the same time, Nigeria's large size, ethnic diversity, and rapid population growth posed major problems, which were exacerbated by the porous nature of its northern border and the spread of fundamentalist terrorism south across the Sahara, not least with arms and fighters from Libya.

Ethnic rivalry was notably an issue in Congo, which became both a failed state and one in which regular forces from other African countries intervened in order to influence the direction of conflict there, dominate neighboring areas, and obtain control over raw materials. Mobutu Sese Seko, the dictator since 1965, fell in 1997 as a result of Rwandan invasion, while another invasion was launched in 1998 by Rwanda and Uganda in an unsuccessful attempt to overthrow his replacement, Laurent Kabila. In Congo, Uganda and Rwanda supported competing rebel factions, Rwanda in part in order to defeat the Hutu militias that staged the genocide of 1994 and took refuge in Congo; while Zimbabwe, Angola, Chad, and Namibia backed Kabila, in part in response to the dynamics of their own internal security situation: Angola wished to stop Congolese support for UNITA, which had been important under Mobutu. Angolan and Zimbabwean intervention stopped the 1998 attempt. The outside powers armed their own Congolese allies, particularly, for Rwanda, the Rally for Congolese Democracy, and the Ugandan-backed Union of Congolese Patriots. These overlapped with tribal militia groups, such as those of the Ugandan-backed Hemas, which competed with the Rwandan-allied Lendus in the northeastern province of Ituri, a major center of conflict. Aside from ethnic rivalries, there was competition for control over gold mines and trade routes.

Probably between 3.1 and 4.7 million people died in Congo in 1998–2003, most of disease and starvation, but many of them in ethnic conflict between tribal militias, as murderous attacks on villages, often accompanied by the rape of the women, proved a particularly common means of waging war. Far from being at the cutting edge of supposedly "new generation" warfare, this conflict saw much of the killing with machetes, and bows and arrows and shotguns were employed, alongside the frequent use of mortars and submachine guns. The conflict also led to cannibalism and to the use of child warriors seen in West Africa, for example by the Union of Patriotic Congolese. Other aspects of African conflict that were distant from Western warfare included the use of traditional charms and spirit mediums.[17] Cannibalism was also seen on Kalimantan (Indonesian Borneo) as native Dayaks fought Muslim migrants from the island of Madura in 1996–2001. Revived violence there in the mid-2010s even more clearly followed religious lines.

Violence in Congo continued after the war officially ended in 2003 when the leading rebel groups joined a transitional government. In the Katanga region in 2004, insurgents reputedly cut off the genitals of victims and drank their blood. Congo's first democratic election, in 2006, was regarded as a possible harbinger of change, but the new government found force a ready response to discontent. Moreover, there were serious security problems with militias, especially in the provinces of North and South Kivu on the eastern border. These problems led to the establishment of village self-defense militias, such as the Angry Villagers, but they also contributed to the violence. In 2016–17, a dispute over the succession to a traditional chief in the region of Kasai became an insurgency against the central government in which over one million people were displaced.

The disorder in Congo also provided a basis for problems elsewhere. Rebel groups opposed to the governments in neighboring Rwanda and Burundi, for example Burundi's National Liberation Front in 2012, were able to find shelter in Congo, where they earned money from criminal activities, such as gold trafficking. Refugees, for example from Kasai in Congo into Angola, have created major problems for governments. Far more benignly in 2016, the movement of troops by ECONWAS (the Economic Community of West African States), and the threat to invade, led Yahya Jammeh, the dictator of Gambia, to abandon attempts to hang on to power after losing an election.

More generally, rivalries between states interacted with insurrections and other civil conflicts elsewhere. Thus, warfare between Eritrea and Ethiopia, which involved large-scale fighting of a conventional type, spilled over into internal conflicts in Somalia where Islamic fundamentalists were opposed to the warlord-dominated Somali transitional government. Foreign intervention, notably by Ethiopia, Kenya, and AMISOM (the African Mission to Somalia), helped limit the Shabab, the fundamentalist militia, who were the key players in the south and center of the country in the late 2000s.

In West Africa, in 2014, the long-standing president of Burkina Faso, Blaise Compaoré (an officer who had come to power in a coup in 1987), was overthrown in a military coup. In turn, in 2015, the former presidential guard mutinied and attempted to replace the government. The president, Michel Kafando, and prime minister were overthrown, but the coup failed to gain momentum. Alongside international criticism and popular demonstrations in the cities of Burkina Faso, the army deployed against the rebels and drove them back into their barracks where, after a siege, they surrendered. This was a "classic" type of attempted coup, one in which rival branches of the military and paramilitaries fought each other, while the fighting focused on the standard places of power: the airport, the presidential compound, and radio and television stations. In 2017 there were mutinies over pay on the part of the army of the Ivory Coast.

Also in 2017, the fifty-six-thousand-man-strong army mounted a coup in Zimbabwe, placing the president, Robert Mugabe, under house arrest, taking over the national broadcaster, and deploying armored vehicles in the center of the capital, Harare. The rival police force was disarmed. The army made much use of Chinese-made Type 89 armored vehicles, notably the armored personnel carrier variant with its heavy machine guns. In the late twentieth century, such coups would have been mounted with American or Soviet armored personnel carriers. China had also paid for the recently opened National Defense College. In an instructive guide to the longevity of conflict, the army justified its military intervention as defending the legacy of the liberation struggle in the 1960s and 1970s. Indeed, the War Veterans Association was a major element in the politics of Zimbabwe.

A different challenge to stability was seen in the Central African Republic, where militias, either mostly Christian or mostly Muslim, proved the key element in politics.[18] By 2017, the UN's chief for humanitarian affairs was reporting the "early warnings of genocide" there. In Zanzibar, part of Tanzania, progovernment militias known as "zombies" attacked the separatist Civic United Front, a party whose 2015 election victory was annulled. Zanzibar is a formerly independent Muslim area.

In states that are not showing this rate of disorder, there is still a use of force. In Kenya in 2017, about 180,000 troops, police, and national park rangers provided a measure of order for the elections. In South Africa, armed gangs "hijacked" buildings extorting rent, leading, in response, to private security, including eviction squads such as the Red Ants.

CONCLUSION

History is what happened in the past and how we, in the present, provide an account of the past. Far from the latter process offering the clarity of panoptic vision, it is understandably shaped by the concerns and views of particular participants in the present. That may account for the degree of anachronism offered during the War on Terror, for it is far from clear that 9/11 had the long-term or global impact that was claimed at the time. There was, indeed, an echo, albeit from a contrasting perspective and with very different conclusions, of the earlier confidence that a Revolution in Military Affairs, indeed the Revolution in Military Affairs, had been similarly transformative. By the nature of considering change, commentators accepted the prospect of different outcomes, although that point was not always to the fore.[19]

A counter, suggesting that the wars following 9/11, particularly those in Afghanistan and Iraq, were a diversion from central geopolitical tensions, notably involving China, India, Japan, and the United States, would have been useful, or one asking about how the naval dimension had changed, or suggesting that the Western interventionist conflicts in the 2000s offered but another instance of the combination of overstretch and asymmetry, and so on. From the context of the late 2010s, when China's rise appears more prominent, the question can also be reformulated to ask how 9/11 would be regarded in, say, 2050 when many current readers will be still alive, but when China may be, if not the leading power, at least one whose military history is regarded as of great significance. Whereas in 2012 the Chinese president, Hu Jintao, told the Chinese Communist Party's seventeenth quinquennial congress that the task of the PLA was "to win a local war in an information age," in 2017, Xi Jinping, a powerful successor as president, at the eighteenth congress, repeated the phrase but without the word *local* and also threatened to destroy Taiwanese independence.

In another global perspective, growing pressure on resources as a result of an unprecedented and continuing rise in the world's population, notably in cities,[20] combined with economic volatility and political instability, suggested that conflict would continue to be a major factor in human history. A decline in bellicosity in many cultures, notably Western Europe, Japan, and Canada, was not matched in many areas in which population was growing rapidly, especially Africa and the Islamic world. It remained normal in these areas to use force to advance political interests. In Nigeria, where in 2009 the Islamic fundamentalist group Boko Haram launched a movement to create an Islamic state, over twenty thousand people have been killed since and over two million people displaced in an insurrection that also affected neighboring Cameroon and Niger. Local people were forcibly recruited. Alongside radical Islam, economic problems were part of the equation of support, as was a rapidly growing population. Already the world's seventh most populous state, Nigeria is predicted to become the third most by 2050, supplanting the United States.

All or some of these factors played a part in the 2000s and 2010s in conflict in other states, including Sudan, Mali, the Ivory Coast, and the Central African Republic. The notions that the world was becoming more peaceful and that population increases were not necessarily creating conflict looked less happy from the perspective of this region, or, indeed, from that of Southwest Asia.

The continued strength of national variety was shown in 2017 with the crisis in Catalonia where the Spanish government used the Civil Guard in an unsuccessful attempt to disrupt an independence referendum. No one was killed, but the use of force was seen as a step that discredited the government. The Civil Guard was withdrawn: "'If there is one lesson from the vote [on October 1] it is that force alone does not work in the internet age,' said one senior politician in Madrid. 'One knitting old lady can stop a whole line of tanks.'"[21]

The primacy in most states of the threat of internal disorder has ensured that countering it is the main challenge for most governments.[22] This threat can lead to the use of the military and to building it up to that end. However, there is also the concern about military loyalty and that of paramilitaries. This is seen in many states. As in Yemen, the continued role of regional tensions, notably in Southwest, South, and East Asia, suggested that conflict, whether direct or proxy, will play an important future part in encouraging, sustaining, and complicating warfare. The use of force to pursue interests within states, and the habit of military intervention in others, implies a continuation from a troubled present to a troubling future.

Chapter Ten

Into the Future

PARALLELS WITH THE FIRST WORLD WAR

History does not repeat itself exactly, but there is guidance in the past to what may happen later. And so for the First World War (1914–18) and the world today. The multiple international rivalries of the early 1910s were organized in terms of great-power systems, notably those of France-Russia and Germany-Austria, in a fashion that is somewhat similar to the situation today. This ensured, and ensures, that the interests of a part of the system may come to affect the remainder. Thus, in 1914, Austria's pressure on Russia's major Balkan protégé, Serbia, caused the crisis that led to war. Today, it is possible that American, Chinese, or Russian support for a protégé may have a similar effect, for example, Russian backing for Syria.

That is a functional guide to international crisis, but there is also the important element of the culture of decision making in the major players. Military history requires an engagement with cultural elements, notably the roles of militarism and bellicosity, and at the strategic and organizational, as well as the operational and tactical levels.

In considering decision making, there tends to be a major contrast between those powers that seek to change arrangements, the revisionists, and others that are essentially content to play within the rules. The clear parallel here is between Germany in 1914 and both China and Russia today. Germany was an aggressive power from the outset, its unification and early expansion the product of three wars in 1864–71 and of a militaristic culture. Although in theory a parliamentary democracy ruled by an emperor, this scarcely described the practice of foreign and military policy in Germany, or, for that matter, in Austria and Russia. The bellicose German leadership was determined to gain the primacy it felt that it deserved. This entailed, in particular, not only keeping France down and Russia at bay, but also an unprovoked naval race with the leading naval power, Britain, an unwise as well as unnecessary choice.

The comparison with the tension between China and the current leading naval power, Britain's successor, the United States, is readily apparent and has attracted attention, both in China and the United States. Moreover, this rivalry has been seen, since the 1990s, in terms of that between a rising and a declining hegemon. And so for Germany and Britain before the First World War. Germany's manufacturing had surpassed that of Britain, even if its service sector was still less prominent. A similar situation can be seen with China and the United States today. In China, there is a clear commitment to revisionism, one directed against what is felt to be the abuses visited on China by foreign powers from the 1830s to the 1940s. This attitude matches the German belief prior to 1914 that their late unification in 1866–71 had denied them their rightful "place in the sun" and that other powers had kept them from it.

In 1914, German leaders opportunistically sought to use the Balkan crisis created by the assassination of Archduke Franz Ferdinand, the heir to the Austro-Hungarian monarchy, in order to change the balance of power in their favor. Encouraging Austria to act, they were willing to risk a war because no other crisis was as likely to produce a favorable constellation of circumstances for Germany. The nature of international relations today, with the large number of crises across the world, and the opportunities, problems, and vulnerabilities created by their interaction, risks creating a similar situation.

Thus, it is misleading to suggest, as has been argued for Germany in 1914, that the war plans of the age, with their dynamic interaction of mobilization and deployment, made war by timetable (a reference to the railway timetables that guided, controlled, and registered the pace of mobilization) difficult to stop once a crisis occurred, that, in short, the powers were victims of circumstances. Such an argument underplays the extent to which leaders in 1914 were not trapped by circumstances. Instead, their own roles, preferences, and choices were important. An underplaying of the importance of choice reflects both an anachronistic, later, sense that no one could have chosen to begin the First World War, as well as a preference for blaming everyone, and no one, in the shape of attributing the causes to "the system."

In fact, in 1914, some decision makers, notably in Germany, believed that war was necessary and could lead to a quick victory.

The danger in the late 2010s is that this view will recur. Thus, Russia, North Korea, China, Iran, Venezuela, or another power, for example the United States against North Korea, may believe that it can profitably launch a local war and control the outcome, as Iraq sought to do against Iran in 1980 and against Kuwait in 1990.

In practice, the course of the campaigning in 1914, as for Iraq, was to reveal that no such control is possible. In 1914, the Germans sought, planned in great detail for, and anticipated a swift and decisive victory in order to avoid the military, political, economic, and social complexities of a large-scale and lengthy war between peoples. As a result of this anticipation, the political dimension was not significant for German military planners, who in any case seriously underestimated their opponents' power, resolve, and resilience.

As a parallel between Europe in 1914 and East Asia today, rising military expenditure encouraged a sense of instability and foreboding and helped drive forward an arms race. In turn, this greater military capability, by lessening earlier weaknesses, made armed diplomacy more plausible to individual powers, as with Russian intervention in Georgia in 2008 and Crimea in 2014, while, at the same time, increasing a sense of vulnerability to the armed diplomacy and cyber intervention of others. As deterrence appeared weaker, so it seemed necessary to identify, and grasp, windows of opportunity for action, which in turn weakened deterrence.

Parallels can be pushed further by suggesting that if a major war occurs anew in the late 2010s, it will have a greater impact than anticipated, not only militarily but also in terms of political, social, and economic disruption. For powers that are not heavily involved, there can notionally be benefits. Thus, in the First World War, the Japanese real gross national product leaped by 40 percent as Japan, which was on the Allied side but only with a limited commitment, profited not only from Western orders for goods but also from the decline of European competition in domestic and Asian markets. However, even so, there was serious disruption as well as grave risk: Japan suffered from inflation and growing economic differences within the country, leading to nationwide rice riots in 1918 and to rising labor and tenant disputes in the 1920s. So also for neutral Spain.

For most countries, the consequences of the First World War were more drastic. Empires fell, revolutions were staged, and inflation, high taxation, and the disruption of trade all wrecked the prewar economic and social order, both at the global level and within individual states.

There is every reason to believe that the situation will be the same today if there is another major conflict, although the war, for example, a new (and very different) Korean War, is likely, at least in its open warfare phase, to be over far faster than in the past due to the nature of the military technology of major powers. Were America to fail, its hegemony might collapse, although the resilience of the American economy and society remains impressive. A defeat for China would probably be the end of Communist rule, an outcome that would be highly disruptive. Such a result might appear inconceivable today, but in early 1914, few believed that war would lead to the disappearance of the Romanov (Russian), Habsburg (Austrian), Ottoman (Turkish), and Hohenzollern (German) Empires by the end of 1918. In practice, the vortex of war was, from 1914, to suck in and destroy much of the established order. Moreover, the resulting instability, not least in the shape of the establishment of a Communist Soviet Union with an adversarial political philosophy and practice, led to a global power politics that remained inherently unstable for many decades.

FRAMEWORKS FOR DISCUSSION

From the perspective of the twenty-first century, and, even more, the developing twenty-first century, which is already more than halfway through its second decade, the military history of the twentieth century changes, and greatly so, or at least should change. In particular, it appears no longer credible to place so much attention in the history of that century on the two world wars when more than seventy years have passed since their close in 1945. These world wars occurred in the twentieth century, but only in its first half. Moreover, although these cataclysmic conflicts greatly affected world history, much since has arisen from different causes. Nor does an account of the post-1945 period focused on the Cold War appear so credible, when that confrontation, and the associated conflicts, ended in 1989 or, as in Angola and El Salvador, shortly thereafter.

Similarly, a discussion of non-Western military history in terms of conflict against Western colonialism seems less plausible given that the last major Western transoceanic colonial presence, that of Portugal in Africa, came to a close in 1975 with the end of an exhausted Portuguese imperialism and independence for Angola, Mozambique, and Portuguese Guinea (although not for an East Timor gobbled by Indonesia). That end, indeed, brought to a close a thirty-year period unprecedented in world history, one, due to decolonization, of a massive transfer of control over a major part of the world and of its population. Russia, of course, remains the colonial power in Siberia (as does China in Tibet), but this element is not generally considered when the colonial period is assessed.

Instead of the established agenda for the military history of the twentieth century, it is appropriate to approach the subject anew, something that many military historians appear to find difficult to do. Here, the focus can be on conflict between non-Western forces, notably, but not only, since 1945. Looking back to the 1910s, non-Western military developments were already significant, particularly in China. Moreover, such a focus on conflict between non-Western forces offers a different analytical approach. This approach does not assume that Western military methods are necessarily paradigmatic but, instead, focuses on specific best practices in a range of very different physical and political environments. Furthermore, to underline the need for, and the possibility of, recentering focus, if once the world is remapped in terms of space-population cartograms, then China and India become the crucial military context and, more generally, East and South Asia do so, as that also included such populous countries as Indonesia, Pakistan, and Japan. In the case of both of these parts of Asia, major cities are a key element of the physical and political environments.

As a related but different point, the military history of much of the world relates not to distant power projection or to state-to-state conflict but instead to conflict within countries, whether insurgencies and counterinsurgency struggles or coups. The related use of the military as an arm of the state, and of the state as a sphere for the military, is highly significant but it also underlines the need to stress the political dimensions of military activity.

This point is especially true of Latin America, within which there has been no major state-to-state war since the 1932–35 conflict between Bolivia and Paraguay over the region of the Gran Chaco, a conflict ably won by Paraguay despite clearly lacking the resources of its opponent. Since 1935, however, there have been numerous conflicts within Latin American states, as well as coups. The two are linked. Thus, in Argentina, a military junta seized power in 1976 and then began a counterinsurgency terror campaign directed against critics and insurgents, one in which many nonengaged civilians were also detained, tortured, and murdered. This campaign, which led to the "disappearance" of thousands, continued until the fall of the junta following its defeat by Britain in the Falklands War in 1982, a conflict that reflected the bellicosity of the regime. More normally, however, coups, for example that in Brazil in 1964, were not followed by foreign war.

There has also been much drug-related violence, notably in Colombia and Mexico. Aside from the struggles of drug cartels with government, they also wage war with each other. The violence used is frequently extreme and demonstrative, as with the prominent display of decapitated heads and tortured bodies. The scale is great. Thus, in 2007–8, the Mexican government deployed close to forty thousand troops, while the cartels' weaponry included antitank rockets and rocket-propelled grenades.[1]

Similarly to Argentina, the military seized power in Greece in a coup in 1967, only to fall in 1974 when its aggressive foreign policy failed in Cyprus in the face of a Turkish invasion. In 1971, an Indian invasion brought a brutal counterinsurgency by the Pakistan army in East Pakistan (since then Bangladesh) to a close. At a more modest level, soldiers and police in riot gear raided the Maldives parliament in 2017, dragging opposition MPs from the building as they attempted to hold a no-confidence vote directed against the government. At the same time, conflicts came to a close. Thus, in 2017, an end to the long-standing FARC rebellion in Colombia was negotiated.

The military frequently emerge as an independent political interest. Iran's 120,000-strong Revolutionary Guards (Army of the Guardians of the Islamic Revolution) have wide-ranging economic interests including in oil, construction, agriculture, petrochemicals, and telecoms. There have been claims that their business wealth is about $100 billion, but the Revolutionary Guards argue that they need the businesses to fund their operations, including in Syria and Iraq. From 2012, the Revolutionary Guards, in the shape of the al-Quds Brigade, its international arm, played a major role in furthering Iran's goals in Iraq and Syria. Major General Qasem Soleimani, the head of the brigade, has been a key military and political player. The Union of Myanmar Economic Holdings Limited and the Myanmar Economic Corporation are army owned and control much of the economy, while the army also controls many land-use decisions.

This conspectus of variety in conflict offers a way to think about war over the last century and a half, as well as into the future. Instead of a central narrative, one in the light of which the remainder of the world can be assessed and its militaries found wanting, there are a number of narratives. Moreover, military history becomes complex when it leads to a situation in which contrasting narratives, as it were, come into conflict. In short, differing views and equations of military success and significance, methods and goals, clash, with combatants who have sharply divergent perceptions of capability and prowess brought into violent conflict. That happened, in the 2000s and 2010s, in the case of bitter and sustained resistance to American-led coalitions in Iraq and Afghanistan. The long-range, large-scale, and speedy force projection offered by modern transport systems ensures that these contrasting military cultures can more rapidly and frequently come into conflict than in the past.

This concern with force projection has led to a restructuring of armies with much more of an emphasis on mobility and related organizational structures. In particular, there has been a stress on brigades not divisions, and on the development of the concept of the strike brigade. Infantry has been made mobile, with vehicles protected notably against ambushes and mines, as in the American Stryker, the Russian R-15 IFV series, and the French VBCI. Tanks and heavy artillery, in contrast, have become relatively less significant.

A last caveat to any easy route into the subject is provided by the nature of military history. While learning from the past is a priority, and notably so in the case of military academies, there is also a framing of questions, and advancing of answers, in terms of the needs of the present. History, indeed, is part of the way in which issues are addressed for current audiences in order to affect the present. Many historians like to suggest that they are somehow separate from this process, but that is not the case. For example, if I, or another, present the key geopolitical and military issues at present (2018) as the nature of Chinese and Russian political, economic, and military power and ambitions, then I will necessarily direct attention away from the problems posed by developments in the Islamic world such as conflict in Afghanistan, Iraq, Syria, and Yemen, or Iranian expansionism.

Moreover, the focus has consequences for the type of military that is required. Confrontation with these powers requires high-spectrum weaponry such as the latest, and highly expensive, fighter aircraft with their advanced avionics. In contrast, intervention in the Islamic world puts the emphasis on an army trained in COIN, the American term for counterinsurgency warfare. However, the deployment and activity of the army very much requires air and naval superiority in both conventional and COIN warfare, and at strategic, operational, and tactical levels.

The role of assessment is also apparent with the reading of the past. This is a reading that is often crucial for the politicization of strategic choice. For example, debate in recent years over the American intervention in Vietnam in the 1960s and early 1970s in part reflects disagreements over the possibilities for COIN today, as well as the bitter politics of vindication with regard to the Vietnam War. There is the argument that American success, both in Vietnam and elsewhere, could have been obtained by better leadership and, more specifically, by policy changes, notably by heavier bombing or by a ground or amphibious invasion of North Vietnam designed to lead to an advance that would cut the Ho Chi Minh Trail.

Conversely, there is the view that these wars were unwinnable, in large part because of political circumstances, both in the United States and in the other country where it projected its force. In the specific case of Vietnam, different American methods may have prolonged the conflict, but the Americans had very few ways to affect the North Vietnamese leadership, and notably so within the constraints of wishing to fight a limited war, one in which there was no ground invasion of North Vietnam. Such a conflict reflected wider strategic parameters, particularly the wish not to wage a full-scale conflict with the Communist bloc, and especially so given the vulnerability of America and its allies in Western Europe, the Mediterranean, and South Korea. There was also an understandable lack of political and public will for the risk of a nuclear confrontation with the Soviet Union and China. A reluctance to use atomic weaponry was also the case with American policy toward North Korea in 2018.

It may have been the case, for the United States in Vietnam and possibly elsewhere, that the political objectives were unattainable by force, especially in light of the political parameters of the time. The difficulty of transforming foreign societies tends to be underplayed, as it also was by the Russians when intervening unsuccessfully in Afghanistan in 1979–89, by the Americans in Afghanistan and Iraq, and, possibly, in a different context, by the Israelis when occupying the Gaza Strip and the West Bank of the Jordan after victory in the Six-Day War in 1967.[2] In part, the underplaying of the problems of transformation is because belief in COIN encourages a sense that foreign intervention can work and that the military accordingly has a role, particularly in establishing the parameters. It does indeed have a role, but the likelihood of success is limited and heavily dependent on political considerations, both in the country in question and in the state sending troops.

The ideological dimension to military history is repeatedly significant, but also far from new. The failure of Habsburg hegemony in Europe was largely the consequence of the Protestant Reformation in the sixteenth century, which was far more deadly for both traditional and novel methods of state creation than the angle-bastion fortifications or any other development in weaponry. There is a clear analogy with the damaging impact of Communism and, more specifically, liberation ideas on the maintenance of European colonial empires in the twentieth century, and also of the impact of liberal consumerism on Communist empires in the 1980s, an impact driven home by television broadcasts and other Western media, notably to East Germany.

These conceptual points underline the need repeatedly to ask questions about what we believe to be significant in causation. More significantly, they also serve as the background for considering where we now are when assessing the standard narrative of the two world wars and the Cold War, and also for discussing the non-Western narrative and the developments over the last quarter century. Military history, in short, needs to be located in a wider context.

For example, the centenary, from 1914, of successive events in the First World War has encouraged possibly extensive attention to this war, but far less of an effort than might have been expected to place it in context, notably, as indicated in chapter 4, in contrast with other significant conflicts in the 1910s, especially the Chinese Revolution of 1911–12 and the Mexican civil war. The standard interpretation of the First World War now focuses, more than in the past, not on an unchanging national style of fighting but on the ability of the armies to improve their fighting effectiveness. In particular, there is a discussion of the ability to deliver results. Serbia was conquered in 1915, Russia was knocked out of the war in 1917, and Romania and Italy were all but knocked out in 1916 and 1917, respectively. Each of these were successes for Germany and its allies, while the takeover of Russia from 1917 by the Bolshevik type of Communism had a major impact on world history. Similarly, in the Second World War, it was possible to deliver results in the shape of knocking out powers.

GEOPOLITICS, POLITICS, AND TECHNOLOGY

Within the context of uncertainty,[3] the future opens up very different perspectives depending on whether the emphasis is on geopolitics or technology. Each is a narrative of change, and not least because of the dynamic consequences of population increases. UN figures suggest an increase in the world's population from 7.3 billion in 2015 to 8.6 billion in 2026 and maybe

11.2 by 2100. It is difficult to see how such a scale and rate of increase can be anything other than greatly destabilizing, both within and between states.

A major rise in population poses significant military problems in terms of subjugating opponents. The balance between regular and irregular forces cannot but be affected by a drastic rise in the potential number of the latter. In response, it is easy to think of governments turning to technology to enhance their position, but that can only bring so much control on the ground. This suggests that land warfare will confront serious issues that are defined more in terms of popular compliance than the deployment of regular forces.

The technological parameters of future warfare are less clear. The future of war may well include the rise and growing use of robotic weaponry, not only drones and mobile mines, but also the use of robotic individual fighters. This use may extend in the future to cloning and to other aspects of genetic manipulation. The frequency of conflict or confrontation today suggests that pressures for change in military proficiency and for acquiring comparative advantage will remain acute.

The cost of technological innovation, let alone leadership, may lead to an emphasis instead on less expensive but still effective weapons, such as the improvised explosive devices used by guerrillas in the 2000s and 2010s. States seek to cut costs. Certainly, current expenditure is high and, in part, only possible due to fiscal loosening and accompanying low interest rates. Expenditure figures can be variously assessed. However, the following, based on Stockholm International Peace Research Institute data, can be used. For the NATO powers, in 2016, the United States spent $597.5 billion on the military, compared to between $35 billion and $50 billion each for Britain, France, and Germany. The NATO guidance is 2 percent of GDP, but Germany does not meet this. Figures for China ($145.8 billion) are more problematic, but expenditure has risen greatly from the 1990s.[4] China in 2016 was followed by $81.9 for Saudi Arabia and $65.6 for Russia. The Japanese defense budget is due to grow to $48 billion in 2018.

Rather than simply pursuing high-specification technology that, as it were, separates land and air capabilities, it may be the case that more modest weaponry will bring the two together. Indeed, land, sea, and air can all be platforms. Cut-price precision weapons using off-the-shelf components, as with the American development of the Sidewinder missile, would be a major contrast with the cost of cruise missiles and other "smart" weaponry of that generation. In particular, the American Army Research Laboratory's Aeromechanics and Flight Control Group is examining the potential of what it terms the Collaborative Cooperative Engagement program. This involves moving the world's leading army from inexpensive, "dumb" weapons to more efficient ones. The plan rests on guiding the "dumb" weapons by means of radio messages from smart munitions. Thus, a swarm of submunitions would be given a guidance system, increasing effectiveness and replacing indiscriminate fire. Precision and speed will be delivered at lower cost than at present and thus be able to hit dispersed targets as well as to counter drones. The nature of artillery would change, and individual soldiers would have maneuvering munitions able to engage snipers and other opponents. 3-D printers, including metal printers, are also interesting indicators for manufacturing as they challenge existing economies of scale.

At the same time, much investment continues to be for existing weapons systems, for example, tanks. Thus, in 2017, Iran began to mass-produce the Karrar (Striker), a battle tank that is similar to the Russian T-90 tank. The Iranian tank, with a top speed of thirty-seven miles per hour, has a 125 mm gun with a laser range finder for a computerized targeting system, as well as a 14.5 mm heavy machine gun, the capability to fire missiles, armor to thwart antitank weapons, and rear slat armor against rocket-propelled grenades. Such investment will continue, not least due to the appeal of using tried-and-tested platforms, as well as to different elements of conservatism in the military.

Weaponry is an important independent variable, but the extent to which it determines outcomes is problematic, and notably so for struggles on land, which is the natural human environment. The key element in the latter is likely to be the major growth in global population and the many difficulties in satisfying resulting aspirations and needs and tackling corresponding divisions and tensions.

PRACTICING FOR THE FUTURE

Land warfare today is all too often treated as a rump of air conflict and even cyber warfare, as a slow-moving, legacy form of warfare that is essentially appropriate for the follow-up operation or for those states (the majority) that lack cutting-edge capabilities. Such commentary may not be explicit, but it can be seen as implicit, and notably as aspects of the unconscious assumptions that are so significant in the world of war and also in military history. Indeed, it is possibly even more so in military history, as the subject tends to focus on what are presented as the cutting edge and on a narrative of modernization. This approach may be of interest for considering the future, but it does not offer much for the present, especially for the majority of countries. Land warfare last engaged this narrative in the case of the tank, and since then, the narrative has apparently been superseded by air and cyber warfare.

This approach may to a degree be appropriate for a leading power, like the United States, where army doctrine has had to pay attention to air force arguments, but the approach does not address the limitations of air power. Nor does it address the nature of the military for most states or for nonstate actors. Looking to the future, it is necessary to do both, alongside the process of considering the major powers. There is no commonality of circumstances for all powers, but there is the significant point that the need for most states and nonstate actors to rely on land warfare perforce has an implication for other states, and more so if the question of control over territory is concerned.

Meanwhile, the future is practiced for. Thus, in 2017, Russia deployed one hundred thousand men in the Zapad-17 military exercise, an intimidation of NATO in the Baltic sphere. This led Sweden to carry out its Aurora-17 war game, which also involved NATO contingents. An increase in Swedish military expenditure by 5 percent annually in real terms in 2018–20 and the reintroduction of conscription in 2018 were part of the equation. Preparations for war scarcely suggest that it is obsolescent. At the same time, experience indicates that victory is far more elusive than generally believed, and notably by those who put their trust in technology.[5] Lesson learning, however, is a key link between past, present, and future.[6]

The costs of military preparations and operations remain high and become ever more formidable, but without guaranteeing success. In the fiscal years 2001–16, military spending on Iraq for the United States was $805 billion, compared to $783 billion for Afghanistan and $127 billion for others, even though none of these were wars of necessity. As a result, the question of obsolescence took on new meanings, not so much that warfare was unlikely but that it was unlikely to achieve the goals anticipated, and not least in the face of unprecedented large populations. And yet the absence, in many contexts, of other political options helped make force appear the likely means of domestic and international policy.

Chapter Eleven

Conclusions

A HISTORICAL CASE STUDY

"The learning curve narrative is perhaps too sanguine or clinical for some of its critics . . . [but] such detachment is necessary for analysis."[1] Written, unsurprisingly, in an analysis of an aspect of the First World War, this remark is more generally relevant to the analysis of war. It is not, however, the sole issue in terms of author and reader concerns over commitment and detachment. So also with the question of sympathy, or straightforward support, for one or the other of the protagonists. For instance, the discussion of the military history of Nicaragua in the twentieth century generally favors the Sandinistas.[2] Ironically, this sympathy for the "underdog" helps to counter other problems, namely that many military historians look only at the "high tech" end of warfare and focus on what appears to happen in, or by, "modern" countries.

Instead, it is apparent from this book that modern warfare is in many respects quite familiar, technological changes notwithstanding, to premodern military history. Linked to this, the book clearly undermines the idea that warfare in the modern age has "graduated" into total warfare. Tactical issues, such as how best to ensure combined-arms effectiveness,[3] continue to play a major role.

All studies are inevitably part of the historical process, a situation outlined in chapter 1. This point has to be underlined at the close. It can best be appreciated by looking at individual books and by realizing that this study itself will also be part of such a sequence of assessment (by the author) and consideration and criticism (by others). Readers are invited to suggest studies they find especially valuable.

As a good example, it is possible to turn to another transatlantic (British author/American publisher) book, Andrew Roe's 2010 study of British operations on the North-West Frontier of British India, which is now the northwest frontier province of modern Pakistan, in the late nineteenth and early twentieth centuries.[4] Roe wrote with a distinctive voice as a British infantry officer who had served in Afghanistan, as well as in Bosnia, Iraq, and Northern Ireland, and to a specific purpose, that of offering what he termed the hard-earned lessons and realities of the British experience in the region of Waziristan on the North-West Frontier, and in pursuit of contemporary parallels and prognostications. His particular theme was the significance of understanding the role of history and culture, and there is, in his book, a discussion not just of the value of containment, but also of how best to practice it.

This work, then, sits in the historicist tradition of British (and other) consideration, notably, but not only, by the military, of assessing past counterinsurgency operations in order to understand best how to succeed anew. Roe is good on the predictable insight that reliance solely on military means was counterproductive in managing the North-West Frontier and that warfare has to be contextualized, particularly with strategy understood as a political purpose, a theme repeatedly seen in this study. Roe, however, takes rather a rosy view that somehow the political officers and negotiation, and establishing a workable system of containment by this means, were more effective than military means. Reminding us of the value of looking at more than one study when considering conflict and its contexts, a different perspective has been provided by Christian Tripodi, who problematized the idea that "Politicals" were effective.[5]

The direction of travel in recent years among military commentators is to be somewhat more skeptical about the recent effectiveness of the (British) military in counterinsurgency warfare, notably, but not only, in Iraq and Afghanistan. This is an approach that opens the way to addressing earlier episodes. Separately, there has come the often ahistorical and tendentious criticism of military methods by nonmilitary specialists, which in practice contributes surprisingly little to the discussion about effectiveness.

Insurgencies against imperial control, both on the North-West Frontier and more generally, coincided, and often overlapped, with resistance to the spread of this control. Indeed, the two were frequently part of the same process, as the nature and extent of imperial control were understood by those upon whom it was imposed. At a different chronological scale, this could also be an aspect of the way in which imperialism and de-imperialism occurred at the same time, which is a key background in which to assess land warfare across much of the world during the period 1860–1975. This may also be a way to consider certain aspects of recent conflict. Imperialism can be seen as a description of policy within large states, for example Sudan after independence in 1956 and Turkey, Iran, and Iraq in Kurdistan.

Frontier conflicts certainly represent and illustrate the power, but also the limits of power, of a state or an empire. In the case of the North-West Frontier, force had a role, but other elements also played a part. The economic dimension was significant, with, prefiguring the situation in much of the world now, overpopulation, unemployment, and structural weaknesses in the local economy all proving important. The role of economics was such that road building served as a counterinsurgency policy for more than military reasons. So also with recent attempts at "state building," notably in Afghanistan.

It is important to be cautious about any cultural "essentialism," an element apparent in most work in the area and, more generally, seen in the discussion of supposed national military styles. This approach can be related to the idea of distinctive strategic cultures, again a valuable approach, but one also that should be employed with caution. While, for example, Waziristan, both past and present, did, and does, indeed exemplify the problem of frontier politics, the Pashtuns did (and do) not always pursue violence as a tool of policy: political lobbying played (and plays) a role, and religious solidarity could (and can) also be significant. The British response, both in Waziristan and elsewhere, was sometimes perceptive and sometimes not.

APPROACHES TO MILITARY HISTORY

The problem, in past policy, of focusing on military options at the expense of a more general approach emerges from Roe's book and others. It appeared particularly appropriate in the late 2000s and early 2010s. In part, this point exemplified the more general issues created by a tendency to downplay strategy. This element of warfare, including the dimension of land warfare, is one that tends to be underplayed in public discussion both of war and of military history, and notably so after the rise of air power. The strategic dimension of the subject is easy to underplay in military history given the conventional focus on conflict in the sense of fighting, both the troops and their weaponry, and the more recent scholarly focus on "War and Society." Both approaches are indeed valuable, but they can lead to a tendency to forget that specific wars were waged for particular reasons, while these reasons affected the means pursued. Instead, there can be a somewhat unproblematic approach based simply on winning battles and wars, an approach that neglects, or at least underplays, the significance of the whys and hows. The Iraq War in 2003 was a classic instance of a failure to plan in a broader context, and it is widely treated in that light.

A challenge ahead in military history, when space is at a premium, is to include this dimension, and to do so as part of an interactive range of factors.[6] For example, strategic factors are affected by political and social change, alongside technological and other factors that affect the nature of conflict. Moreover, the question of national styles and cultures in conflict and effectiveness remains significant, but also difficult.[7] Many of the arguments made about national style and culture are crude, limited, and overly reductionist, a point that can be clearly indicated by looking at past examples. An instance of the role of prejudiced stereotyping was provided by a disparaging British military report on Italian army maneuvers in 1894:

> the evil traits of character generated by despotism and superstition. There is no wholesome spirit of patriotism and religious morality in the country—no sense of duty—nor any adequate infusion of the military virtues which are indispensable to form a solid army.[8]

In practice, the commitment shown in 1915–18 during the First World War by Italian forces, ready on the Isonzo front to attack repeatedly and despite heavy casualties, disproves this argument. So also will be the case with some of our current glib assessments. In addition, at the level of smaller units than that of the nation, the analysis may differ as well as vary.[9]

Understanding land warfare going into the future is in part a matter of assessing goals and means of analysis, including the use of history, as well as considering the more conventional agenda of weaponry and geopolitics. There will also be a dynamic engagement with concepts. Hybrid warfare is one such. It was earlier described also as compound warfare, and the Afghan intervention led the American Army Command and General Staff College Press to publish in 2002 a collection produced by its Combat Studies Institute, the preface of which declared that "knowing how the dynamics of compound warfare have affected the outcome of past conflicts will better prepare us to meet both present crises and future challenges of a similar nature."[10] In this and other instances, recent decades show the serious analytical work done in military and government bureaucracies in order to assess conflict. This work counters the old line about armies fighting the last war, even if there is a tendency, notably among politicians, to look back for "lessons."

POLITICS AND MILITARY HISTORY

Another dynamic element of change is presented by the political nature of history. This is a situation that very much includes military history, as in the use of historical analogies,[11] although many of its practitioners do not accept this point. What to cover, how to cover it, and the conclusions that are drawn are explicitly or implicitly political. This thesis may be better appreciated if debates within both the military and government over procurement, tasking, strategy, and doctrine are understood as, at least in part, political. Due to the nature, particularly accessibility, of the archival record and the related weight of scholarship, these points are more apparent for the nonrecent past, for example the appeasement of Germany, Italy, and Japan in the 1930s, rather than for more recent periods and episodes.

Public moods, moreover, are significant contexts for scholarly inquiry, as with the move from militarism to antimilitarism in Germany after the Second World War. Japan provides a good example, one that can be more widely applied. In Japan, from the end of the Russo-Japanese War in 1905 until the 1920s, the two conflicting trends in military history were a consequence of rapid industrialization and urbanization. On the one hand, in response to the challenges these posed, the military itself promoted the idea of a unique Japanese military spirit, commonly known as *Bushidō* or *Yamato damashii*. This emphasis on spirit was reflected in official writings and more popular works by sympathetic authors.

On the other hand, there was a continuing reaction against the economic costs of the military, and, during the 1920s, the public mood of Japan was largely antimilitarist. This mood changed with the Manchurian incident of 1931 and the rising influence of the armed forces in Japanese politics. As a result, it became far more difficult (and dangerous) to be openly critical of the Japanese military, either then or in earlier conflicts. Instead, the trend once again was to emphasize the unique spirit both of the Japanese and, especially, of the Japanese military. The nationalist character of most scholarship became more pronounced in the 1930s and 1940s, as censorship effectively made it impossible for more liberal scholars to publish anything for fear of prosecution.

In turn, total defeat in the Second World War transformed the situation. From its creation in 1954, the Japan Self-Defense Force rejected any direct link with the imperial military, while left-wing scholars, silenced by the war years, completely occupied the field until the 1970s. Thereafter, there was a contest with revisionists, many but not all nationalists, a contest that has continued to the present. This situation has been studied, notably in the case of the Nanjing Massacre of 1937.

In other countries, the situation is frequently less explicit and obvious, but that does not mean that politics plays a lesser role in military history. Land warfare is no exception. In Germany, revisionism was to the fore in 2017. Alexander Gauland, a leader of the far-right AFD group that entered the Bundestag, having done well in the elections, spoke of wishing to "restore" the honor of German soldiers in both world wars.[12]

This political dimension is particularly salient if due attention is paid to strategy, and the prioritization, tasking, doctrine, and procurement involved in it, as context, cause, and consequence. In each chapter, more could have been said on the topic had there been more space. That is a challenge for the ongoing discussion of the topic. Politics also played a major role in command styles and choices, and in military patronage. This was abundantly clear in the American Civil War, notably so for the Union side, with McClellan, George Meade, and some other Democratic commanders backing limited-war strategies that differed from Lincoln's Republican emphasis on a more uncompromising conflict aimed at the clear defeat of the Confederacy.[13] This contrast was also linked to (although not completely coincident with) differences in military theory at the time of the Civil War, with the limited-war figures regarded as generals of "intellect" and their rivals as generals of "genius."[14]

To return to the point made in the preface about history being a movable feast, the past, present, and future exist on, and in, a continuum. Yet the present is an illusion as we move from the past toward the future. The present cannot exist but for an infinitesimal moment because it always tends toward zero. Mostly, what is termed the present is, in fact, the very recent past. The past begins a picosecond after now (whenever now is). Hence, the term *the present* refers to an indistinct time span: of the past as of the present. As a result, the sole data set for the future, including what will briefly become the present, is the past, and it is that which we must scrutinize.

Notes

1. INTRODUCTION

1. Mark Grimsley, "The American Military History Master Narrative: Three Textbooks on the American Military Experience," *JMH* 79 (2015): 800.

2. John Nagl, "Let's Win the Wars We're In," *Joint Force Quarterly* 52 (2009); Giuseppe Caforio, "Italian Empirical Research on Asymmetric Warfare: Data from Soldiers Experiences," *Rivista di Studi Militari* 2 (2013): 189–203.

3. David Fitzgerald, *Learning to Forget: U.S. Army Counterinsurgency Doctrine and Practice from Vietnam to Iraq* (Stanford, CA: Stanford University Press, 2013).

4. Thomas Huber, ed., *Compound Warfare: That Fatal Knot* (Fort Leavenworth, KS: US Army Command and General Staff College Press, 2002); Williamson Murray and Peter Mansoor, eds., *Hybrid Warfare: Fighting Complex Opponents from the Ancient World to the Present* (Cambridge: Cambridge University Press, 2012); Ethan Rafuse, "'Little Phil,' a 'Bad Old Man,' and the 'Gray Ghost': Hybrid Warfare and the Fight for the Shenandoah Valley, August–November 1864," *JMH* 81 (2017): 775–801.

5. Steven Morewood, *The British Defence of Egypt, 1935–1940* (London: Frank Cass, 2005); Mark Stoler, "George C. Marshall and the 'Europe-First' Strategy, 1939–1951: A Study in Diplomatic as well as Military History," *JMH* 79 (2015): 293–316.

6. *The National Defense Program: Unification and Strategy: Hearings before the U.S. House of Representatives Committee on the Armed Services*, 81st Cong., 1st Sess., October 1949 (Washington, DC: US Government Printing Office, 1949), 521.

7. Jeremy Black, *Combined Operations: A Global History of Amphibious and Airborne Warfare* (Lanham, MD: Rowman and Littlefield, 2018).

2. A NEW AGE OF WAR? 1860–80

1. For a pro-Southern view, see Frederic Trautmann, ed., *A Prussian Observes the American Civil War: Military Studies of Justus Scheibert* (Columbia: University of Missouri Press, 2001).

2. W. J. Hail, *Tsêng Kuo-Fan and the Taiping Rebellion* (New Haven, CT: Yale University Press, 1927), 125.

3. Prosper Giquel, *A Journal of the Chinese Civil War*, ed. Steven Leibo (Honolulu: University of Hawaii Press, 1985).

4. Edward Longacre, *The Early Morning of War: Bull Run, 1861* (Norman: University of Oklahoma Press, 2014).

5. Donald Stoker, *The Grand Design: Strategy and the U.S. Civil War* (Oxford: Oxford University Press, 2010); Daniel Canfield, "Opportunity Lost: Combined Operations and the Development of Union Military Strategy, April 1861–April 1862," *JMH* 79 (2015): 686–87.

6. Gary Joiner, *Through the Howling Wilderness: The 1864 Red River Campaign and Union Failure in the West* (Knoxville: University of Tennessee Press, 2006).

7. Timothy Smith, *Rethinking Shiloh: Myth and Memory* (Knoxville: University of Tennessee Press, 2013).

8. Lawrence Kreiser, *Defeating Lee: A History of the Second Corps, Army of the Potomac* (Bloomington: Indiana University Press, 2012).

9. Gary Ecelbarger, *Slaughter at the Chapel: The Battle of Ezra Church, 1864* (Norman: University of Oklahoma Press, 2016).

10. Jennifer Weber, *Copperheads: The Rise and Fall of Lincoln's Opponents in the North* (New York: Oxford University Press, 2006).

11. Michael Ballard, *Grant at Vicksburg: The General and the Siege* (Carbondale: Southern Illinois Press, 2013).

12. D. H. Dilbeck, *A More Civil War: How the Union Waged a Just War* (Chapel Hill: University of North Carolina Press, 2016); Bradley Clampitt, *Occupied Vicksburg* (Baton Rouge: Louisiana State University Press, 2016).

13. Mark Grimsley, *The Hard Hand of War: Union Military Policy toward Southern Civilians, 1861–1865* (Cambridge: Cambridge University Press, 1995).

14. Williamson Murray and Wayne Hsieh, *A Savage War: A Military History of the Civil War* (Princeton, NJ: Princeton University Press, 2016).

15. Earl J. Hess, *The Union Soldier in Battle: Enduring the Ordeal of Combat* (Lawrence: University Press of Kansas, 1997).

16. Peter Scarlett, British envoy in Mexico, to John Earl Russell, Foreign Secretary, May 10, June 9, 1865, NA. FO. 50/386, fols. 186, 209; Alfred Jackson Hanna and Kathryn Abbey Hanna, *Napoleon III and Mexico: American Triumph over Monarchy* (Chapel Hill: University of North Carolina Press, 1971).

17. Richard Bassett, *For God and Kaiser: The Imperial Austrian Army* (New Haven, CT: Yale University Press, 2015).

18. John Merriman, *Massacre: The Life and Death of the Paris Commune of 1871* (New Haven, CT: Yale University Press, 2014), 249–52.

19. Dennis Showalter, *The Wars of German Unification* (New York: Bloomsbury, 2015).

20. J. P. Clark, *Preparing for War: The Emergence of the Modern U.S. Army, 1815–1917* (Cambridge, MA: Harvard University Press).

21. John Laband, *Zulu Warriors: The Battle for the South African Frontier* (New Haven, CT: Yale University Press, 2014).

22. Brian Robson, *The Road to Kabul: The Second Afghan War, 1878–81* (London: Arms and Armour, 1986).

23. Douglas Richmond, *Conflict and Carnage in Yucatán: Liberals, the Second Empire and Maya Revolutionaries, 1856–1876* (Tuscaloosa: University of Alabama Press, 2015).

24. Pekka Hämäläinen, *The Comanche Empire* (New Haven, CT: Yale University Press, 2008).

25. David J. Silverman, *Thundersticks: Firearms and the Violent Transformation of Native America* (Cambridge, MA: Belknap Press, 2016).

26. Adam Smith, *An Inquiry into the Nature and Causes of the Wealth of Nations* (Oxford: Oxford University Press, 1976), 691–92.

27. Debra Buchholtz, *The Battle of the Greasy Grass/Little Bighorn: Custer's Last Stand in Memory, History, and Popular Culture* (New York: Routledge, 2012).

3. DIFFERENT TYPES OF CONFLICT, 1880–1913

1. Dominic Green, *Three Empires on the Nile: The Victorian Jihad, 1809–1899* (New York: Free Press, 2007).

2. D. Colin Jaundrill, *Samurai to Soldier: Remaking Military Service in Nineteenth-Century Japan* (Ithaca, NY: Cornell University Press, 2016).

3. Sally Paine, *The Sino-Japanese War of 1894–1895: Perceptions, Power, and Primacy* (Cambridge: Cambridge University Press, 2003).

4. Jerry Cooper, *The Rise of the National Guard: The Evolution of the American Militia, 1865–1920* (Lincoln: University of Nebraska Press, 1997).

5. Brian Linn, *The Philippine War, 1899–1902* (Lawrence: University Press of Kansas, 2000).

6. Tim Moreman, *The Army in India and the Development of Frontier Warfare, 1849–1947* (London: Palgrave, 1998), 68–71.

7. Sally Paine, *The Japanese Empire: Grand Strategy from the Meiji Restoration to the Pacific War* (Cambridge: Cambridge University Press, 2017).

8. Michael Welch, "The Centenary of the British Publication of Jean de Bloch's *Is War Now Impossible?* (1899–1999)," *War in History* 7 (2000): 281.

9. David Morgan-Owen, *The Fear of Invasion: Strategy, Politics, and British War Planning, 1880–1914* (Oxford: Oxford University Press, 2017), 45.

10. NA. WO. 32/2816, p. 43.

11. Nicholas Murray, *The Rocky Road to the Great War: The Evolution of Trench Warfare to 1914* (Washington, DC: Potomac Books, 2013).

12. Dominik Geppert, William Mulligan, and Andreas Rose, eds., *The Wars before the Great War: Conflict and International Politics before the Outbreak of the First World War* (Cambridge: Cambridge University Press, 2015).

13. Ryan Gingeras, *Fall of the Sultanate: The Great War and the End of the Ottoman Empire, 1908–1922* (Oxford: Oxford University Press, 2016).

14. Antulio J. Echevarria II, "The 'Cult of the Offensive' Revisited: Confronting Technological Change before the Great War," *Journal of Strategic Studies* 25 (2002): 199–214, esp. 209–10.

4. THE FIRST WORLD WAR, 1914–18

1. Alan McPherson, *A Short History of U.S. Interventions in Latin America and the Caribbean* (Hoboken, NJ: Wiley-Blackwell, 2016).
2. Alan Knight, *The Mexican Revolution*, 2 vols. (Cambridge: Cambridge University Press, 1986).
3. Christopher Clark, *The Sleepwalkers: How Europe Went to War in 1914* (London: Allen Lane, 2012).
4. Lawrence Sondhaus, *Franz Conrad von Hötzendorf: Architect of the Apocalypse* (Boston, MA: Humanities Press, 2000).
5. Thomas Otte, *July Crisis: The World's Descent into War, Summer 1914* (Cambridge: Cambridge University Press, 2014).
6. Gordon Martel, *The Month That Changed the World, July 1914* (Oxford: Oxford University Press, 2014), 428.
7. Dominic Lieven, *Towards the Flame: Empire, War and the End of Tsarist Russia* (London: Allen Lane, 2015).
8. Hans Ehlert, Michael Epkenhans, and Gerhard Gross, eds., *The Schlieffen Plan: International Perspectives on the German Strategy for World War I* (Lexington: University Press of Kentucky, 2014).
9. James Lyon, *Serbia and the Balkan Front, 1914: The Outbreak of the Great War* (London: Bloomsbury, 2015).
10. Frank Buchholz, Janet Robinson, and Joe Robinson, *The Great War Dawning: Germany and Its Army at the Start of World War I* (Vienna: Verlag Militaria, 2013).
11. William Astore, "Loving the German War Machine: America's Infatuation and *Blitzkrieg*, Warfighters, and Militarism," in *Arms and the Man*, ed. Michael Neiberg (Leiden: Brill, 2011), 5–30.
12. "Great War Stories," *RUSI* 162, no. 3 (June–July 2017): 7.
13. Keith Jeffery, *1916: A Global History* (London: Bloomsbury, 2016).
14. Nick Lloyd, "'With Faith and Without Fear': Sir Douglas Haig's Command of First Army during 1915," *JMH* 71 (2007): 1068–76.
15. Robert Foley, *German Strategy and the Path to Verdun: Erich von Falkenhayn and the Development of Attrition, 1870–1916* (Cambridge: Cambridge University Press, 2005).
16. Hew Strachan, "The Battle of the Somme and British Strategy," *Journal of Strategic Studies* 21 (1998): 79.
17. Mark Grotelueschen, *The AEF Way of War: The American Army and Combat in World War I* (New York: Cambridge University Press, 2007); Richard Faulkner, *The School of Hard Knocks: Combat Leadership in the American Expeditionary Forces* (College Station: Texas A and M University Press, 2012); David Woodward, *The American Army and the First World War* (Cambridge: Cambridge University Press, 2014).
18. Nicholas Hall, "The French 75 mm Modèle 1897 Field Gun," *Arms and Armour* 12, no. 1 (April 2015): 4–21.
19. George Cassar, *Trial by Gas: The British Army at the Second Battle of Ypres* (Lincoln, NE: Potomac Books, 2014); Jean Pascal Zanders, ed., *Innocence Slaughtered: Gas and the Transformation of Warfare and Society* (London: Uniform Press, 2016).
20. Roger Lee, *British Battle Planning in 1916 and the Battle of Fromelles: A Case Study of Evolving Skill* (Farnham: Ashgate, 2015).
21. Sidney Rogerson, *Twelve Days on the Somme: A Memoir of the Trenches, 1916* (London: Greenhill Books, 2006).

22. Jonathan Krause, *Early Trench Tactics in the French Army: The Second Battle of Artois, May–June 1915* (Farnham: Ashgate, 2013).

23. Elizabeth Greenhalgh, *The French Army and the First World War* (Cambridge: Cambridge University Press, 2014).

24. May 30, 1915, AWM. 3DL/2316, 1/1, p. 72.

25. Nick Lloyd, *Passchendaele: The Lost Victory of World War I* (New York: Basic Books, 2017).

26. Richard DiNardo, *Invasion: The Conquest of Serbia, 1915* (Santa Barbara, CA: Praeger, 2015).

27. Michael Barrett, *Prelude to Blitzkrieg: The 1916 Austro-German Campaign in Romania* (Bloomington: Indiana University Press, 2013).

28. Geoffrey Wawro, *A Mad Catastrophe: The Outbreak of World War I and the Collapse of the Habsburg Empire* (New York: Basic Books, 2014).

29. Graydon Tunstall, *Written in Blood: The Battles for Fortress Przemyśl in WWE* (Bloomington: Indiana University Press, 2016), 301, 333.

30. Mark Thompson, *The White War: Life and Death on the Italian Front, 1915–1919* (London: Faber and Faber, 2008).

31. Neil Faulkner, *Lawrence of Arabia's War: The Arabs, the British, and the Remaking of the Middle East in WWI* (New Haven, CT: Yale University Press, 2010).

32. Edward Erickson, *Palestine: The Ottoman Campaigns of 1914–1918* (Barnsley: Pen and Sword, 2016); Metin Gürcan and Robert Johnson, eds., *The Gallipoli Campaign: The Turkish Perspective* (Farnham: Ashgate, 2016).

33. Kristian Coates Ulrichsen, *The First World War in the Middle East* (London: Hurst, 2014); T. G. Fraser, ed., *The First World War and Its Aftermath: The Shaping of the Middle East* (Chicago, IL: University of Chicago Press, 2015); Rob Johnson, *The Great War and the Middle East* (Oxford: Oxford University Press, 2016).

34. Bruce Gudmundsson, *Stormtroop Tactics: Innovation in the German Army, 1914–1918* (New York: Praeger, 1989); Martin Samuels, *Command or Control? Command, Training, and Tactics in the British and German Armies, 1888–1918* (London: Frank Cass, 1995).

35. David Zabecki, *The German 1918 Offensives: A Case Study in the Operational Level of War* (New York: Routledge, 2006).

36. Tim Cook, *Vimy: The Battle and the Legend* (London: Allen Lane, 2017), 67.

37. David Aubin and Catherine Goldstein, eds., *The War of Guns and Mathematics: Mathematical Practices and Communities in France and Its Western Allies around World War I* (Providence, RI: American Mathematical Society, 2014).

38. Paddy Griffith, ed., *British Fighting Methods in the Great War* (London: Frank Cass, 1996); Jonathan Boff, *Winning and Losing on the Western Front: The British Third Army and the Defeat of Germany in 1918* (Cambridge: Cambridge University Press, 2012).

39. Jean Bou, ed., *The AIF in Battle: How the Australian Imperial Force Fought, 1914–1918* (Melbourne: Melbourne University Publishing, 2016).

40. Alexander Nordlund, "'Done My Bit': British Soldiers, the 1918 Armistice, and Understanding the First World War," *JMH* 81 (2017): 425–46.

41. "Characteristics and Tactics of the Mark V, Mark V One Star and Medium 'A' Tanks," June 27, 1918, AWM. 3 DRL 6643, 5/27, p. 1–3.

42. Tim Gale, *The French Army's Tank Force in the Great War: The "Artillerie Spéciale"* (Farnham: Ashgate, 2013).

43. Stephen Biddle, *Military Power: Explaining Victory and Defeat in Modern Battle* (Princeton, NJ: Princeton University Press, 2004).

44. Robert Stevenson, *To Win the Battle: The 1st Australian Division in the Great War, 1914–1918* (Cambridge: Cambridge University Press, 2013).

45. Mark Monmonier, *Rhumb Lines and Map Wars: A Social History of the Mercator Projection* (Chicago, IL: University of Chicago Press, 2004).

46. Exeter, Devon Record Office, 5277M/F3/29.

47. *Daily Telegraph*, July 25, 1917.

48. Corey Reigel, *The Last Great Safari: East Africa in World War I* (Lanham, MD: Rowman and Littlefield, 2015).

49. Edward Gutiérrez, *Doughboys on the Great War: How American Soldiers Viewed Their Military Experience* (Lawrence: University of Kansas Press, 2014).

50. Joshua Sanborn, *Imperial Apocalypse: The Great War and the Destruction of the Russian Empire* (Oxford: Oxford University Press, 2014).

5. BETWEEN THE WARS, 1918–39

1. Robert Citino, *The Path to Blitzkrieg: Doctrine and Training in the German Army, 1920–1939* (Boulder, CO: Lynne Rienner, 1999).

2. Thomas Faith, *Behind the Gas Mask: The U.S. Chemical Warfare Service in Peace and War* (Urbana: University of Illinois Press, 2014).

3. LH., Liddell Hart papers, 7/1920/167.

4. Peter Whitewood, *The Red Army and the Great Terror: Stalin's Purge of the Soviet Military* (Lawrence: University Press of Kansas, 2015).

5. Roger Reese, *Stalin's Reluctant Soldiers: A Social History of the Red Army, 1925–1941* (Lawrence: University Press of Kansas, 1996).

6. Laura Engelstein, *Russia in Flames: War, Revolution, Civil War, 1914–1921* (Oxford: Oxford University Press, 2017).

7. A. G. Park, *Bolshevism in Turkestan, 1917–1927* (New York: Columbia University Press, 1957).

8. Jonathan Smele, *The "Russian" Civil Wars, 1916–1926: Ten Years That Shook the World* (New York: Oxford University Press, 2015); focusing on 1928–32: Lynne Viola, *Peasant Rebels under Stalin: Collectivisation and the Culture of Peasant Resistance* (Oxford: Oxford University Press, 1996).

9. Michael Malet, *Nestor Makhno in the Russian Civil War* (London: Palgrave, 1982).

10. Robert Gerwarth and John Horne, eds., *War in Peace: Paramilitary Violence in Europe after the Great War* (Oxford: Oxford University Press, 2013).

11. Michael Neiberg, *The Treaty of Versailles: A Concise History* (New York: Oxford University Press, 2017), 9–10.

12. Robert Gerwarth, *The Vanquished: Why the First World War Failed to End, 1917–1923* (London: Allen Lane, 2016); Jochen Böhler, Włodimierz Borodziej, and Joachim von Puttkamer, eds., *Legacies of Violence: Eastern Europe's First War* (Munich: Oldenbourg, 2014).

13. Matthew Butler, *Popular Piety and Political Identity in Mexico's Cristero Rebellion: Michoacán, 1927–1929* (Oxford: Oxford University Press, 2004).

14. Nick Lloyd, "Colonial Counter-insurgency in Southern India: The Malabar Rebellion, 1921–1922," *Contemporary British History* 29 (2015): 297–317.

15. Michael Russ, "The Marine Air-Ground Task Force in Nicaragua, 1927–33: A Campaign against Sandino's Counterinsurgency," *Marine Corps History* 2 (2016): 55–64.

16. Peter Lieb, "Suppressing Insurgencies in Comparison: The Germans in the Ukraine, 1918, and the British in Mesopotamia, 1920," *Small Wars and Insurgencies* 23 (2012): 627–47.

17. Brian Robson, *Crisis on the Frontier: The Third Afghan War and the Campaign in Waziristan, 1919–20* (Staplehurst: Spellmount, 2004).

18. Gyanesh Kudaisya, "'In Aid of Civil Power': The Colonial Army in Northern India, c. 1919–42," *Journal of Imperial and Commonwealth History* 32 (2004): 41–68.

19. Adam Zamoyski, *Warsaw 1920: Lenin's Failed Conquest of Europe* (London: Harper Press, 2008).

20. Leon Poullada, "Political Modernisation in Afghanistan: The Amanullah Reforms," in *Afghanistan: Some New Approaches*, ed. G. Grassmack and L. W. Adamec, 97–129 (Ann Arbor: Center for Near Eastern and North African Studies, University of Michigan, 1969); Rhea Stewart, *Fire in Afghanistan, 1914–1929: Faith, Hope and the British Empire* (New York: Doubleday, 1973).

21. Amin Banani, *The Modernization of Iran, 1921–1941* (Stanford, CA: Stanford University Press, 1961).

22. Peter Hart, *The IRA and Its Enemies: Violence and Community in Cork, 1916–1923* (Oxford: Oxford University Press, 1998).

23. William Sheehan, *A Hard Local War: The British Army and the Guerrilla War in Cork, 1919–1921* (Staplehurst: Spellmount, 2011).

24. Gerry White, "Free State *versus* Republic: The Opposing Armed Forces in the Civil War," in *Atlas of the Irish Revolution*, ed. John Crowley, Donal Ó Drisceoil, and Mike Murphy (Cork: Cork University Press, 2017), 692.

25. Arthur Waldron, "The Warlord: Twentieth Century Chinese Understandings of Violence, Militarism, and Imperialism," *American Historical Review* 96 (1991): 1073–110.

26. Arthur Waldron, *From War to Nationalism: China's Turning Point, 1924–1925* (Cambridge: Cambridge University Press, 1995).

27. Donald Jordan, *The Northern Expedition: China's National Revolution of 1926–1928* (Honolulu: University of Hawaii Press, 1976).

28. Peter Worthing, "Continuity and Change: Chinese Nationalist Army Tactics, 1925–1938," *JMH* 78 (2014): 995–1016.

29. Peter Harmsen, *Shanghai 1937: Stalingrad on the Yangtze* (Havertown, PA: Casemate, 2013).

30. Hans van de Ven, *War and Nationalism in China, 1925–1945* (London: Routledge, 2003), and *The Battle for China: Essays on the Military History of the Sino-Japanese War of 1937–1945* (Stanford, CA: Stanford University Press, 2011); Rana Mitter, *China's War with Japan, 1937–1945: The Struggle for Survival* (London: Penguin, 2013).

31. José Alvarez, "Tank Warfare during the Rif Rebellion," *Armor* 106, no. 1 (January–February 1997): 26–28.

32. LH., Montgomery-Massingberd papers, 10/6.

33. David Edgerton, *England and the Aeroplane: Militarism, Modernity and Machines* (London: Penguin, 2013).

34. NA. WO. 33/1512, p. 3.

35. David Stone, "Tukhachevsky in Leningrad: Military Politics and Exile, 1928–31," *Europe-Asia Studies* 48 (1996): 1382.

36. Joe Maiolo, *Cry Havoc: The Arms Race and the Second World War, 1931–1941* (London: John Murray, 2010).

37. Michael Alpert, "The Clash of Spanish Armies: Contrasting Ways of War in Spain, 1936–1939," *War in History* 6 (1999): 349–50.

38. Martin Alexander, *The Republic in Danger: General Maurice Gamelin and the Politics of French Defence, 1933–1940* (Cambridge: Cambridge University Press, 1992).

39. David Zook, *The Conduct of the Chaco War* (New York: Bookman Associates, 1960); Paul Robinson, "Forgotten Victors: White Russian Officers in Paraguay during the Chaco War, 1932–35," *Journal of Slavic Military Studies* 12 (1999): 178–85.

40. Helen Graham, ed., *Interrogating Francoism: History and Dictatorship in Twentieth-Century Spain* (London: Bloomsbury, 2016).

41. Michael Alpert, *The Republican Army in the Spanish Civil War, 1936–1939* (Cambridge: Cambridge University Press, 2013).

6. THE SECOND WORLD WAR, 1939–45

1. NA. PREM 3/328/5, pp. 23–26.

2. John Kiszely, *Anatomy of a Campaign: The British Fiasco in Norway, 1940* (Cambridge: Cambridge University Press, 2017), 293.

3. William Bartsch, *Victory Fever on Guadalcanal: Japan's First Land Defeat of WWII* (College Station: Texas A and M University Press, 2014).

4. Alfred Rieber, *Stalin and the Struggle for Supremacy in Eurasia* (New York: Cambridge University Press, 2015).

5. Jeffrey Gunsburg, "*La Grande Illusion*: Belgian and Dutch Strategy Facing Germany, 1919–May 1940," *JMH* 78 (2014): 668–69.

6. BL. Add. 49699, fols. 53–55.

7. General Staff Report, "The Military Situation in Russia," NA. CAB. 24/84, fol. 285.

8. Glen Jeansonne and David Luhrssen, *War on the Silver Screen: Shaping America's Perception of History* (Lincoln: University of Nebraska Press, 2014).

9. James Corum, "Myths of *Blitzkrieg*," *Historically Speaking* 6 (2005): 11–13.

10. Larry Addington, *The Blitzkrieg Era and the German General Staff, 1865–1941* (New Brunswick, NJ: Rutgers University Press, 1971), xi, 216–17.

11. Andrew Stewart, *The First Victory: The Second World War and the East Africa Campaign* (New Haven, CT: Yale University Press, 2016).

12. Simon Anglim, *Orde Wingate and the British Army, 1922–1944* (London: Pickering and Chatto, 2010).

13. John Gooch, *Mussolini and His Generals: The Italian Armed Forces and Fascist Foreign Policy, 1922–1940* (Cambridge: Cambridge University Press, 2007).

14. Craig Stockings and Eleanor Hancock, *Swastika over the Acropolis: Re-interpreting the Nazi Invasion of Greece in World War II* (Brill: Leiden, 2013); David Horner, "Britain and the Campaigns in Greece and Crete in 1941," *Proceedings of the NIDS International Forum on War History*, 2014, 40–41.

15. Callum MacDonald, *The Lost Battle: Crete 1941* (New York: Free Press, 1993).

16. Roger Reese, "Lessons of the Winter War: A Study in the Military Effectiveness of the Red Army," *JMH* 72 (2008): 825–52.

17. David Stahel, *Operation Barbarossa and Germany's Defeat in the East* (Cambridge: Cambridge University Press, 2009).

18. David Stahel, *Kiev 1941: Hitler's Battle for Supremacy in the East* (Cambridge: Cambridge University Press, 2012).

19. David Stahel, *Operation Typhoon: Hitler's March on Moscow, October 1941* (Cambridge: Cambridge University Press, 2013).

20. David Stahel, *The Battle for Moscow* (Cambridge: Cambridge University Press, 2015).

21. Evan Mawdsley, *Thunder in the East: The Nazi-Soviet War 1941–1945*, 2nd ed. (New York: Bloomsbury Academic, 2016).

22. John A. English, *Marching Through Chaos: The Descent of Armies in Theory and Practice* (Westport, CT: Praeger, 1996), 105.

23. Christian Hartmann, *Operation Barbarossa: Nazi Germany's War in the East, 1941–1945* (Oxford: Oxford University Press, 2013).

24. Vincent O'Hara, *Torch: North Africa and the Allied Path to Victory* (Annapolis, MD: Naval Institute Press, 2015).

25. Mungo Melvin, *Manstein: Hitler's Greatest General* (London: Weidenfeld and Nicolson, 2010).

26. Steven Newton, ed., *Kursk: The German View* (Boston, MA: Da Capo Press, 2002).

27. Noburo Tajima, "The Japanese Perspective on Germany's War," *Proceedings of the NIDS International Forum on War History*, 2011, 62–63.

28. Raymond Callahan, *Triumph at Imphal-Kohima: How the Indian Army Finally Stopped the Japanese Juggernaut* (Lawrence: University Press of Kansas, 2017): 126–27.

29. Andrew Holborn, *The D-Day Landing on Gold Beach* (London: Bloomsbury, 2015).

30. Penney to Major General Sinclair, Director of Military Intelligence, War Office, May 2, 1945, LH., Penney papers, 5/1.

31. Russell Hart, *Clash of Arms: How the Allies Won in Normandy* (Boulder, CO: Lynne Rienner, 2001); John Buckley, ed., *The Normandy Campaign 1944: Sixty Years On* (London: Routledge, 2006).

32. Walter Dunn, *Stalin's Keys to Victory: The Rebirth of the Red Army* (Westport, CT: Praeger, 2006).

33. Shimon Naveh, *In Pursuit of Military Excellence: The Evolution of Operational Theory* (London: Frank Cass, 1997).

34. Bastiaan Willems, "Defiant Breakwaters or Desperate Blunders? A Revision of the German Late-War Fortress Strategy," *Journal of Slavic Military Studies* 28 (2015): 353–78.

35. David Glantz, *Red Storm over the Balkans: The Failed Soviet Invasion of Romania, Spring 1944* (Lawrence: University Press of Kansas, 2007).

36. Manchester, John Rylands Library, Special Collections, GOW 1/2/2/2, pp. 33, 54; 1/2/1, p. 6.

37. O'Connor to Major General Allan Adair, July 24, 1944, LH., O'Connor papers, 5/3/22.

38. John Buckley, *Monty's Men: The British Army and the Liberation of Europe* (New Haven, CT: Yale University Press, 2013).

39. A. D. Harvey, "The Bayonet on the Battlefield," *RUSI* 150, no. 2 (April 2005): 62–63.

40. LH., Alanbrooke papers, 6/2/37.

41. Douglas Nash, *Victory Was beyond Their Grasp: With the 272nd Volks-Grenadier Division from the Hürtgen Forest to the Heart of the Reich* (Bedford, PA: Casemate, 2008).

42. Peter Schrijvers, *Those Who Hold Bastogne: The True Story of the Soldiers and Civilians Who Fought in the Biggest Battle of the Bulge* (New Haven, CT: Yale University Press, 2014).

43. Ben Shepherd, *Hitler's Soldiers: The German Army in the Third Reich* (New Haven, CT: Yale University Press, 2016).

44. Jeremy Crang, "The British Soldier on the Home Front: Army Morale Reports, 1940–45," in *Time to Kill: The Soldier's Experience of War in the West, 1939–1945*, ed. Paul Addison and Angus Calder (London: Pimlico, 1997), 74.

45. Rick Atkinson, "Projecting American Power in the Second World War," *JMH* 80 (2016): 349.

46. Peter Caddick-Adams, *Show and Steel: The Battle of the Bulge, 1944–45* (Oxford: Oxford University Press, 2017), 527.

47. Russell Weigley, *History of the United States Army* (New York: Macmillan, 1967), 467–69.

48. O'Connor to Major General Sir Percy Hobart, August 24, 1944, LH., O'Connor papers, 5/3/41.

49. J. M. Vernet, "The Army of the Armistice 1940–1942: A Small Army for a Great Revenge," in *Proceedings of the 1982 International Military History Symposium: The Impact of Unsuccessful Military Campaigns on Military Institutions, 1860–1980*, ed. Charles R. Shrader (Washington, DC: US Army Center of Military History, 1984), 241–42, 246–47.

50. Mark Wilson, *Destructive Creation: American Business and the Winning of World War II* (Philadelphia: University of Pennsylvania Press, 2016).

51. Douglas Nash, "Army Boots on Volcanic Sands: The 147th Infantry Regiment at Iwo Jima," *Army History* 105 (Fall 2017): 10.

52. Hugh Rockoff, *America's Economic Way of War: War and the US Economy from the Spanish-American War to the Persian Gulf War* (Cambridge: Cambridge University Press, 2012).

53. Stephen Hart, *Montgomery and "Colossal Cracks": The 21st Army Group in Northwest Europe, 1944–45* (Westport, CT: Praeger, 2000); John Buckley, *Monty's Men: The British Army and the Liberation of Europe* (New Haven, CT: Yale University Press, 2013).

54. Charles Forrester, "Field Marshal Montgomery's Role in the Creation of the British 21st Army Group's Combined Arms Doctrine for the Final Assault on Germany," *JMH* 78 (2014): 1319–20.

55. See, impressively, Isaak Kobylyanskiy, *From Stalingrad to Pillau: A Red Army Artillery Officer Remembers the Great Patriotic War* (Lawrence: University Press of Kansas, 2014).

56. H. Nelson, "Kokada: And Two National Histories," *Journal of Pacific History* 42 (2007).

57. AWM. 3 DRL/6643 3/9, p. 1.

7. THE COLD WAR, 1945–71

1. Ted Hopf, *Reconstituting the Cold War: The Early Years, 1945–1958* (New York: Oxford University Press, 2012).

2. Peter Worthing, *General He Yingqin: The Rise and Fall of Nationalist China* (Cambridge: Cambridge University Press, 2016).

3. Kevin Peraino, *A Force So Swift: Mao, Truman and the Birth of Modern China, 1949* (New York: Crown, 2017).

4. Harold Tanner, *The Battle for Manchuria and the Fate of China: Siping, 1946* (Bloomington: Indiana University Press, 2013), and *Where Chiang Kai-shek Lost China: The Liao-Shen Campaign, 1948* (Bloomington: Indiana University Press, 2015); Odd Westad, *Decisive Encounters: The Chinese Civil War, 1946–1949* (Stanford, CA: Stanford University Press, 2003).

5. Allan Millett, *The War for Korea, 1945–1950* (Lawrence: University of Kansas Press, 2005).

6. Stephen Taaffe, *MacArthur's Korean War Generals* (Lawrence: University Press of Kansas, 2016).

7. Xiaobing Li, *China's Battle for Korea: The 1951 Spring Offensive* (Bloomington: Indiana University Press, 2014).

8. Seth Johnston, *How NATO Adapts: Strategy and Organisation in the Atlantic Alliance since 1950* (Baltimore, MD: Johns Hopkins University Press, 2017).

9. Donald Alan Carter, "Eisenhower versus the Generals," *JMH* 71 (2017): 1169–99.

10. Martin Windrow, *The Last Valley: Dien Bien Phu and the French Defeat in Vietnam* (London: Weidenfeld and Nicolson, 2004). For an important corrective to the established emphasis on Viet Minh artillery, see Kevin Boylan, "No 'Technical Knockout': Giap's Artillery at Dien Bien Phu," *JMH* 78 (2014): 1349–83.

11. Aragorn Miller, *Precarious Paths to Freedom: The US, Venezuela, and the Latin American Cold War* (Albuquerque: University Press of New Mexico, 2016).

12. Dennis Showalter, ed., *Forging the Shield: Eisenhower and National Security for the 21st Century* (Chicago: Imprint Publications, 2005).

13. Martin Thomas, *Fight or Flight: Britain, France, and Their Roads from Empire* (Oxford: Oxford University Press, 2014).

14. Gregory Daddis, "Mired in a Quagmire: Popular Interpretations of the Vietnam War," *Orbis* 57 (2013): 532–48.

15. Andrew Ross, *The Search for Tactical Success in Vietnam: An Analysis of Australian Task Force Combat Operations* (Cambridge: Cambridge University Press, 2015).

16. Gregory Daddis, "Out of Balance: Evaluating American Strategy in Vietnam, 1968–72," *War and Society* 32 (2013): 252–70.

17. Thomas Richardson, *Destroy and Build: Pacification in Phuoc Tuy, 1966–72* (Cambridge: Cambridge University Press, 2017), esp. 204–11; Kevin Boylan, *Losing Binh Dinh: The Failure of Pacification and Vietnamization, 1969–71* (Lawrence: University Press of Kansas, 2016).

18. James Willbanks, *The Battle of An Loc* (Bloomington: Indiana University Press, 2015).

19. Shuja Nawaz, *Crossed Swords: Pakistan, Its Army, and the Wars Within* (Oxford: Oxford University Press, 2008).

20. Tristan Moss, *Guarding the Periphery: The Australian Army in Papua New Guinea, 1951–75* (Cambridge: Cambridge University Press, 2017), 186.

21. Yezid Sayigh, *Armed Struggle and the Search for State: The Palestinian National Movement, 1949–1993* (Oxford: Oxford University Press, 1997).

22. Beatrice Heuser and Eitan Shamir, eds., *Insurgencies and Counterinsurgencies: National Styles and Strategic Cultures* (Cambridge: Cambridge University Press, 2016); Jeff Moore, *The Thai Way of Counterinsurgency* (Muir Analytics, 2014); Ehud Eilam, *Israel's Way of War: A Strategic and Operational Analysis, 1948–2014* (Jefferson, NC: McFarland, 2015).

23. Brian Linn, *Elvis's Army: Cold War GIs and the Atomic Battlefield* (Cambridge, MA: Harvard University Press, 2016).

8. THE COLD WAR, 1972–89

1. William Taylor, *Military Service and American Democracy: From World War II to the Iran and Afghanistan Wars* (Lawrence: University of Kansas Press, 2016).

2. Xiaoming Zhang, *Deng Xiaoping's Long War: The Military Conflict between China and Vietnam, 1979–1991* (Chapel Hill: University of North Carolina Press, 2015).

3. Geraint Hughes, "Demythologising Dhofar: British Policy, Military Strategy, and Counter-Insurgency in Oman, 1963–1976," *JMH* 79 (2015): 423–56.

4. J. L. Young, "The Heights of Ineptitude: The Syrian Army's Assault on the Golan Heights," *JMH* 74 (2010): 852–70.

5. Asaf Siniver, ed., *The October War: Politics, Diplomacy, Legacy* (London: Hurst, 2013).

6. Dan Strode and Rebecca Strode, "Diplomacy and Defense in Soviet National Security Policy," *International Security* 8, no. 2 (1983): 91–116.

7. Harold Winston, "Partnership and Tension: The Army and Air Force between Vietnam and Desert Shield," *Parameters*, Spring 1996, 100–19; Robert Doughty, *The Evolution of US Army Tactical Doctrine, 1946–76* (Fort Leavenworth, KS: Combat Studies Institute, 2001); Benjamin Jensen, *Forging the Sword: Doctrinal Change in the U.S. Army* (Stanford, CA: Stanford University Press, 2016).

8. Bernd Lemke, ed., *Periphery or Contact Zone? The NATO Flanks 1961 to 2013* (Freiburg: Rombach Verlag, 2015).

9. Fred Bridgland, *The War for Africa: Twelve Months That Transformed a Continent*, 2nd ed. (Havertown, PA: Casemate, 2017).

10. Ali Ahmad Jalai and Lester W. Grau, *Afghan Guerrilla Warfare: In the Words of the Mujahideen Fighters* (St. Paul, MN: MBI Publishing, 2001); Russian General Staff, *The Soviet-Afghan War: How a Superpower Fought and Lost*, trans. and ed. Lester W. Grau and Michael A. Gress (Lawrence: University Press of Kansas, 2002); Gregory Feifer, *The Great Gamble: The Soviet War in Afghanistan* (New York: HarperCollins, 2009); William Maley, *The Afghanistan Wars*, 2nd ed. (Basingstoke: Palgrave, 2009); Rodric Braithwaite, *Afghantsy: The Russians in Afghanistan, 1979–89* (Oxford: Oxford University Press, 2011); Gregory Fremont-Barnes, *The Soviet Afghan War, 1979–1989* (Oxford: Osprey, 2012).

11. Brynjar Lia, "The Islamist Uprising in Syria, 1976–82: The History and Legacy of a Failed Revolt," *British Journal of Middle Eastern Studies* 43 (2016): 541–59.

12. Pierre Razoux, *The Iran-Iraq War* (Cambridge, MA: Harvard University Press, 2015).

13. Thomas Walker and Christine Wade, *Nicaragua: Living in the Shadow of the Eagle*, 5th ed. (Boulder, CO: Westview, 2011), 40–54.

14. Holger Albrecht, "The Myth of Coup-Proofing: Risk and Instances of Military Coups d'État in the Middle East and North Africa, 1950–2013," *Armed Forces and Society* 41 (2015): 659–87.

9. AFTER THE COLD WAR, 1990–TODAY

1. Emil Souleimanov and Huseyn Aliyev, "Asymmetry of Values, Indigenous Forces, and Incumbent Success in Counterinsurgency: Evidence from Chechnya," *Journal of Strategic Studies* 38 (2015): 678–703.

2. Paul Robinson, "'Ready to Kill but Not to Die,' NATO Strategy in Kosovo," *International Journal*, Autumn 1999, 680.

3. Dan Lake, "The Limits of Coercive Airpower: NATO's 'Victory' in Kosovo Revisited," *International Security* 34 (2009): 83–112.

4. Mary Kaldor, *New and Old Wars: Organized Violence in a Globalized Era* (Cambridge: Polity, 2012).

5. Henry McDonald, *Gunsmoke and Mirrors: How Sinn Féin Dressed Up Defeat as Victory* (Dublin: Gill and MacMillan, 2008).

6. Beth Bailey and Richard Immerman, eds., *Understanding the U.S. Wars in Iraq and Afghanistan* (New York: New York University Press, 2015).

7. Francis Hoffman, "Strategic Assessment and Adaptation: Reassessing the Afghanistan Surge Decision," *Naval War College Review* 69, no. 3 (Summer 2016): 45–64; Theo Farrell, *Unwinnable: Britain's War in Afghanistan, 2001–2014* (London: Penguin, 2017).

8. David Hendrickson and Robert Tucker, "Revisions in Need of Revising: What Went Wrong in the Iraq War," *Survival* 47 (2005): 7–32, esp. 27.

9. Emma Sky, *The Unraveling: High Hopes and Missed Opportunities in Iraq* (New York: PublicAffairs, 2015); Nicholas Schlosser, *The Battle for Al-Qaim and the Campaign to Secure the Western Euphrates River Valley, September 2005–March 2006* (Washington, DC: United States Marine Corps, 2013), and *The Surge, 2007–2008* (Washington, DC: Center for Military History, 2017).

10. David Ucko, *The New Counterinsurgency Era* (Washington, DC: Georgetown University Press, 2009).

11. Jessica Stern and J. M. Berger, *ISIS: The State of Terror* (London: William Collins, 2015).

12. Dmitri Trenin, *What Is Russia Up To in the Middle East?* (Cambridge: Polity, 2017).

13. Rod Thornton, "The Russian Military's New 'Main Emphasis': Asymmetric Warfare," *RUSI* 162, no. 4 (August/September 2017): 18–28.

14. Igor Sutyagin with Justin Bronk, *Russia's New Ground Forces: Capabilities, Limitations and Implications for International Security* (London: RUSI, 2017).

15. Timothy Thomas, "Russia's Military Strategy and Ukraine: Indirect, Asymmetric- and Putin-Led," *Journal of Slavic Military Studies* 28 (2015): 445–61.

16. June Teufel Dreyer, *Middle Kingdom and Empire of the Rising Sun: Sino-Japanese Relations, Past and Present* (Oxford: Oxford University Press, 2016).

17. See also re Sierra Leone 1991–2002, Kieran Mitton, *Rebels in a Rotten State: Understanding Atrocity in Sierra Leone* (London: Hurst, 2015).

18. C. Varin and D. Abubakar, eds., *Violent Nonstate Actors in Africa: Terrorists, Rebels, and Warlords* (Basingstoke: Palgrave, 2017).

19. James Burk, ed., *How 9/11 Changed Our Ways of War* (Palo Alto, CA: Stanford University Press, 2013).

20. Nelida Fuccaro, ed., *Violence and the City in the Modern Middle East* (Stanford, CA: Stanford University Press, 2016).

21. *Financial Times*, October 10, 2017, 4.

22. "Civil Wars and Global Disorder: Threats and Opportunities," ed. Karl Eikenberry and Stephen Krasner, special issue of *Daedalus* 146, no. 4 (Fall 2017).

10. INTO THE FUTURE

1. Mark Joyce, "Mexico's Security Crisis and Implications for US Policy," *RUSI* 154, no. 1 (February 2009): 66–70.

2. Stuart Cohen, *Israel and Its Army: From Cohesion to Confusion* (London: Routledge, 2007).

3. Paul Cornish and Kingsley Donaldson, *2020: World of War* (London: Hodder and Stoughton, 2017).

4. Xiaobing Li, *A History of the Modern Chinese Army* (Lexington: University Press of Kentucky, 2007).

5. Lawrence Freedman, *The Future of War: A History* (London: Allen Lane, 2017).

6. Raphael Marcus, "Military Innovation and Tactical Adaptation in the Israel-Hizballah Conflict: The Institutionalization of Lesson-Learning in the IDF," *Journal of Strategic Studies* 38 (2015): 500–528.

11. CONCLUSIONS

1. William Westerman, *Soldiers and Gentlemen: Australian Battalion Commanders in the Great War, 1914–1918* (Cambridge: Cambridge University Press, 2017), 201.

2. See, for example, Thomas Walker and Christine Wade, *Nicaragua: Living in the Shadow of the Eagle*, 6th ed. (Boulder, CO: Westview, 2016).

3. Jonathan House, *Combined Arms Warfare in the Twentieth Century* (Lawrence: University Press of Kansas, 2001).

4. Andrew M. Roe, *Waging War in Waziristan: The British Struggle in the Land of Bin Laden, 1849–1947* (Lawrence: University Press of Kansas, 2010).

5. Christian Tripodi, *Edge of Empire: The British Political Officer and Tribal Administration on the North-West Frontier, 1877–1947* (Farnham: Ashgate, 2011).

6. Stephen Morillo and Michael Pavkovic, *What Is Military History?*, 3rd ed. (Cambridge: Polity, 2018).

7. Paul Addison and Angus Calder, eds., *Time to Kill: The Soldier's Experience of War in the West, 1939–1945* (London: Pimlico, 1997).

8. NA. WO. 30/40/14, fol. 90.

9. L. P. Devine, *The British Way of War in Northwest Europe, 1944–5: A Study of Two Infantry Divisions* (London: Bloomsbury, 2016).

10. Anon. preface to T. Huber, ed., *Compound Warfare: That Fatal Knot* (Fort Leavenworth, KS: Army Command and General Staff College Press, 2002), x.

11. Paul Miller, "Graveyard of Analogies: The Use and Abuse of History for the War in Afghanistan," *Journal of Strategic Studies* 39 (2016): 446–76.

12. http://www.haz.de/Nachrichten/Politik/Deutschland-Welt/Gauland-fordert-Stolz-auf-Weltkriegs-Leistungen, accessed September 29, 2017.

13. Allen Guelzo, *Gettysburg: The Last Invasion* (New York: Knopf, 2013).

14. Carol Reardon, *With a Sword in One Hand and Jomini in the Other: The Problem of Military Thought in the Civil War* (Chapel Hill: University of North Carolina Press, 2012).

Selected Further Reading

Addison, Paul, and Angus Calder, eds. *Time to Kill: The Soldier's Experience of War in the West, 1939–1945*. London: Pimlico, 1997.
Alexander, Martin. *The Republic in Danger: General Maurice Gamelin and the Politics of French Defence, 1933–1940*. Cambridge: Cambridge University Press, 1992.
Alpert, Michael. *The Republican Army in the Spanish Civil War, 1936–1939*. Cambridge: Cambridge University Press, 2013.
Anglim, Simon. *Orde Wingate and the British Army, 1922–1944*. London: Pickering and Chatto, 2010.
Aubin, David, and Catherine Goldstein, eds. *The War of Guns and Mathematics: Mathematical Practices and Communities in France and Its Western Allies around World War I*. Providence, RI: American Mathematical Society, 2014.
Bailey, Beth, and Richard Immerman, eds. *Understanding the U.S. Wars in Iraq and Afghanistan*. New York: New York University Press, 2015.
Ballard, Michael. *Grant at Vicksburg: The General and the Siege*. Carbondale: Southern Illinois Press, 2013.
Banani, Amin. *The Modernization of Iran, 1921–1941*. Stanford, CA: Stanford University Press, 1961.
Bartsch, William. *Victory Fever on Guadalcanal: Japan's First Land Defeat of WWII*. College Station: Texas A and M University Press, 2014.
Bassett, Richard. *For God and Kaiser: The Imperial Austrian Army*. New Haven, CT: Yale University Press, 2015.
Biddle, Stephen. *Military Power: Explaining Victory and Defeat in Modern Battle*. Princeton, NJ: Princeton University Press, 2004.
Black, Jeremy. *Insurgency and Counterinsurgency: A Global History*. Lanham, MD: Rowman and Littlefield, 2016.
———. *Combined Operations: A Global History of Amphibious and Airborne Warfare*. Lanham, MD: Rowman and Littlefield, 2018.
———. *Fortifications and Siegecraft: Defense and Attack through the Ages*. Lanham, MD: Rowman and Littlefield, 2018.
Boff, Jonathan. *Winning and Losing on the Western Front: The British Third Army and the Defeat of Germany in 1918*. Cambridge: Cambridge University Press, 2012.

Böhler, Jochen, Włodimierz Borodziej, and Joachim von Puttkamer, eds. *Legacies of Violence: Eastern Europe's First War*. Munich: Oldenbourg, 2014.
Bou, Jean, ed. *The AIF in Battle: How the Australian Imperial Force Fought, 1914–1918*. Melbourne: Melbourne University Publishing, 2016.
Boylan, Kevin. *Losing Binh Dinh: The Failure of Pacification and Vietnamization, 1969–71*. Lawrence: University Press of Kansas, 2016.
Braithwaite, Rodric. *Afghantsy: The Russians in Afghanistan, 1979–89*. Oxford: Oxford University Press, 2011.
Bridgland, Fred. *The War for Africa: Twelve Months That Transformed a Continent*. 2nd ed. Havertown, PA: Casemate, 2017.
Buchholtz, Debra. *The Battle of the Greasy Grass/Little Bighorn: Custer's Last Stand in Memory, History, and Popular Culture*. New York: Routledge, 2012.
Buchholz, Frank, Janet Robinson, and Joe Robinson. *The Great War Dawning: Germany and Its Army at the Start of World War I*. Vienna: Verlag Militaria, 2013.
Buckley, John, ed. *The Normandy Campaign 1944: Sixty Years On*. London: Routledge, 2006.
———. *Monty's Men: The British Army and the Liberation of Europe*. New Haven, CT: Yale University Press, 2013.
Burk, James, ed. *How 9/11 Changed Our Ways of War*. Palo Alto, CA: Stanford University Press, 2013.
Butler, Matthew. *Popular Piety and Political Identity in Mexico's Cristero Rebellion: Michoacán, 1927–1929*. Oxford: Oxford University Press, 2004.
Caddick-Adams, Peter. *Show and Steel: The Battle of the Bulge, 1944–45*. Oxford: Oxford University Press, 2017.
Callahan, Raymond. *Triumph at Imphal-Kohima: How the Indian Army Finally Stopped the Japanese Juggernaut*. Lawrence: University Press of Kansas, 2017.
Cassar, George. *Trial by Gas: The British Army at the Second Battle of Ypres*. Lincoln, NE: Potomac Books, 2014.
Chickering, Roger, Dennis Showalter, and Hans van de Ven, eds. *War and the Modern World*. Vol. 4 of *The Cambridge History of War*. Cambridge: Cambridge University Press, 2012.
Citino, Robert. *The Path to Blitzkrieg: Doctrine and Training in the German Army, 1920–1939*. Boulder, CO: Lynne Rienner, 1999.
Clampitt, Bradley. *Occupied Vicksburg*. Baton Rouge: Louisiana State University Press, 2016.
Clark, Christopher. *The Sleepwalkers: How Europe Went to War in 1914*. London: Allen Lane, 2012.
Clark, J. P. *Preparing for War: The Emergence of the Modern U.S. Army, 1815–1917*. Cambridge, MA: Harvard University Press.
Coates Ulrichsen, Kristian. *The First World War in the Middle East*. London: Hurst, 2014.
Cook, Tim. *Vimy: The Battle and the Legend*. London: Allen Lane, 2017.
Cooper, Jerry. *The Rise of the National Guard: The Evolution of the American Militia, 1865–1920*. Lincoln: University of Nebraska Press, 1997.
Cornish, Paul, and Kingsley Donaldson. *2020: World of War*. London: Hodder and Stoughton, 2017.
Devine, L. P. *The British Way of War in Northwest Europe, 1944–5: A Study of Two Infantry Divisions*. London: Bloomsbury, 2016.
Dilbeck, D. H. *A More Civil War: How the Union Waged a Just War*. Chapel Hill: University of North Carolina Press, 2016.
DiNardo, Richard. *Invasion: The Conquest of Serbia, 1915*. Santa Barbara, CA: Praeger, 2015.
Doughty, Robert. *The Evolution of US Army Tactical Doctrine, 1946–76*. Fort Leavenworth, KS: Combat Studies Institute, 2001.

Dreyer, June Teufel. *Middle Kingdom and Empire of the Rising Sun: Sino-Japanese Relations, Past and Present*. Oxford: Oxford University Press, 2016.

Ecelbarger, Gary. *Slaughter at the Chapel: The Battle of Ezra Church, 1864*. Norman: University of Oklahoma Press, 2016.

Edgerton, David. *England and the Aeroplane: Militarism, Modernity and Machines*. London: Penguin, 2013.

Ehlert, Hans, Michael Epkenhans, and Gerhard Gross, eds. *The Schlieffen Plan: International Perspectives on the German Strategy for World War I*. Lexington: University Press of Kentucky, 2014.

Eilam, Ehud. *Israel's Way of War: A Strategic and Operational Analysis, 1948–2014*. Jefferson, NC: McFarland, 2015.

Engelstein, Laura. *Russia in Flames: War, Revolution, Civil War, 1914–1921*. Oxford: Oxford University Press, 2017.

Erickson, Edward. *Palestine: The Ottoman Campaigns of 1914–1918*. Barnsley: Pen and Sword, 2016.

Faith, Thomas. *Behind the Gas Mask: The U.S. Chemical Warfare Service in Peace and War*. Urbana: University of Illinois Press, 2014.

Farrell, Theo. *Unwinnable: Britain's War in Afghanistan, 2001–2014*. London: Penguin, 2017.

Faulkner, Neil. *Lawrence of Arabia's War: The Arabs, the British, and the Remaking of the Middle East in WWI*. New Haven, CT: Yale University Press, 2010.

Faulkner, Richard. *The School of Hard Knocks: Combat Leadership in the American Expeditionary Forces*. College Station: Texas A and M University Press, 2012.

Feifer, Gregory. *The Great Gamble: The Soviet War in Afghanistan*. New York: Harper, 2009.

Foley, Robert. *German Strategy and the Path to Verdun: Erich von Falkenhayn and the Development of Attrition, 1870–1916*. Cambridge: Cambridge University Press, 2005.

Fraser, T. G., ed. *The First World War and Its Aftermath: The Shaping of the Middle East*. Chicago, IL: University of Chicago Press, 2015.

Freedman, Lawrence. *The Future of War: A History*. London: Allen Lane, 2017.

Fremont-Barnes, Gregory. *The Soviet Afghan War, 1979–1989*. Oxford: Osprey, 2012.

Fuccaro, Nelida, ed. *Violence and the City in the Modern Middle East*. Stanford, CA: Stanford University Press, 2016.

Gambone, Michael. *Small Wars: Low-Intensity Threats and the American Response since Vietnam*. Knoxville: University of Tennessee Press, 2012.

Geppert, Dominik, William Mulligan, and Andreas Rose, eds. *The Wars before the Great War: Conflict and International Politics before the Outbreak of the First World War*. Cambridge: Cambridge University Press, 2015.

Gerwarth, Robert, and John Horne, eds. *War in Peace: Paramilitary Violence in Europe after the Great War*. Oxford: Oxford University Press, 2013.

———. *The Vanquished: Why the First World War Failed to End, 1917–1923*. London: Allen Lane, 2016.

Gingeras, Ryan. *Fall of the Sultanate: The Great War and the End of the Ottoman Empire, 1908–1922*. Oxford: Oxford University Press, 2016.

Giquel, Prosper. *A Journal of the Chinese Civil War, 1864*. Edited by Steven Leibo. Honolulu: University of Hawaii Press, 1985.

Gooch, John. *Mussolini and His Generals: The Italian Armed Forces and Fascist Foreign Policy, 1922–1940*. Cambridge: Cambridge University Press, 2007.

Graham, Helen, ed. *Interrogating Francoism: History and Dictatorship in Twentieth-Century Spain*. London: Bloomsbury, 2016.

Green, Dominic. *Three Empires on the Nile: The Victorian Jihad, 1809–1899*. New York: Free Press, 2007.
Greenhalgh, Elizabeth. *The French Army and the First World War*. Cambridge: Cambridge University Press, 2014.
Griffith, Paddy, ed. *British Fighting Methods in the Great War*. London: Frank Cass, 1996.
Grimsley, Mark. *The Hard Hand of War: Union Military Policy toward Southern Civilians, 1861–1865*. Cambridge: Cambridge University Press, 1995.
Gudmundsson, Bruce. *Stormtroop Tactics: Innovation in the German Army, 1914–1918*. New York: Praeger, 1989.
Guelzo, Allen. *Gettysburg: The Last Invasion*. New York: Knopf, 2013.
Gürcan, Metin, and Robert Johnson, eds. *The Gallipoli Campaign: The Turkish Perspective*. Farnham: Ashgate, 2016.
Gutiérrez, Edward. *Doughboys on the Great War: How American Soldiers Viewed Their Military Experience*. Lawrence: University of Kansas Press, 2014.
Hail, William James. *Tsêng Kuo-Fan and the Taiping Rebellion*. New Haven, CT: Yale University Press, 1927.
Hämäläinen, Pekka. *The Comanche Empire*. New Haven, CT: Yale University Press, 2008.
Hanna, Alfred Jackson, and Kathryn Abbey Hanna. *Napoleon III and Mexico: American Triumph over Monarchy*. Chapel Hill: University of North Carolina Press, 1971.
Harmsen, Peter. *Shanghai 1937: Stalingrad on the Yangtze*. Havertown, PA: Casemate, 2013.
Hart, Peter. *The IRA and Its Enemies: Violence and Community in Cork, 1916–1923*. Oxford: Oxford University Press, 1998.
Hart, Russell. *Clash of Arms: How the Allies Won in Normandy*. Boulder, CO: Lynne Rienner, 2001.
Hart, Stephen. *Montgomery and "Colossal Cracks": The 21st Army Group in Northwest Europe, 1944–45*. Westport, CT: Praeger, 2000.
Hess, Earl J. *The Union Soldier in Battle: Enduring the Ordeal of Combat*. Lawrence: University Press of Kansas, 1997.
Heuser, Beatrice, and Eitan Shamir, eds. *Insurgencies and Counterinsurgencies: National Styles and Strategic Cultures*. Cambridge: Cambridge University Press, 2016.
Holborn, Andrew. *The D-Day Landing on Gold Beach*. London: Bloomsbury, 2015.
Hopf, Ted. *Reconstituting the Cold War: The Early Years, 1945–1958*. New York: Oxford University Press, 2012.
House, Jonathan. *Combined Arms Warfare in the Twentieth Century*. Lawrence: University Press of Kansas, 2001.
Huber, Thomas, ed. *Compound Warfare: That Fatal Knot*. Fort Leavenworth, KS: Army Command and General Staff College Press, 2002.
Jalai, Ali Ahmad, and Lester W. Grau. *Afghan Guerrilla Warfare: In the Words of the Mujahideen Fighters*. St. Paul, MN: MBI Publishing, 2001.
Jeansonne, Glen, and David Luhrssen. *War on the Silver Screen: Shaping America's Perception of History*. Lincoln: University of Nebraska Press, 2014.
Jeffery, Keith. *1916: A Global History*. London: Bloomsbury, 2016.
Jensen, Benjamin. *Forging the Sword: Doctrinal Change in the U.S. Army*. Stanford, CA: Stanford University Press, 2016.
Johnson, Rob. *The Great War and the Middle East*. Oxford: Oxford University Press, 2016.
Johnston, Seth. *How NATO Adapts: Strategy and Organisation in the Atlantic Alliance since 1950*. Baltimore, MD: Johns Hopkins University Press, 2017.
Kaldor, Mary. *New and Old Wars: Organized Violence in a Globalized Era*. Cambridge: Polity, 2012.

Kiszely, John. *Anatomy of a Campaign: The British Fiasco in Norway, 1940.* Cambridge: Cambridge University Press, 2017.

Knight, Alan. *The Mexican Revolution.* 2 vols. Cambridge: Cambridge University Press, 1986.

Kobylyanskiy, Isaak. *From Stalingrad to Pillau: A Red Army Artillery Officer Remembers the Great Patriotic War.* Lawrence: University Press of Kansas, 2014.

Krause, Jonathan. *Early Trench Tactics in the French Army: The Second Battle of Artois, May–June 1915.* Farnham: Ashgate, 2013.

Kreiser, Lawrence. *Defeating Lee: A History of the Second Corps, Army of the Potomac.* Bloomington: Indiana University Press, 2012.

Laband, John. *Zulu Warriors: The Battle for the South African Frontier.* New Haven, CT: Yale University Press, 2014.

Ledwidge, Frank. *Losing Small Wars: British Military Failure in Iraq and Afghanistan.* New Haven, CT: Yale University Press, 2011.

Lee, Roger. *British Battle Planning in 1916 and the Battle of Fromelles: A Case Study of Evolving Skill.* Farnham: Ashgate, 2015.

Lieven, Dominic. *Towards the Flame: Empire, War and the End of Tsarist Russia.* London: Allen Lane, 2015.

Linn, Brian. *The Philippine War, 1899–1902.* Lawrence: University Press of Kansas, 2000.

———. *Elvis's Army: Cold War GIs and the Atomic Battlefield.* Cambridge, MA: Harvard University Press, 2016.

Lloyd, Nick. *Passchendaele: The Lost Victory of World War I.* New York: Basic Books, 2017.

Longacre, Edward. *The Early Morning of War: Bull Run, 1861.* Norman: University of Oklahoma Press, 2014.

Lyon, James. *Serbia and the Balkan Front, 1914: The Outbreak of the Great War.* London: Bloomsbury, 2015.

MacDonald, Callum. *The Lost Battle: Crete 1941.* New York: Free Press, 1993.

Maiolo, Joe. *Cry Havoc: The Arms Race and the Second World War, 1931–1941.* London: John Murray, 2010.

Malet, Michael. *Nestor Makhno in the Russian Civil War.* London: Palgrave, 1982.

Maley, William. *The Afghanistan Wars.* 2nd ed. Basingstoke: Palgrave, 2009.

Martel, Gordon. *The Month That Changed the World, July 1914.* Oxford: Oxford University Press, 2014.

Mawdsley, Evan. *Thunder in the East: The Nazi-Soviet War, 1941–1945.* 2nd ed. New York: Bloomsbury Academic, 2016.

McPherson, Alan. *A Short History of U.S. Interventions in Latin America and the Caribbean.* Hoboken, NJ: Wiley-Blackwell, 2016.

Melvin, Mungo. *Manstein: Hitler's Greatest General.* London: Weidenfeld and Nicolson, 2010.

Merriman, John. *Massacre: The Life and Death of the Paris Commune of 1871.* New Haven, CT: Yale University Press, 2014.

Mitter, Rana. *China's War with Japan, 1937–1945: The Struggle for Survival.* London: Penguin, 2013.

Mitton, Kieran. *Rebels in a Rotten State: Understanding Atrocity in Sierra Leone.* London: Hurst, 2015.

Monmonier, Mark. *Rhumb Lines and Map Wars: A Social History of the Mercator Projection.* Chicago: University of Chicago Press, 2004.

Moore, Jeff. *The Thai Way of Counterinsurgency.* Muir Analytics, 2014.

Moreman, Tim. *The Army in India and the Development of Frontier Warfare, 1849–1947.* London: Palgrave, 1998.

Morewood, Steven. *The British Defence of Egypt, 1935–1940*. London: Frank Cass, 2005.

Morgan-Owen, David. *The Fear of Invasion: Strategy, Politics, and British War Planning, 1880–1914*. Oxford: Oxford University Press, 2017.

Morillo, Stephen, and Michael Pavkovic. *What Is Military History?* 3rd ed. Cambridge: Polity, 2018.

Moss, Tristan. *Guarding the Periphery: The Australian Army in Papua New Guinea, 1951–75*. Cambridge: Cambridge University Press, 2017.

Murray, Williamson, and Wayne Hsieh. *A Savage War: A Military History of the Civil War*. Princeton, NJ: Princeton University Press, 2016.

Murray, Williamson, and Peter Mansoor, eds. *Hybrid Warfare: Fighting Complex Opponents from the Ancient World to the Present*. Cambridge: Cambridge University Press, 2012.

Nagl, John. "Let's Win the Wars We're In." *Joint Force Quarterly* 52 (2009).

Nash, Douglas. *Victory Was beyond Their Grasp: With the 272nd Volks-Grenadier Division from the Hürtgen Forest to the Heart of the Reich*. Bedford, PA: Casemate, 2008.

Naveh, Shimon. *In Pursuit of Military Excellence: The Evolution of Operational Theory*. London: Frank Cass, 1997.

Newton, Steven, ed. *Kursk: The German View*. Boston, MA: Da Capo Press, 2002.

O'Hara, Vincent. *Torch: North Africa and the Allied Path to Victory*. Annapolis, MD: Naval Institute Press, 2015.

Otte, Thomas. *July Crisis: The World's Descent into War, Summer 1914*. Cambridge: Cambridge University Press, 2014.

Park, Alexander Garland. *Bolshevism in Turkestan, 1917–1927*. New York: Columbia University Press, 1957.

Peraino, Kevin. *A Force So Swift: Mao, Truman and the Birth of Modern China, 1949*. New York: Crown, 2017.

Razoux, Pierre. *The Iran-Iraq War*. Cambridge, MA: Harvard University Press, 2015.

Reardon, Carol. *With a Sword in One Hand and Jomini in the Other: The Problem of Military Thought in the Civil War*. Chapel Hill: University of North Carolina Press, 2012.

Reese, Roger. *Stalin's Reluctant Soldiers: A Social History of the Red Army, 1925–1941*. Lawrence: University Press of Kansas, 1996.

Reigel, Corey. *The Last Great Safari: East Africa in World War I*. Lanham, MD: Rowman and Littlefield, 2015.

Richardson, Thomas. *Destroy and Build: Pacification in Phuoc Tuy, 1966–72*. Cambridge: Cambridge University Press, 2017.

Richmond, Douglas. *Conflict and Carnage in Yucatán: Liberals, the Second Empire and Maya Revolutionaries, 1856–1876*. Tuscaloosa: University of Alabama Press, 2015.

Rieber, Alfred. *Stalin and the Struggle for Supremacy in Eurasia*. New York: Cambridge University Press, 2015.

Robson, Brian. *The Road to Kabul: The Second Afghan War, 1878–81*. London: Arms and Armour, 1986.

———. *Crisis on the Frontier: The Third Afghan War and the Campaign in Waziristan, 1919–20*. Staplehurst: Spellmount, 2004.

Rockoff, Hugh. *America's Economic Way of War: War and the US Economy from the Spanish-American War to the Persian Gulf War*. Cambridge: Cambridge University Press, 2012.

Roe, Andrew M. *Waging War in Waziristan: The British Struggle in the Land of Bin Laden, 1849–1947*. Lawrence: University Press of Kansas, 2010.

Ross, Andrew. *The Search for Tactical Success in Vietnam: An Analysis of Australian Task Force Combat Operations*. Cambridge: Cambridge University Press, 2015.

Samuels, Martin. *Command or Control? Command, Training, and Tactics in the British and German Armies, 1888–1918.* London: Frank Cass, 1995.

Sanborn, Joshua. *Imperial Apocalypse: The Great War and the Destruction of the Russian Empire.* Oxford: Oxford University Press, 2014.

Sayigh, Yezid. *Armed Struggle and the Search for State: The Palestinian National Movement, 1949–1993.* Oxford: Oxford University Press, 1997.

Schlosser, Nicholas. *The Battle for Al-Qaim and the Campaign to Secure the Western Euphrates River Valley, September 2005–March 2006.* Washington, DC: United States Marine Corps, 2013.

———. *The Surge, 2007–2008.* Washington, DC: Center for Military History, 2017.

Schrijvers, Peter. *Those Who Hold Bastogne: The True Story of the Soldiers and Civilians Who Fought in the Biggest Battle of the Bulge.* New Haven, CT: Yale University Press, 2014.

Sheehan, William. *A Hard Local War: The British Army and the Guerrilla War in Cork, 1919–1921.* Staplehurst: Spellmount, 2011.

Shepherd, Ben. *Hitler's Soldiers: The German Army in the Third Reich.* New Haven, CT: Yale University Press, 2016.

Showalter, Dennis, ed. *Forging the Shield: Eisenhower and National Security for the 21st Century.* Chicago, IL: Imprint Publications, 2005.

———. *The Wars of German Unification.* New York: Bloomsbury, 2015.

Silverman, David J. *Thundersticks: Firearms and the Violent Transformation of Native America.* Cambridge, MA: Belknap Press, 2016.

Sky, Emma. *The Unraveling: High Hopes and Missed Opportunities in Iraq.* New York: PublicAffairs, 2015.

Smele, Jonathan. *The "Russian" Civil Wars, 1916–1926: Ten Years That Shook the World.* New York: Oxford University Press, 2015.

Smith, Timothy. *Rethinking Shiloh: Myth and Memory.* Knoxville: University of Tennessee Press, 2013.

Sondhaus, Lawrence. *Franz Conrad von Hötzendorf: Architect of the Apocalypse.* Boston, MA: Humanities Press, 2000.

Stahel, David. *Operation Barbarossa and Germany's Defeat in the East.* Cambridge: Cambridge University Press, 2009.

———. *Kiev 1941: Hitler's Battle for Supremacy in the East.* Cambridge: Cambridge University Press, 2012.

———. *Operation Typhoon: Hitler's March on Moscow, October 1941.* Cambridge: Cambridge University Press, 2013.

———. *The Battle for Moscow.* Cambridge: Cambridge University Press, 2015.

Stern, Jessica, and J. M. Berger. *ISIS: The State of Terror.* London: William Collins, 2015.

Stewart, Andrew. *The First Victory: The Second World War and the East Africa Campaign.* New Haven, CT: Yale University Press, 2016.

Stewart, Rhea. *Fire in Afghanistan, 1914–1929: Faith, Hope and the British Empire.* New York: Doubleday, 1973.

Stockings, Craig, and Eleanor Hancock. *Swastika over the Acropolis: Re-interpreting the Nazi Invasion of Greece in World War II.* Brill: Leiden, 2013.

Stoker, Donald. *The Grand Design: Strategy and the U.S. Civil War.* Oxford: Oxford University Press, 2010.

Sutyagin, Igor, with Justin Bronk. *Russia's New Ground Forces: Capabilities, Limitations and Implications for International Security.* London: RUSI, 2017.

Taaffe, Stephen. *MacArthur's Korean War Generals.* Lawrence: University Press of Kansas, 2016.

Tanner, Harold. *The Battle for Manchuria and the Fate of China: Siping, 1946*. Bloomington: Indiana University Press, 2013.

———. *Where Chiang Kai-shek Lost China: The Liao-Shen Campaign, 1948*. Bloomington: Indiana University Press, 2015.

Taylor, William. *Military Service and American Democracy: From World War II to the Iran and Afghanistan Wars*. Lawrence: University of Kansas Press, 2016.

Thomas, Martin. *Fight or Flight: Britain, France, and Their Roads from Empire*. Oxford: Oxford University Press, 2014.

Trautmann, Frederic, ed. *A Prussian Observes the American Civil War: Military Studies of Justus Scheibert*. Columbia: University of Missouri Press, 2001.

Tripodi, Christian. *Edge of Empire: The British Political Officer and Tribal Administration on the North-West Frontier, 1877–1947*. Farnham: Ashgate, 2011.

Ucko, David. *The New Counterinsurgency Era*. Washington, DC: Georgetown University Press, 2009.

Varin, Caroline, and Dauda Abubakar, eds. *Violent Nonstate Actors in Africa: Terrorists, Rebels, and Warlords*. Basingstoke: Palgrave, 2017.

Ven, Hans van de. *War and Nationalism in China, 1925–1945*. London: Routledge, 2003.

Viola, Lynne. *Peasant Rebels under Stalin: Collectivisation and the Culture of Peasant Resistance*. Oxford: Oxford University Press, 1996.

Waldron, Arthur. *From War to Nationalism: China's Turning Point, 1924–1925*. Cambridge: Cambridge University Press, 1995.

Walker, Thomas, and Christine Wade. *Nicaragua: Living in the Shadow of the Eagle*. 6th ed. Boulder, CO: Westview, 2016.

Wawro, Geoffrey. *A Mad Catastrophe: The Outbreak of World War I and the Collapse of the Habsburg Empire*. New York: Basic Books, 2014.

Weigley, Russell. *History of the United States Army*. New York: Macmillan, 1967.

Westerman, William. *Soldiers and Gentlemen: Australian Battalion Commanders in the Great War, 1914–1918*. Cambridge: Cambridge University Press, 2017.

Whitewood, Peter. *The Red Army and the Great Terror: Stalin's Purge of the Soviet Military*. Lawrence: University Press of Kansas, 2015.

Willbanks, James. *The Battle of An Loc*. Bloomington: Indiana University Press, 2015.

Wilson, Mark. *Destructive Creation: American Business and the Winning of World War II*. Philadelphia: University of Pennsylvania Press, 2016.

Windrow, Martin. *The Last Valley: Dien Bien Phu and the French Defeat in Vietnam*. London: Weidenfeld and Nicolson, 2004.

Woodward, David. *The American Army and the First World War*. Cambridge: Cambridge University Press, 2014.

Worthing, Peter. *General He Yingqin: The Rise and Fall of Nationalist China*. Cambridge: Cambridge University Press, 2016.

Xiaobing Li. *China's Battle for Korea: The 1951 Spring Offensive*. Bloomington: Indiana University Press, 2014.

Xiaoming Zhang. *Deng Xiaoping's Long War: The Military Conflict between China and Vietnam, 1979–1991*. Chapel Hill: University of North Carolina Press, 2015.

Zamoyski, Adam. *Warsaw 1920: Lenin's Failed Conquest of Europe*. London: HarperPress, 2008.

Zanders, Jean Pascal, ed. *Innocence Slaughtered: Gas and the Transformation of Warfare and Society*. London: Uniform Press, 2016.

Zook, David. *The Conduct of the Chaco War*. New York: Bookman Associates, 1960.

Index

Afghanistan, 4, 55, 99, 186, 190, 191, 204, 210–213, 215, 231, 240, 244
Afghan Wars, 37, 96, 189–193
Africa, 202, 203, 226–230, 231, 236; East, 121, 192; North, 116, 127, 128–134, 138, 146, 147; Sub-Saharan, 152, 184–185; West, 16, 41
air power, 8, 84, 100, 104–106, 105, 112–113, 116, 118, 122, 123, 131, 132–133, 137, 153, 156, 161, 162, 174, 180, 182, 183, 189, 193, 194, 211, 215, 217, 218, 219; antiaircraft defenses, 90, 129, 161, 182, 183, 218
al-Qaeda, 211, 212, 213, 219
American Civil War, 11, 13, 14, 19–28, 49, 50, 73, 250
Amin, Idi, 193
amphibious operations, 7–10, 45, 46, 51, 103, 118, 129, 130, 135, 155. *See also* Operation Overlord
Angola, 185, 189, 192, 210, 228, 229, 236
Arab-Israeli Wars, 152, 164, 165, 166, 172–176, 186, 188, 194. *See also* Six-Day War; Yom Kippur War
army size, 10, 13, 31, 35, 42, 45, 48, 70, 98, 102, 105, 126, 131, 133, 137, 141, 145, 170, 181, 191, 197, 214, 215, 216, 219, 223, 225, 238
artillery, 16, 20, 31, 42, 44, 46, 47, 69, 71, 72, 76, 113, 120, 128, 129, 143, 146, 147, 183, 221; field, 50, 53, 69, 71;
mortars, 49, 71, 78, 142, 143, 193, 196, 224; naval, 8, 48, 133; quick-firing, 49, 50, 53; tactics, 48, 52, 53, 54, 74, 79, 81, 82, 84, 108, 113, 215
Asia: Central, 34, 37, 87, 92; Southeast, 116, 160, 180–182, 191, 204, 237
Atatürk, Kemal, 98, 99, 101
Australia, 74, 121, 165, 168, 210, 214
Austria, 33, 35, 36, 54, 61, 62, 64, 66, 68, 72, 75, 76, 156, 233, 234, 236. *See also* Austro-Prussian War; Wars of German Unification
Austro-Hungarian Empire, 60, 92, 94, 103, 234
Austro-Prussian War, 21, 31–32

Balkan Wars, 21, 37, 51, 54, 58, 62, 208
Baltic, 5, 98, 136, 191, 221, 244
barbed wire, 48, 53
bayonet, 36, 51–52, 139
Bazaine, Achille, 17–18
Beijing, 16, 38, 42, 59, 101, 102, 103, 198, 202
Belgium, 58, 62, 63, 65, 83, 84, 113–114, 115, 120
Benedek, Ludwig, 31
Berlin Wall, 186, 202
blitzkrieg, 105, 119–120, 136, 188
blockades, 23, 27, 115, 220
Boer War, Second, 42, 47–48, 50, 83

bombardment, 8, 33, 42, 67, 68, 74, 81, 118, 133, 135, 143, 221
bombing, 8, 97, 109, 114, 142, 148, 161, 170, 171, 174, 207, 219, 240
Bosnia, 35, 54, 206, 208–209
Brazil, 28–29, 52, 91, 160, 168, 222, 238
Britain, 7; after the Cold War, 204, 205, 209, 234, 238, 242; before the First World War, 13, 14, 15, 25, 35, 42, 44, 49, 50, 52; between the Wars, 100, 106; the Cold War and, 149, 150, 172, 173, 182, 188, 192; the First World War and, 58, 62, 63, 66, 68, 76, 77, 80, 85, 86, 86–87; the Second World War and, 111–112, 114, 114–115, 116, 117, 118, 130, 135. *See also* Boer War, Second; England
brutality, 33, 35, 44, 45, 91, 92, 93, 97, 99, 108, 124, 148, 161, 198, 203, 206, 207, 208, 220, 226, 227, 238, 250

Calais, 117, 132
Canada, 14, 22, 73, 87, 231
Caribbean, 42, 46, 59, 96, 160. *See also* Cuba
casualties, attitudes toward, 9, 12, 18, 19, 21, 38, 60, 73, 74, 75, 114, 122, 126, 159, 163, 174, 183, 186, 216, 217
Caucasus, 4, 82, 98, 125, 126, 140, 198, 202, 206, 208
cavalry, 18, 31, 44, 52, 53, 80, 90, 106, 138, 163
Central African Republic, 202, 226, 230, 231
Central America, 46, 52, 149, 179, 196–197
Chaco War, 29, 107–110, 168, 237
Chechnya, 189, 206–207
chemical weapons, 196, 213, 221, 227
China, viii, 4, 5, 233, 234, 236, 237, 242; after the Cold War, 201, 203, 220–221, 225–226, 230, 231; before the First World War, 11, 15, 15–17, 27, 43–45, 48, 49, 52; between the Wars, 90, 91, 95, 96, 99, 101–104, 108; the Cold War and, 180, 181, 195, 198; the First World War and, 58–60; the Second World War and, 152, 152–153, 154, 158, 159, 161, 167. *See also* Beijing

Chinese Civil War, 101, 150, 154
Chorrillos, 45
civil conflict, viii, 87, 91, 108, 197–198, 222, 230, 232. *See also* coup
civilians, 5, 27, 34, 36, 44, 100, 103, 114, 124, 148, 151, 156, 161, 198, 204, 216, 219, 220, 227
climate. *See* environmental factors
coastal protection, 45, 109, 132–133, 134, 163. *See also* amphibious operations; naval power; Operation Overlord
Cold War, 2, 98; doctrines of, 186–189; end of, 198, 202–203. *See also* Chinese Civil War; Korean War; nuclear confrontation; Vietnam War
colonies, 22, 33, 47, 58, 82, 103, 116, 149, 157, 171, 184, 185, 192
combined-arms operations, 7, 54, 73, 81, 86, 144, 146, 173, 183, 245
compound warfare. *See* hybrid warfare
conscription, 4, 5, 18, 43, 59, 87, 179, 186, 197, 207, 221, 244
counterinsurgency, 6, 15, 45, 46, 48, 159–161, 161, 169, 170, 191, 192, 207, 208, 216, 237, 238, 239, 246, 247. *See also* irregular warfare; guerilla warfare
coup, 59, 76, 108, 156, 168, 169, 170, 173, 174, 193, 203, 216, 222, 227, 229, 230, 238. *See also* civil conflict
Crimea, 5, 6, 13, 47, 83, 92, 201, 202, 221, 223, 235. *See also* Ukraine
Croatia, 208
Cuba, 46, 151, 159, 160, 168, 189
cultural factors, 17, 19, 21, 51, 52, 54, 61, 62, 105, 142, 145, 162, 215, 233, 247, 248
cyber warfare, 10, 235, 243, 244
Cyprus, 161, 193, 238
Czechs, 94, 117, 156, 172, 190
Czechoslovakia, 104, 156, 190, 191

D-Day. *See* Operation Overlord
desertion, 28, 59, 93
diplomacy, 61, 62, 171, 205, 208, 235. *See also* negotiations
disease, 12, 29, 76, 191, 219, 227, 228
doctrine, military, 2, 51, 54, 89, 186–189, 223, 225
Dunkirk, 116, 117–118

Dutch, 114, 154. *See also* Netherlands

Eastern Front, 68, 73, 75–76, 126, 127–128, 134, 136, 143
economic factors, 11–13, 17, 37, 86, 107, 124, 146, 174, 181, 195, 198, 202, 203, 231, 235, 236, 238, 247, 249
education, 2, 6, 15
Egypt: after the Cold War, 219, 222; before the Cold War, 34, 41, 82, 90, 96, 121, 127, 147; the Cold War and, 151, 152, 160, 164, 165, 166, 168–171, 189, 194. *See also* Arab-Israeli Wars; Yom Kippur War
encirclement, 97, 127, 136, 219
England, 3, 118, 132. *See also* Britain
environmental factors, 15, 46, 76, 96, 105, 108, 113, 121, 145, 163, 167, 170, 193–194. *See also* terrain, influence of
Ethiopia, 41–42, 106, 121, 161, 192, 203, 229
ethnic cleansing, 54, 92, 97, 99, 172, 203, 204, 208, 209, 220, 227, 228, 230. *See also* wars among the people
explosives, 45, 53, 67, 71, 220, 221, 242

Faidherbe, Louis, 33
Falkenhayn, Erich von, 68–69
field armies, 23, 24, 48
financing, 157, 195, 196, 203, 235; expenditure, 31, 156, 173, 220, 224, 235, 242, 244
Finland, 47, 98, 104, 113, 137. *See also* Winter War
First World War, 49, 104, 105, 195, 241; Face of Battle paradigm and, 71–73; modern parallels with, 233–236; strategies of, 60–66. *See also* Eastern Front; trench warfare; Western Front
fitness-for-purpose, 82, 102
force: and politics, 36, 54, 87, 202, 203, 222–223, 232; purposes of, 59, 104, 107
fortifications, 49, 54, 105, 113, 131, 182, 241
France: 1940 fall of, 112, 118, 119–120; after the Cold War, 209, 214, 242; before the First World War, 13, 14, 20, 21, 28, 29, 35, 36, 44; between the Wars, 96, 105; the Cold War and, 150, 151, 157, 158, 160, 173, 188, 195; the First World War and, 57, 58, 62, 63, 80, 83; the Second World War and, 111, 115, 116, 120, 129. *See also* Franco-German War; Maginot Line; Napoleonic Wars; Operation Overlord; Paris; Western Front
Franco-German War, 2, 11, 14, 32–33, 33, 34, 36, 57, 83

Gaddafi, Muammar, 216–217, 217
General Staffs, 14, 15, 30, 31, 34, 43, 53, 72, 85, 115, 248. *See also* war preparations
genocide. *See* ethnic cleansing
Germany: after the Cold War, 209, 234, 241, 242, 249, 250; before the First World War, 14, 15, 18, 31, 32, 33–34, 36, 44, 49, 53; between the Wars, 104, 105, 106; the Cold War and, 160, 188; the First World War and, 58, 62, 63, 66, 80; the Second World War and, 111–112, 114–115, 118, 119, 124, 136–137, 137, 140, 141, 148, 241. *See also* Berlin Wall; Eastern Front; Franco-German War; Operation Barbarossa; Operation Blue; Operation Overlord; Prussia; Wars of German Unification; Western Front
Gorbachev, Mikhail, 192, 202
Great Power confrontations, 4, 14, 151, 220–221
Greece, 51, 97, 120, 120–122, 137, 159, 193, 209, 238
guerrilla warfare, 29, 35, 45, 46, 93, 101, 159, 161, 170, 171, 173, 181, 182, 184–185, 189, 191, 192, 196–197, 204, 207, 210, 215, 216, 242. *See also* counterinsurgency; irregular warfare
Gulf Wars, 205–206, 206, 213–216

Habsburgs, 87, 236, 240. *See also* Austria
Haftar, Khalifa, 217
Hezbollah, 218, 220, 221
Hindenburg Line, 70, 74, 77
history: approaches to, viii, 1–6, 10, 14, 90, 101, 103, 157, 188, 230–231, 233, 236–241, 243, 245, 247–249; politics

and, 15, 249–250
Hitler, Adolf, 62, 104, 116, 121, 122, 123, 124, 126, 127, 129, 132, 140, 141
Huerta, Victoriano, 59, 95
Hundred Days Offensive, 79
hybrid warfare, 5, 210, 216, 223, 248

imperialism, 11, 12, 41, 42, 90, 92, 97, 111, 157, 161, 236, 246–247
Inchon, American landing at, 9, 155
India, 160, 161, 198, 204, 213, 221, 222, 231, 237; British rule of, 41, 47, 90, 96, 97, 112, 139, 246; Chinese conflicts with, 153, 181, 220–221, 225; North-West Frontier, 47, 96, 246–247; Indian Mutiny, 13, 44. *See also* India-Pakistan wars
India-Pakistan wars, 164, 167–168, 175, 238
Indochina, French, 116, 157–159
internal security, 43, 44, 55, 92, 168, 202, 213, 227, 228, 229, 232
interwar period: interpretations of, 89–99; means of waging war, 105–107
Iran, 90, 98, 99, 161, 166, 167, 179, 182, 212, 217, 218–219, 220, 238, 243
Iran-Iraq War, 73, 148, 194–196, 235
Ireland, 99–101, 210
irregular warfare, 6, 17, 34, 35, 93, 172, 193, 242. *See also* counterinsurgency; guerrilla warfare
Islamic State, 9, 216, 217, 219, 231
Islamic world, 90, 181, 182, 194, 195, 206, 216–220, 229, 231, 239. *See also* Middle East
Israel, 151, 167, 168, 169, 182, 186, 188, 204; Gaza strip and, 174, 198, 240. *See also* Arab-Israeli Wars; Six-Day War; Yom Kippur War
Italy, 8, 42, 96, 106, 195, 197, 249; the First World War and, 66, 76, 77, 241; the Second World War and, 115, 116, 120, 128–134. *See also* Wars of Italian Unification
Ivory Coast, viii, 227, 230, 231

Japan, 5, 249–250; after the Cold War, 201, 220, 225, 226, 231, 242; before the First World War, 43–45, 50; between the Wars, 91, 96, 102, 103–104, 107, 109, 110; the Cold War and, 153; the First World War and, 66, 235; the Second World War and, 8, 9, 111, 112, 113, 115, 125, 126, 128, 134, 139, 142, 144, 145, 148, 150. *See also* Russo-Japanese War; War of the Pacific
Jordan, 164, 169, 171–173, 174, 175–176, 240

Korea, 5, 43–44, 48, 185, 201, 221, 235, 236, 240
Korean War, 9, 129, 151, 155–157, 158, 196
Kosovo, 206, 209, 210
Kuwait, 195, 196, 203, 205, 206, 235

Latin America, 14, 15, 28–31, 42, 52, 95, 108, 160, 168, 196, 197, 237
logistics, 12, 16, 17, 29, 33, 34, 42, 45, 64, 86, 93, 108, 120, 142, 144–145, 163, 167
Libya, 5, 50, 90, 121, 152, 193, 202, 203, 216–217, 217, 227

machine guns, 53, 90, 139, 143, 243
Maduro, Nicolás, 222–223
Maginot Line, 113, 114
Manchuria, 43, 48–49, 50, 51, 54, 102, 153, 154, 249
Mao Zedong, 154, 159, 162, 225, 226
maps, 42, 43, 58, 82–86, 216, 237
Mediterranean, 8, 120–123, 127, 129, 133, 165, 174
Mexico, 15, 28, 29, 30, 32, 37, 90, 92, 95–96, 222, 238, 241; The First World War and, 58–60
Mexican-American War, 21–22
Middle East, 76–77, 83, 90, 97, 116, 138, 149, 160, 169, 220. *See also* Islamic world
militias, 46, 59, 156, 197, 203, 210, 217, 219, 223, 226–227, 228–229, 230
missiles, 150–151, 156, 157, 163, 182–183, 186–187, 192, 195, 195–196, 201, 218, 221, 242, 243
Mongols, 3, 44
morale, 24, 27, 31, 45, 52, 54, 60, 64, 79, 80, 117, 121, 142, 148, 165, 174, 176

Moscow, 124–125, 202, 207, 224
Mugabe, Robert, 184–185, 230

Nanjing, 16, 59, 250
Napoleon III of France, 29, 32, 33
Napoleonic warfare, 14–15, 17, 21, 24, 31, 32, 63, 76
Native Americans, 22, 37–38, 42, 49
naval power, 7, 8, 27, 42, 46, 48, 51, 111, 118, 122, 131, 133, 231, 234, 239. *See also* amphibious operations; coastal protection
negotiation, 16, 87, 100, 116, 155, 160, 171, 180, 208, 238, 246. *See also* diplomacy
Netherlands, 113, 114, 115, 120. *See also* Dutch
Normandy landings. *See* Operation Overlord
North American Treaty Organization, 2, 5, 151, 152, 156, 187, 188, 191, 209, 212, 221, 224, 242, 244
nuclear confrontation, 150–153, 156–157, 161, 166, 176, 180, 187, 188, 240

Operation Barbarossa, 123–125, 131, 141
Operation Blue, 125–127
Operation Overlord, 130–135
operational factors, 7, 8, 10, 24, 30, 47, 62, 82, 86, 137, 145, 154, 163, 166, 175, 183, 187, 188, 193
Ottomans, 87, 90, 236. *See also* Russo-Turkish War; Turkey

Pakistan, 160, 167, 182, 210, 211, 213, 237, 238, 246. *See also* India-Pakistan wars
Palestine, 76, 82, 171, 172, 173, 174, 176, 194, 198
Paris, 33, 83, 138
Passchendaele, 70, 72, 73, 75
Persia. *See* Iran
Philippines, 46, 50, 118, 157, 159, 198, 222
Piedmont, 13, 35–36
poison gas, 72, 77, 87, 89, 218, 222
Poland, 68, 75, 104, 112–113, 115, 120, 140, 186

Portugal, 184, 186, 197; Portuguese Empire, 108, 161, 179, 184, 209, 210, 236
prisoners, 33, 59, 76, 100, 117, 126, 150, 206
Prussia, 13, 14, 15, 18, 29, 34, 36, 38, 63, 65. *See also* Austro-Prussian War; Franco-German War; Wars of German Unification
Putin, Vladimir, 207, 221, 223–224

raiding, 19, 27, 38, 77, 78, 93, 99, 100, 207, 208, 227
rebellion, 35, 42, 44, 47, 87, 95, 100, 161, 167, 171, 190, 226, 227, 238. *See also* Taiping Rebellion
refugees, 173, 176, 227, 229
religious conflicts, 4, 54, 92, 97, 99, 182, 204, 206, 209, 211, 213, 218, 228
resource targeting, 140
revolts, 59, 90, 95, 97, 99, 198
Revolution in Military Affairs, 4, 204, 211, 230
Rhodesia. *See* Zimbabwe
rockets, 143, 160, 193, 214, 238, 243
Roe, Andrew, 246, 247
Russia, 6, 13, 42, 44, 49, 54, 90, 92, 94, 101, 104, 111, 114–115, 150, 202, 212, 217–218, 220, 221, 223–224, 233, 234, 235, 237, 241, 242, 244. *See also* Chechnya; Cold War; Crimea; Eastern Front; First World War; Moscow; Soviet Union
Russian Civil War, 92, 93, 94, 98, 109, 150
Russo-Japanese War, 2, 41, 42, 48–50, 50, 51, 53, 54, 63, 249
Russo-Polish War, 98
Russo-Turkish War, 35
Rwanda, 4, 203, 228, 229

Saudi Arabia, 90, 169, 170, 170–171, 195, 218–219, 220, 242
Scandinavia, 112–113, 140, 221
Second World War, 8, 23, 25, 64, 69, 73, 104, 110, 153, 249, 250; close of, 140–142; developments during, 123–148; movement in, 144–145; overview of, 111–112; resources in, 146; weaponry of, 142–144. *See also*

Dunkirk; Eastern Front; Operation Overlord; Western Front
Serbia, 35, 51, 54, 58, 64, 66, 75, 203, 206, 208–209, 233, 241
Sicily, 9, 35–36, 96, 129, 132
sieges, 26, 33, 35, 47, 49, 125, 163, 170, 171, 207, 229
Six-Day War, 164, 165, 171, 194, 240
South Africa, 185, 192, 198, 230
Soviet Union, 91, 105, 107, 112, 116, 148, 149, 150–152, 153, 159, 166, 171, 176, 181, 198, 202, 214, 225, 236, 240; offensives in 1943-45, 135–137. *See also* Afghan Wars; Cold War; Eastern Front; Moscow; Operation Barbarossa; Russia; Second World War; Warsaw Pact
Spain, 51, 96, 105, 108, 179, 197, 235. *See also* Cuba; Mexico; Spanish-American War; Spanish Civil War
Spanish-American War, 42, 46–47
Spanish Civil War, 89, 102, 107–110
Sri Lanka, 161, 227
Stalin, Josef, 62, 91, 107, 113, 115, 123, 124, 160
starvation, 37, 125, 219, 227, 228
Stalingrad, 126, 127, 140
submarines, 63, 77, 87, 148, 151
surveillance, 84, 193, 198, 207
Sweden, 221, 244
Syria: after the Cold War, viii, 3, 5, 201, 216, 217–218, 219, 220, 221, 238; before the Cold War, 90, 96, 97, 116, 122; the Cold War and, 151, 152, 160, 164, 165, 166, 171, 172, 173–174, 176, 182, 183, 184, 194

Taiping Rebellion, vii, 11, 15, 15–17, 44
Taliban, 211–213, 215
Tamil Tigers. *See* Sri Lanka
tanks, 166, 167, 175, 180, 183, 184, 194, 195, 206, 214, 219, 232, 239, 243; before the Second World War, 80–81, 87, 105, 107, 108; defenses against, 8, 81, 128, 138, 142, 143, 144, 148, 183, 193, 203, 238, 243; in the Second World War, 114, 117, 119, 123, 133, 135, 138, 140, 142, 144

technology: influence of, 4, 5, 12, 24, 32, 42, 49, 50, 58, 65, 81, 213, 242, 244, 248; innovation in, 17–18, 38, 41, 79, 150, 179, 221, 225, 241–243
terrain, influence of, 8, 24, 36, 42, 44, 46, 72, 75, 82, 121, 129, 143, 167, 169, 170, 191, 193, 207, 209, 215, 217. *See also* environmental factors
terrorism, 94, 176, 179, 198, 204, 210, 213, 216, 220, 227
total war, viii, 2, 4, 21, 80, 155
trench warfare, 13, 19, 29, 46, 47, 49, 53, 155; in the First World War, 58, 71, 72, 74–75, 79, 81, 83, 84. *See also* Western Front
Turkey, 13, 50, 51, 55, 58, 66, 68, 87, 90, 96, 97–98, 99, 101, 193, 197, 203, 220. *See also* Ottomans

Ukraine, 5–6, 98, 124, 128, 132, 191, 201, 223, 224
United States of America, 4, 5, 7, 10, 46, 111; after the Cold War, 201, 202, 203, 204, 206, 207, 209, 211, 212, 213, 218, 220, 221, 222, 234, 235, 242, 244; between the Wars, 96, 100; the First World War and, 63, 66, 77. *See also* American Civil War; Cold War; First World War; Gulf Wars; Korean War; Mexican-American War; Second World War; Vietnam War; Western Expansionism; War of the Pacific

Venezuela, 52, 125, 160, 222, 235
Vicksburg, 26–27
Vietnam War, 5, 149, 157, 158, 161–166, 170, 176, 180, 186, 192, 240
von Moltke, Helmuth: the elder, 30–31, 33, 68; the younger, 53, 64

War of the Pacific, 8, 45, 51, 113, 133, 135, 143, 145, 213
War on Terror, 204, 230
war preparations, 10, 14, 30, 31, 49, 52–55, 61, 63, 107, 131, 133, 135, 153, 188, 189, 215, 244
wars among the people, viii, 4, 204, 206–210. *See also* ethnic cleansing

Wars of German Unification, vii, 13, 14, 28, 30–34, 44, 53, 233, 234
Wars of Italian Unification, 13, 35–36
Warsaw, 98, 136
Warsaw Pact, 2, 4, 152, 187, 189
water supplies, 17, 41, 108
Western expansion, 37–38, 42
Western Front, 9, 58, 63, 65, 66–71, 71, 73, 77–80, 84, 85, 86, 91, 112, 113–117, 119, 140, 195

Winter War, 47, 113

Yemen, 168–171, 174, 175, 182, 218, 219, 220, 232, 239
Yom Kippur War, 182–184
Yugoslavia, 4, 51, 94, 120, 121–122, 137, 203, 207, 208

Zhang Zuolin, 102
Zimbabwe, 184–185, 192, 228, 230

About the Author

Jeremy Black graduated from Cambridge University with a Starred First and did graduate work at Oxford University before teaching at the University of Durham and then at the University of Exeter, where he is professor of history. He is a 2018 Templeton Fellow of the Foreign Policy Research Institute. He has held visiting chairs at the United States Military Academy at West Point, Texas Christian University, and Stillman College. Black received the Samuel Eliot Morison Prize from the Society for Military History in 2008. *Land Warfare since 1860* is the capstone book in Black's global warfare series, which includes *Air Power: A Global History*, *Naval Warfare: A Global History since 1860*, *Insurgency and Counterinsurgency: A Global History*, *Combined Operations: A Global History of Amphibious and Airborne Warfare*, and *Fortifications and Siegecraft: Defense and Attack through the Ages*.